THE NEW ERA OF WEALTH

HOW INVESTORS CAN PROFIT FROM THE 5 ECONOMIC TRENDS SHAPING THE FUTURE

THE NEW ERA OF WEALTH

HOW INVESTORS CAN PROFIT FROM THE 5 ECONOMIC TRENDS SHAPING THE FUTURE

B RIAN S. W ESBURY

New York San Francisco Washington, D.C. Auckland Bogotá
Caracas Lisbon London Madrid Mexico City Milan
Montreal New Delhi San Juan Singapore
Sydney Tokyo Toronto

McGraw-Hill

A Division of The McGraw-Hill Companies

Copyright © 2000 by The McGraw-Hill Companies, Inc. All rights reserved.
Printed in the United States of America. Except as permitted under the United
States Copyright Act of 1976, no part of this publication may be reproduced or
distributed in any form or by any means, or stored in a data base or retrieval
system, without the prior written permission of the publisher.

Library of Congress Cataloging-in-Publication Data

Wesbury, Brian S.
    The new era of wealth : how investors can profit from the 5
economic trends shaping the future / by Brian S. Wesbury.
        p.   cm.
    Includes bibliographical references.
    ISBN 0-07-135180-9
    1. Portfolio management—United States.   2. Investments—United
States.   3. Securities—United States.   4. Wealth—United States.
5. United States—Economic conditions—1981-   I. Title.
HG4529.5.W47   1999
332.6—dc21   99-40337
                                                                              CIP

  2 3 4 5 6 7 8 9 0 DOC/DOC   0 9 8 7 6 5 4 3 2 1 0

ISBN 0-07-135180-9

*The sponsoring editor for this book was Kelli Christiansen, the editing supervisor was
John M. Morriss, and the production supervisor was Elizabeth J. Strange.*

Printed and bound by R. R. Donnelley & Sons Company.

McGraw-Hill books are available at special quantity discounts to use as
premiums and sales promotions, or for use in corporate training programs. For
more information, please write to the Director of Special Sales, McGraw-Hill, 11
West 19th Street, New York, NY 10011. Or contact your local bookstore.
This publication is designed to provide accurate and authoritative information in
regard to the subject matter covered. It is sold with the understanding that
neither the author nor publisher is engaged in rendering legal, accounting, or
other professional service. If legal advice or other expert assistance is required,
the services of a competent professional person should be sought.
—From a Declaration of Principles jointly adopted by a Committee of the American Bar
Association and a Committee of Publishers.

This book is printed on recycled, acid-free paper containing a
minimum of 50% recycled, de-inked fiber.

To the Lord who made me,
my parents, Stuart and June
and my wife, Brenda.

"A wife of noble character is her husband's crown..."
                                                    Proverbs 12:4

CONTENTS

PART 2
--- -- -- -- -- --

PREPARING YOUR PORTFOLIO FOR THE COMING BOOM

7

FOUR THREATS TO THE NEW ERA   87

8

SHIFTING PERCEPTIONS   97

9

STRATEGIES FOR CREATING PERSONAL WEALTH   105

PART 3
INVESTMENT IMPLICATIONS FOR THE NEW ERA OF WEALTH

10
PICKING STOCKS FOR THE FUTURE—THE TOP-DOWN APPROACH

11

PICKING THE RIGHT STOCKS AND MUTUAL FUNDS

12

USING BONDS FOR LONG-TERM REWARD

ACKNOWLEDGMENTS

My life changed in the early 1980s when, as a young college graduate, Robert Genetski, chief economist at the Harris Bank in Chicago, hired me as an economics assistant. The experience of the real world and the patient mentoring that Genetski provided allowed me to learn the way the world really worked.

Early in my career, I met Beryl Sprinkel, Arthur Laffer, Jack Kemp, Alan Reynolds, Larry Kudlow, Victor Canto, Bob Mottice, Joe Bast and David Padden. I cannot thank each of them enough for the wisdom that they imparted.

Of many things, they directed me to the writings of Milton Friedman, F. A. Hayek, and Ludwig von Mises. Reading the writing of these great men has shaped my life as much as it taught me economic knowledge. They provided the inspiration for this book by teaching me the power of ideas.

One of the most powerful ideas is that when freedom prevails, the ingenuity and inventiveness of people creates incredible wealth. This is the source of the natural improvement of the human condition. This idea has become the cornerstone of my economic thinking. If this book allows one other person to understand and profit from this idea, then it was worth it.

Freedom and entrepreneurial activity have transformed the U.S. economy from the miserable 1970s to the booming 1980s and 1990s. Because of this, the United States is experiencing a New Era of unprecedented growth, rivaled only by the Industrial Revolution. This New Era of Wealth is being driven forward by 5 key trends, which are defined in this book.

Some of those trends were put in place in Washington, D.C., and I had the good fortune to work closely with Senator Connie Mack, one of the great political leaders of our time. During my tenure as the Chief Economist for the Joint Economic Committee, chaired by Senator Mack, I gained invaluable knowledge of how politics and economics work together and I will benefit from that knowledge for the rest of my life.

Needless to say, the others I worked with in Washington, D.C., Bruce Bartlett, Paul Merski, Dan Mitchell, Steve Moore, Bob Stein, Phaedon Sinis, Missy Shorey, Melissa Cortese Foxman, and Jeff Given, will see pieces of their thoughts and work in these pages.

In addition to those mentioned above, my education in financial markets would have been incomplete without many others. At the Harris Bank, Bob Davis, John Kirscher, Dave Mead, Bud Bruffee, Willie McNickle and Jerry Jurs helped mold me into a good banker. Walter Fitzgerald, whom I met at the Chicago Corporation, will never know how much he has helped me grow.

At Griffin, Kubik, Stephens & Thompson, Inc. in Chicago, I have had the chance to work for some of the finest men in the bond industry. Gary Griffin, Jim Kubik and David Thompson not only gave me the freedom to write this book, but along with Larry Stephens, they allowed me to develop as a public figure under their guidance and wisdom.

Friends and coworkers who helped in every aspect of this book from editing to content, Bob Kengott, Jay Fairbanks, Wayne Morkes, Larry Kohls, and Gregg Riley, should know that I value their friendship and loyalty immensely. My assistant, Aleksandrs Kalnins, put up with endless editing jobs, carried the ball while I was buried under work and, for him, I am truly grateful.

Moreover, this book would not have been hatched without the recognition that I gained by being published on the editorial page of *The Wall Street Journal*. I thank Robert Bartley, Amity Shlaes, Max Boot, Claudia Rosett, and James Taranto for that opportunity. Not only have I learned by reading their editorials, but the opportunity to write on their pages remains a high honor.

Paul Sperry at *Investors' Business Daily*, humbled me by including me in the "IBD Brain Trust" and has always supported my efforts. His knowledge of economics and markets is only equaled, not surpassed and I am proud to count him as a friend.

Without the efforts and sacrifices of my parents, Stuart and June Wesbury, I would never have grown up loving to learn and would never have written this book. The same goes for my brothers, Brent, Bruce and Brad, who have always loved me and supported any task that I have undertaken.

Finally, without my wife Brenda, this book would still be a dream. I love her very much, she is a gift from God and she should see much of herself in these pages. Not only did she give up a social life for a half a year, she helped edit the very thing that was keeping us from enjoying our wonderful friends together.

Brian Wesbury
September 21, 1999

THE NEW ERA OF WEALTH

HOW INVESTORS CAN PROFIT FROM THE 5 ECONOMIC TRENDS SHAPING THE FUTURE

INTRODUCTION

When I graduated from the University of Montana in the early 1980s, the economy was in recession and finding a job that fully utilized my education and training was almost impossible. Today, a single college graduate can start a bidding war between two companies and computer scientists can virtually write their own ticket. Not only have jobs become more plentiful, but wages are rising faster than inflation, the stock market has soared, interest rates have fallen, and the United States has become the most powerful economy the world has ever seen. This begs a simple question. And from that simple question, this entire book flows. How did the U.S. economy turn from the miserable stagflation of the 1970s, into a New Era economy that continues to create wealth at an astounding rate? The answer means everything, especially for investors. This book, and the analysis that it contains, will help you understand the forces that created this New Era. By understanding these forces you and your portfolio will be better prepared for the next 20 or 30 years of prosperity.

Something special has happened to the economy and, more importantly, its foundation seems solid. As the biblical parable tells us, a house built on a rock can withstand a storm, but a house built on sand cannot. So our one question leads us to others. Is the U.S. economy built on a rock, or on the sand? Are we lucky or have we truly done something right? Can the boom disappear as fast as it came? While the answers to these questions are important for our future investment strategy, this book is about more than making money; it is about creating wealth. It is about what conditions make it easier for all of us to create wealth. Wealth is more satisfying when it is widespread, and when wealth is widespread, creating our own personal wealth is that much easier.

I know my job search experience in the early 1980s was shared by many. Interest rates, inflation, and unemployment were in the double digits, stocks were stagnant, and the economy was like a yo-yo with one recession after another. Today, it is hard to remember how bad those times were, but many forecast that the bad times were here for good. In 1979, even before the recessions of the early 1980s, Robert Lekachman, a prominent economist and frequent editorial writer for *The New York Times* warned, "The Era of Growth is over and the era of limits is upon us."[1] He was wrong and those dismal times have now become a distant memory.

In what seems like no time, the United States has entered a New Era of Wealth. Historically the U.S. economy has ridden an up-and-down pattern of growth with constant battles against inflation, but the New Era economy has been and will be different. It will be characterized by strong growth, low inflation, low interest rates, and rising stock prices. The New Era economy is being driven upward by innovation and ideas and as a result, its closest comparison would be the Industrial Revolution. However, because of the unique technology of the Internet and telecommunications this New Era will be even more powerful. The risk of owning stocks will decline and great wealth will be accumulated.

An analysis of a simple set of five trends suggests that this New Era of wealth creation will continue for decades. How can I be so sure? History shows, that when these five trends work together, rapid accumulation of wealth occurs. These five trends are self-reinforcing and have momentum. They are here to stay and so is the New Era in which they thrive.

These five trends, listed here, are discussed at length in Part I.

- *Technology*—While the history of the world is one of innovation and improvement, the advancements made in computers and telecommunications in recent years are special. They operate using the law of increasing returns and have increased productivity faster than at any time in U.S. history.
- *Globalization*—As technology makes the world smaller, the United States benefits because of its relatively free markets and sound currency. Not only does the U.S. economy benefit because of increased capital flow, but an increase in global trade also increases efficiency while holding down prices. An integrated global economy makes everyone better off.
- *Fiscal policy*—It is not a coincidence that the New Era began in the early 1980s. Government policy, which for so long was focused on redistributing a larger share of U.S GDP and regulating business, shifted in the early 1980s toward a smaller and less intrusive style.
- *A shift in our political culture*—The shift in U.S. policy during the early 1980s and the collapse of socialism in the late 1980s reflect the ascendance of market capitalism. From the United States to Bangladesh, citizens have begun to believe that individual responsibility, rather than government responsibility, is the best way to improve living standards. In addition, more Americans own stocks than ever before. These two facts make it almost impossible for politicians to reverse course. As a result, the positive fiscal policy environment is likely to remain in place.
- *Monetary policy and inflation*—The huge decline in inflation from over 13 percent in 1980 to less than 1.5 percent in 1998 and 1999 has boosted stocks and lowered interest rates. The drop in inflation is the result of two forces: rising productivity and an improved Federal Reserve policy. Low inflation and price stability are essential to the creation of wealth.

THE PESSIMISTS ARE WRONG

In the mid-1980s, the eternal optimist Don Zimmer was managing the Chicago Cubs. The team returned from an eight-game road trip after splitting their games with opponents. As I recall, the Chicago sportswriters were not impressed with this .500 record and gave Zimmer a hard time. At one point in the press conference, Zimmer got frustrated and said, "I know we were 4–4 on the trip, but you should understand that it could have easily gone the other way."

To Zimmer, it all depended on how you looked at the situation. The economy and financial markets are no different. Both optimistic and pessimistic investors can find evidence to support their moods. Recently, the optimists have found support in the data. Today, many individuals finally believe that they are better off than their parents were and the economy continues to blow away dismal projections. Optimists are having a field day.

But the pessimists have loaded bats too. The Asian economic miracle turned into the Asian economic nightmare. Russia has collapsed and South America is stumbling. Fears of both inflation and deflation strangely exist at the same time and according to some analysts, the Year 2000 (Y2K) problem threatens a worldwide recession. All of this, some argue, has pushed frothy U.S. financial markets to the brink of collapse.

Pessimists, thinking that it could have "easily gone the other way," and may do so shortly, are everywhere. This group views every stumble in the markets as the beginning of the end. They also believe that if it were not for a few temporary "fortuitous circumstances," inflation would be bubbling while financial markets tumbled.

In April 1998, a cover story in *The Economist* highlighted "America's bubble economy"[2] and suggested that a market and economic collapse were on their way. Four months later, *The New Yorker* magazine published an article titled "Pricking the Bubble" in which its author, John Cassidy, wrote that "the parallels [between 1929 and today] are striking."[3]

In October 1998 another magazine, *Esquire*, not known for its business acumen, published an article titled "The Coming Economic Collapse."[4] In that article, Walter Mead wrote that the economy was experiencing a "storm of the century, an economic cataclysm as big or bigger than the Great Depression of the thirties."[5]

Granted, most of these articles were written during the global financial crisis of 1998, but underlying their analysis was a forecast that the New Era had to end soon. With forecasts like these, optimists begin to look like Pollyanna. But optimists have history on our side. For over 200 years, the United States has consistently created wealth faster than any other nation on earth. The reason for this is our belief in individual initiative, entrepreneurship, and the Rule of Law. Despite the consistency of wealth creation, the United States has gone through long periods of both stagnation and growth. Typically these periods last 20 years or so; however, every once in a while, we enter a period of 40 years or longer when wealth creation accelerates such as it did during the Industrial Revolution between 1870 and 1910. Today is one of those times, which is why the U.S. economy remained virtually untouched by the 1998 global financial crisis.

The optimists are right and the pessimists are wrong. Bad bounces or broken bats may affect the final score of a single baseball game, but over a 162-game season the quality of pitching, hitting, and defense become the deciding factors. The economy is no different. Underlying economic strength is not determined by luck, but by the fundamental economic factors of investment, entrepreneurial innovation, and risk-taking. And the best way to encourage these developments is for policymakers to strive toward free markets and price stability.

THE SEEDS FOR THE BOOM

If we step back 18 years and look forward it is easy to see why the current economic boom was so hard to imagine. In the early 1980s, the U.S. economy was in deep recession and pessimism was rampant. Inflation and unemployment were in double digits and Ronald Reagan became president by asking the question, "Are you better off today than you were four years ago?"[6]

This question rang true. In the early 1980s, after adjusting for inflation, stock prices were between 60 percent and 70 percent lower than they were in 1965. Even after including dividends, total returns for large corporate stocks were negative between 1965 and the end of 1981. More importantly, incomes were sliding and interest rates shot above 20 percent. Even President Carter used the word *malaise* to describe the economy he presided over.

While it has become popular to blame President Carter for the bad economic times, they did not sprout up overnight. The problems had been building since 1965. The Lyndon Johnson–driven Great Society programs of the mid-1960s expanded government spending rapidly. Taxes rose to pay for that spending and the increased military budget for fighting the Vietnam War. It was in the early 1970s, however, under President Nixon that redistributionist government spending grew the most.

As the economy stumbled under the weight of higher taxes and bigger government, the Federal Reserve began to stimulate the economy to keep it moving. Eventually the burdens of government drove up unemployment and easy money boosted inflation. This forced Nixon to close the gold window and initiate wage and price controls. While many want to blame outside forces such as OPEC for our problems, they were entirely homegrown. Nonetheless, the U.S. economy has completely rebounded from those depressing times and has now reached what Federal Reserve Board Chairman Alan Greenspan said is "as impressive a performance as any I have witnessed in my nearly half-century of daily observation of the American economy."[7]

During the past 17 years, inflation-adjusted, *per capita* net worth rose by nearly 70%—from $80,700 in 1982 to $136,250 in 1998. That bears repeating.

In 1998 the average net worth of every man, woman, and child in America was $136,250.

More U.S. citizens own stocks today than ever before in our history. In addition, inflation-adjusted incomes have climbed for 5 consecutive years. The United States has become a wealth-creating machine all over again and the whole world will eventually benefit.

WHERE DOES WEALTH COME FROM? ASK ABE LINCOLN

Where does wealth come from? Does it come from government programs and spending? Does it come from low interest rates? Or does it come from entrepreneurial innovation?

If you picked the third answer you were right. Ideas create wealth. Finding more efficient ways to produce goods and services produces wealth. So does the invention of new products that others need, want, or desire.

While many economists have studied wealth, most answer this question in the wrong way. More importantly, most of these economists taught us in Economics 101 that wealth comes from astute government management of the economy. However, government intervention, because it often interferes with individual initiative and incentives, may actually hinder growth.

Fortunately many economists have described the wealth creation process in the right way. One of the most important was Adam Smith. In 1776, he published his famous book, *An Inquiry into the Nature and Causes of the Wealth of Nations*. Smith did a remarkable job of explaining what wealth is, and most importantly what it is not.

He wrote that wealth is not money (or gold in his day), but instead is productive resources—people, knowledge, and capital. He spent a great deal of time describing how the "division of labor" increases productivity and wealth. By letting bakers be bakers and butchers be butchers we all benefit when they attempt to increase their own standard of living.

When a baker finds a more productive way of delivering or producing bread the world benefits in three ways. First, the cost of bread falls. Second, the baker uses fewer resources in the production and distribution of bread and those resources can then be used to produce other goods. Third, the baker makes a larger profit that will be used to invest in his or her business or in some other business. Moreover, when the baker's profits rise, others are drawn into the industry, which increases the odds of further innovation and a further decline in prices.

All serious students of economics should read Smith's book. But there are others who have eloquently described the same processes. Abraham Lincoln, in a speech given 83 years after the publication of Smith's book, explained with simple clarity the wealth creation process throughout history.

Michael Novak should be credited for calling attention to Lincoln's 1859 speech. In his 1997 book, *The Fire of Invention*,[8] Novak summarized Lincoln's speech into a detailed list of the six great human steps toward wealth accumulation and higher standards of living.

The six steps are development of a language, refinement of the powers of observation, inventing the written word, inventing the printing press, discovering America which allowed the emancipation of ideas, and the writing of the U.S. Constitution. Specifically, Lincoln focused on the Constitution's protection of inventions and writing through patents and copyrights that, according to Lincoln, added the "fuel of interest" to the "fire of genius."

The "fire of genius" brings the entrepreneurial process alive and explains perfectly the wealth creation process. For example, Thomas Edison reportedly said that he found "5000 ways how not to make a light bulb." But, his one success changed the world forever and created tremendous wealth. The wealth that is important is not the wealth that Edison created for himself, but the wealth that he created for the world as light bulbs boosted productivity and raised living standards.

Lincoln's most important point focused on the Constitution. By protecting ideas through the Rule of Law (specifically copyrights and patents), the government protects the intellectual capital of the entrepreneur. Because *things* are worthless without a way to use them, *ideas* are the key to wealth creation. For example, sand is just sand until it is used to create a silicon wafer. It is the idea, not the sand, that holds the value.

It is important to understand that when Abraham Lincoln gave his 1859 speech, the United States was beginning its move into the Industrial Revolution. While interrupted by the Civil War, the industrial era was born in the second half of the nineteenth century. The first transatlantic telegraph cable was laid in 1865 and the railroad spread like a wildfire. Over the next 40 years, the electric light, the electric motor, the automobile, the phonograph, and the telephone were all put into use.

This process of discovery and invention led to a noninflationary boom in economic growth that lasted for 40 years. Today the same type of phenomenon is occurring. The fax machine, computer, Internet, cellular telephone, and satellite communication system all emanate from the "fire of genius." These developments are also producing a noninflationary boom. The United States has entered a "New Era of Wealth."

OPPOSING FORCES: ACCUMULATION AND REDISTRIBUTION OF WEALTH

While inventions have changed our world, the history of man is also a history of politics. Throughout history, as wealth has been accumulated, the political force of redistribution has also gained strength. Investors and politicians should know that these are opposing forces.

Redistribution limits the benefits of economic growth. The real political lesson of the past century is that free markets, governed by the Rule of Law, work best at raising living standards. America is the shining success, while Russia is the tarnished failure. More importantly for investors, the U.S. market performs much better when government interference is kept to a minimum. With spending falling as a share of GDP, tax rates much lower than in the 1970s, and regulations becoming less onerous, the economy and financial markets are much more buoyant.

THE STOCK MARKET BAROMETER

This buoyancy can be seen in the stock market. It is the best barometer of U.S. economic health and its future wealth creation capacity. Why? The stock market allows millions of investors to express their opinions (using their own money) on the outlook for the future on a daily basis. Collectively we are much more prescient than we are individually.

The following chart shows the Dow Jones Industrial Average back to 1920. It shows that U.S. wealth has shot up like a rocket. One look at the chart on the top of the next page and everyone can understand why Alan Greenspan called U.S. investors "irrationally exuberant" back in December 1996.

This chart is misleading, however. A move in the Dow from 100 to 200 appears very small even though it is the same percentage point change as a move from 5,000 to 10,000. Logarithmic scales fix this problem. As can be seen in the next chart, the market looks much more rational when it is plotted logarithmically. It also paints an interesting history of the U.S. economy. The market and the economy boomed in the 1920s, only to collapse in the 1930s. The boom returned from 1941 to 1965, but then stagnated from 1965 to 1982. Since 1982, the economy and the market have been booming again.

These periods show that poor market performance occurred during periods of government activism. The stock market in 1929 and the early 1930s was hammered by deflationary mistakes in monetary policy, the passage of the Smoot-Hawley Tariff Act and New Deal tax increases, spending, and regulation.

The poor performance of the stock market and the economy between 1965 and 1982 was correlated with the Great Society programs of Lyndon Johnson and inflationary mistakes in monetary policy. As U.S. stock market history shows, redistribution and government policy mistakes hurt wealth creation.

Dow Jones Industrial Average – Close at End of Year

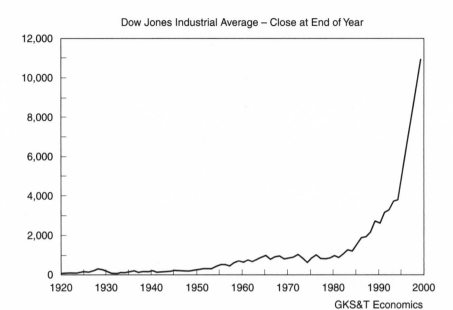

GKS&T Economics

Dow Jones Industrial Average – Close at End of Year
Logarithmic Scale

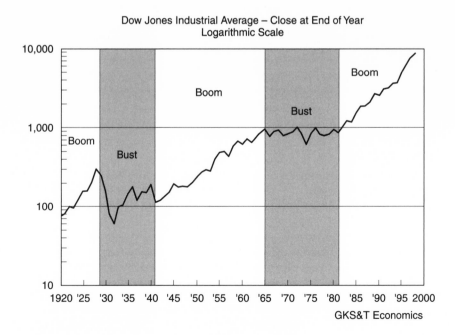

GKS&T Economics

So it should come as no surprise that since 1982 the markets have boomed. As President Clinton stated in 1996, "The era of big government is over."[9] This bodes well for investors in the years ahead and the five key trends, discussed in Part I, suggest that the boom is here to stay. As long as the United States can avoid repeating the mistakes of the past, the future is decidedly against the doomsayers.

BENEFITING FROM THE NEW ERA

Part II of this book focuses on preparing your portfolio to benefit from the boom and how to recognize the potential threats to prosperity. The New Era could end if protectionism, an increasing role of government in the economy, or a sharp swing to deflation or inflation inhibit the wealth creation process. Recognizing these developments before they hurt markets is a key to safeguarding your wealth.

This said, the goal of this book is to provide a framework for understanding the New Era and develop strategies to benefit from it. Starting a business and investing in education or your career can often create more wealth than investing in stocks. The New Era will reward risk-taking and initiative, not the status quo.

Part III, which builds an investment strategy based on the five key trends, details how you can profit from the New Era. Invest in ideas not commodities, think small, not big and remember that nimble and dynamic is better than static and staid.

If you take the time to understand why this age has prospered, you will understand that it will inevitably continue. While there will be winners and losers in the New Era of Wealth, there will be mostly winners. By using the framework explained in this book, your future can be as bright as you want it to be.

The framework suggests some simple strategies for creating personal wealth in the years ahead:

1. Exposure to equities is absolutely essential.
2. Do not be afraid to invest in bonds, even at today's seemingly low yields.
3. Save, stay out of debt, and pay down your mortgage. Deflation is a reality of the New Era.
4. Trust serendipity. A dynamic economy increases opportunity and diversity. Trust the market and its mysterious ways. Be optimistic.

The future is always a question mark, however, a solid framework for understanding and forecasting will wipe away many of the uncertainties. By improving the base of your investment knowledge better outcomes are ensured. After all, even baseball's homerun Kings, Mark McGwire and

Sammy Sosa, take batting practice. Without working on the fundamentals, success cannot be guaranteed.

References

[1] Lekachman, Robert. 1979. Testimony to the Joint Economic Committee of Congress, October 29.

[2] No Author. 1998. America's dangerous bubble. *The Economist,* 18 April, pp. 15, 67, 68, 69.

[3] Cassidy, John. 1998. Annals of finance; Pricking the bubble. *The New Yorker,* 17 August, pp. 37–41.

[4] Mead, Walter Russell. 1998. The coming economic collapse; What did you do after the crash daddy? *Esquire,* October, pp. 92–105, 162, 165.

[5] Ibid.

[6] The Carter–Reagan Presidential Debate, October 28, 1990.

[7] Greenspan, Alan. 1998. *Monetary policy testimony and report to the Congress,* July 21. Washington, DC: Federal Reserve Board.

[8] Novak, Michael, 1997, The fire of invention: Civil society and the future of the corporation, Lanham, Maryland, Rowman & Littlefield.

[9] Clinton, William Jefferson, State of the Union Address, January 1995.

PART 1

THE FRAMEWORK FOR PROFITING IN THE NEW ERA

1

THE TECHNOLOGY REVOLUTION

Technology is the key to the New Era of Wealth. By definition, technology and innovation come from ideas, and ideas create wealth. The concept is as simple and miraculous as that. Throughout history, the human condition has been one of slow improvement in living standards from subsistence to the comfort enjoyed today. Although there have been setbacks, sometimes for hundreds of years, the general direction of economic growth and wealth creation has been up. The "human condition" is always to push forward for the better and economics is the study of that process. In fact, one of the greatest economists of the twentieth century, Ludwig Von Mises, wrote the book, *Human Action*. In it, he described how humans act to make their world more comfortable. Those actions, which Mises called entrepreneurial and Abraham Lincoln termed the "fire of genius" result in finding production processes that utilize fewer resources and increase efficiency. By creating more goods and services at lower cost, the economy increases its wealth. Economists calculate this output and wealth any number of ways, but the most widely visible measure is the gross domestic product (GDP), which measures the total output of all goods and services in any economy. As such, it is the broadest measure of our economy's production available.

Over time, as any economy increases its GDP, it also increases the share of its production that it saves for the future. In the days of subsistence living, by definition, there was nothing left over for the future. Once individuals found ways to increase output with fewer resources, savings became possible. Excess grain was stored, and time was freed up because of this saving. This allowed the construction of shelter and the invention of new goods and services that made life easier, safer, and more comfortable.

These inventions, in turn, freed up time for more research, and living standards continued to rise. Eventually, we found that resources were so plentiful that we could take time for leisure activities and more people developed tastes for sports, music, art, and theater. At first, these things were available only to the rich, but eventually they became so plentiful that all could enjoy them.

As resources, ideas, and potential proliferated, an economic system develops institutions and conventions to help these processes along. One of the most important innovations of all time was that of money and the resulting financial system that made certain that money flows to its best use. Financial markets enabled the profits from farming to finance the building of washing machines, and the profits from building washing machines to finance the invention of the computer. In essence, money is just grease in the wheels of commerce. Without innovation and human effort, money is worthless.

Stock and bond markets, credit cards, banks, finance companies, pension funds, and mutual funds are the institutions and inventions that allow individuals to direct the wealth that is not used for subsistence into areas that will increase output for the future. By investing our savings in ideas that will increase wealth we can share in the profits of those endeavors. Capital accumulation is essential for wealth creation and vibrant and dynamic economies tend to accumulate capital rapidly.

In this regard, the United States has clearly done something right. With the exception of 1991, U.S GDP has increased every year since 1982. Most importantly, this increase has occurred without an increase in the rate of inflation, making it the longest period of noninflationary growth since the Industrial Revolution. During these years, the U.S. stock market has increased more than 12-fold and capital from around the globe has flowed into U.S. investments.

New ideas and, specifically technology, are at the heart of the U.S. economic miracle. Predictably, even though technology is available to everyone on the face of the earth, the center of its proliferation is in America. There are two reasons for this. First, the United States has historically attempted to keep the government's role in the economy limited. This does not mean that the United States has been entirely successful or that our government sector is small; but when compared with the rest of the world, U.S. interference in the entrepreneurial process has actually declined since the early 1980s.

The second reason for the proliferation of technology in the United States is its time-honored tradition of respecting individual freedom; thus, the United States is uniquely suited to a technology boom. Abraham Lincoln explained this in his February 1859 speech detailed in the Introduction. Lincoln knew instinctively that ideas were the most powerful thing on earth. He also understood that taking ideas and transforming them into products was a difficult process.

The breathtaking inventiveness of the human experience has been recorded for thousands of years and is not solely an American trait; however, the freedom and the market orientation of U.S. constitutional law have magnified the power of innovation. In fact, you could say that the United

States is an invention in its own right. Free spirits invented America so that they would have a place to invent and prosper. Nonetheless, it took thousands of years to achieve the material well-being that we enjoy today.

Slowly, and intermittently, ideas have created a more productive world and along with it, higher living standards. In his 1998 book, *The Wealth and Poverty of Nations,* David S. Landes traces many of the life-altering inventions of our history in economic terms. According to Landes, the Middle Ages were peppered with inventions of great magnitude—the water wheel (tenth and eleventh century), eyeglasses (late in the thirteenth century), the mechanical clock (last quarter of the thirteenth century), the printing press (1452–1455), and gunpowder (refined in England during the sixteenth century).[1] Each increased the efficiency and productivity of our world. Eyeglasses increased the productive working life of craftsmen, the printing press allowed the broad dissemination of knowledge and ideas, and as Landes puts it, "the very notion of productivity is a by-product of the clock."

Each of these inventions led to further inventions and it is now clear that the pace of productivity enhancing ideas has accelerated for thousands of years. In other words, knowledge begets new knowledge. As productivity increases, resources are released for the further advancement of society. Once sustenance was no longer an issue, society could invest in its future. Once investment in new ideas began, the world was launched on an upward course that few could have foreseen.

Following the inventions of the Middle Ages, industrial era developments began to take center stage. The first steam-powered engine was developed in 1705 by Thomas Newcomen in England.[2] More than 60 years passed before James Watt invented a steam engine with a separate condenser that could be used outside of the mining industry, and it took another 15 years to "adapt the machine to rotary motion, so that it could drive the wheels of industry."[3] In 1884, Charles A. Parsons once again raised the efficiency and power of steam engines by inventing the steam turbine. Each of these processes took time; in all, steam engine development took 200 years.

During this same period, iron smelting and steel production were invented beginning in 1709 when Abraham Darby completed the first coke smelt of iron. Not until 1856, however, did Henry Bessemer develop cheap steel. Until then, steel was used for small things. In the latter half of the nineteenth century, steel was finally ready for such "prime time" uses as building steel rails and ships. During this same period, powered machinery and its uses in cotton spinning took off as well. This increased textile output and productivity dramatically.

As Landes wrote, "all these gains, plus, the invention of machines to build machines, came together in the last third of the eighteenth century— a period of contagious novelty."[4] This "contagious novelty" is reflected in the economic data. Starting sometime between 1760 and 1770, economic historians can show a clear acceleration in economic growth and living standards. This coincides perfectly with what is known as the British Industrial Revolution (1770–1870). Interestingly, while this boom was ending, another was just beginning.

In 1859, Abraham Lincoln stood at the sunset of one great industrial era and at the dawn of an even greater era of inventiveness. He marveled at the material progress humans had already made, but was optimistic that the future would be even brighter. He was right and the Industrial Revolution was born. However, even before it began, the United States was already beating the world in terms of economic growth. According to Landes, "a recent comparison of productivity in manufacturing shows America well ahead of Britain by the 1820s."[5] By the mid-1800s, ". . . American mills paid higher wages [than in England]," and "hours were long, but shorter for example than in Japanese mills at the same stage."[6]

How did America achieve the leading role in world economic development? Well, the answers are not absolute, but the culture of competition that America developed allowed it to shake off the shackles of great landlords and peasants that Europe held on to so tightly. The European system, with all of its vested interests built up over hundreds of years, did not allow change to happen rapidly. The entrepreneurial spirit was suppressed in Europe, but encouraged in America. And when competition increases, vested interests break down quickly.

The Industrial Revolution blossomed in America and the pace of wealth creation truly began to accelerate. In the 1830s, railroad miles could be measured in the hundreds and by the 1850s in the thousands; but the invention of cheap steel accelerated their proliferation and by 1916 there were 254,000 miles of track in the United States.[7]

During those same years, the electric light, the electric motor, the telegraph, the telephone, and the automobile all came of age. The result was a tremendous period of change that had an impact on every industry in America. Landes quotes a letter from the July 1900 edition of *Scientific American* that said, "Indeed there is scarcely a thing done on the farm of today in which patented machinery does not perform the greater part of the labor."[8] These patents, and their power to force change, are what Lincoln described in 1859 as being a key ingredient of wealth creation.

The U.S. Industrial Revolution lead to a noninflationary boom in the economy that lasted for more than 40 years. Between 1869 and 1911, U.S. real GDP (after adjustment for inflation) grew by an annual average of 4.0 percent per year while the Consumer Price Index *fell* 0.6 percent per year.[9] This deflationary boom led to a surge in living standards, boosted stock prices to very high levels, and made the U.S. economy the largest in the world.

This boom reflected the ascendancy of the American model of free market capitalism and "by 1913, American output was two and a half times that of the United Kingdom or Germany, four times that of France. Measured per person, American GDP surpassed that of the United Kingdom by 20 percent, France 77, Germany by 86."[10] The wealth that was created during this period allowed ordinary people, not just the rich, to enjoy the use of all kinds of consumer goods only dreamed of a few short years before.

THE INFORMATION AGE

Today, the United States is leading the world in another economic revolution and is once again in the midst of a surge in technology and productivity that will increase living standards. This revolution is different from the past, in that it is even more powerful and will increase wealth more rapidly than the world has ever seen.

As we can see in history, the pace of change has consistently accelerated. In the information age, however, change is coming more rapidly than ever before. The impact can be seen everywhere: outdated Old Era economic models, which cannot comprehend this New Era, are breaking down; competition is increasing exponentially; the world is becoming smaller; and opportunity has exploded. Understanding these trends is of paramount importance in our quest for wealth creation. Do not underestimate the power of the high-tech boom.

While the recent explosion of Internet stocks seems to have developed overnight, the new information age economy has been a long time coming. As George Gilder wrote in his prophetic 1989 book, *Microcosm*, "the seeds [of the information age] were sown in 1959 in Pasadena, at the California Institute of Technology."[11] At the institute, Carver Mead experimented and failed to perfect the tunnel diode, a crude precursor to the microchip. Nonetheless, by delving into what Gilder called the "Microcosm," Mead was able to discern in a deeper way than anyone before him, the problems of large mainframe computers and the future of personal computing. As Mead described it, the computer industry had a dilemma: "It has enormous investment in big machines and big software programs, and the only thing the industry can do right now is to use the new microelectronics as it fits into the existing system. . . . "[12] Through his research, "Mead foresaw in 1968—three years before it was done—it would soon be possible to put an entire computer on a chip and sell it for a few dollars."[13]

Again in 1968, Mead wrote, " 'We have computer power coming out of our ears. What we need is the kind of systems we would like to have in our automobiles, in our telephones, in our typewriters—where people now spend vast amounts of time on the repetitive and mundane. . . .' "[14] Mead predicted "that the new silicon technologies would allow the creation of small computers that brought power to the people as automobiles did, rather than bringing it to large institutions and sophisticated programmers like mainframe computers did."[15]

Carver Mead was a visionary who predicted what would happen in the information age well before its technologies were commonplace. He advised Gordon Moore, one of the founders of Intel, to prepare for the era of decentralized computing power and personal computers. At first, Moore and his colleagues decided to exploit the market for big computers and go against Mead's advice. However, Intel eventually changed its strategy as Mead's philosophy of "small is better" began to come true. In November 1971, Intel announced the development of a microprocessor— essentially a computer on a chip—and advertised it as a "New Era of integrated electronics."[16] Since developing this market in 1971, Intel has dominated the chip market.

More importantly, during the early days of microprocessor development, Gordon Moore developed what has become known as "Moore's law," which stated that computer chips would halve in price or double in power every 18 months. Moore felt that these advances would taper off in the mid-1980s, but they did not. Chip capacity and price still continue to follow Moore's law. By 1998, microchip prices had fallen to just 1 percent of their cost in 1980. If automobile prices had followed the same path, a $20,000 car in 1980 would cost just $200 today.

These declining chip prices have fostered a new and potent growth force in the economy. Faster and more reliable machines are increasing productivity in every industry worldwide. From CAD/CAM design, to inventory control and checkout scanners, the economy is experiencing revolutionary developments that are lowering costs and increasing incomes for the entire world.

Despite the obvious increases in our living standards and the clear impact of the computer in that process, there are naysayers. Even an award-winning *Wall Street Journal* reporter, Bob Davis, wrote as recently as January 1999 that, "PCs have yet to produce *any* discernible productivity boost. Indeed, the rate of productivity growth has slowed substantially since 1973, around the time the PC was invented."[17]

This pessimism is a typical response to revolutionary developments, but is horribly wrong. We are now living in an era of "increasing returns" that is boosting growth and living standards more rapidly than at any time in the past 30 years and possibly in history. Even more disturbing to the pessimists, who continue to view the world through economic models built over 60 years ago, is the fact that while the economy's growth rate is accelerating, the rate of inflation is falling.

This goes against nearly every popular economic theory in existence. Most Economics 101 classes teach that the economy has certain "limits to growth." For example, the "law of diminishing returns" states: "[A]s extra units of one factor of production are employed, with all others held constant, the output generated by each additional unit will eventually fall."[18] In everyday language this law says that as more cars enter a highway, the speed of traffic declines or traffic jams appear. An offshoot of the law of diminishing returns is the "Phillips Curve." This theory suggests that if unemployment falls below a certain level, then inflation will accelerate.

Computer and telecommunication systems are nonetheless breaking down all of these cherished theories. Progress in computing power and speed has followed Moore's law and the world is becoming networked. The fax machine, cellular phone, and Internet have proliferated rapidly. As they have grown in use and power their value has increased, not diminished. In essence, the information superhighway moves faster and becomes more valuable as more people and businesses join it. We are building a "networked economy" which defies many of our long-standing rules of economics.

The networked economy is reducing the cost of information while increasing its value. As John Browning and Spencer Reiss in *Wired Magazine*[19] have pointed out, the very first fax machine ever built was worth absolutely nothing (even though it may have cost a bundle to build). The reason: There were no other machines to fax to, or to receive faxes from; however, the second fax machine was worth something and it made the first machine worth something as well. From that point on, every fax machine that is added to the worldwide network of fax machines not only increases the value of the very first fax machines, but it also increases the value of the entire network of fax machines.

As Santa Fe Institute economist Brian Arthur, one of the pioneers of modern-day "increasing returns" analysis, wrote, "Not only do the costs of producing high-technology products fall as a company makes more of them, but the benefits of using them increase."[20] When the cost of something falls, while its value increases, by definition that is an increase in productivity and the law of diminishing returns is repealed. In fact, it is not just repealed it is replaced. Today, the "law of increasing returns" is the appropriate economic theory. As Kevin Kelly put it in his must-read book, *New Rules for the New Economy*, "The value of a network explodes as its membership increases, and the value explosion sucks in yet more members, compounding the result."[21]

Think about it. In a world with only 3 fax machines, there are 6 possible faxes that can be accomplished. If we add 3 more fax machines to increase the number to 6, we more than double the number of possible connections to 30; 9 makes 72. If we double this number again to 18 fax machines, then there are 306 different connections possible. As can be seen, the number of possible connections rises much faster than the rate at which new members are added to the network. The number of possible connections is equal to = $N \times (N-1)$. Each additional member (N) of the network boosts the value of the network in a nearly exponential fashion.

This process creates an interesting problem for economists, especially those steeped in old-style, industrial age economic theory. Economic statistics that were designed in the industrial age cannot measure the increase in value of any of the New Era networks. We could put all the economists from the Federal Reserve Board, World Bank, IMF, Bureau of Labor Statistics, and the Department of Commerce together and give them unlimited time to measure the productivity of the network of fax machines and they could not do it. Simply put, the value of the network is embedded in the economy and is therefore inseparable from it. The sharing of information at a more rapid rate and the plummeting cost of sharing that information add to growth in ways that we have no way of calculating.

In some sectors of the economy, however, it is possible to calculate productivity growth accurately. For example, in durable goods manufacturing industries we can measure how many hours of work it takes to produce an automobile or any other good. As a result, it is possible to compare relatively accurate measures of productivity with the past. As can be seen in the following chart, durable goods manufacturing productivity growth has been twice as strong during the current recovery as it was during an average of the previous eight recoveries since World War II. In fact, productivity growth in the current recovery is even stronger than it was during the Industrial Revolution.

There are both obvious, and not so obvious, reasons for the productivity boom. First, computer-controlled robotic assembly systems have come of age. These robots take mundane tasks and mechanize them, working faster, and with fewer defects than before. Less obvious is the dramatic reduction in waste. Just-in-time inventory systems, computer-assisted quality control, computer-aided design, and new computer-generated algorithms for handling inventory and controlling production schedules all contribute by increasing productivity.

Interestingly, the minute we move away from durable goods manufacturing, productivity becomes more ephemeral. For example, measuring

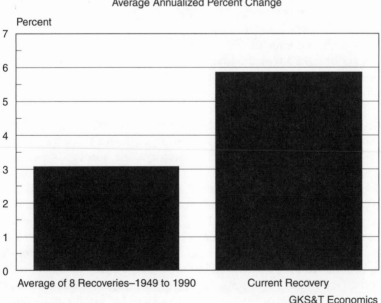

Durable Goods Manufacturing Productivity Growth
Average Annualized Percent Change

Percent

Average of 8 Recoveries–1949 to 1990   Current Recovery

GKS&T Economics

productivity in service sectors of the economy is impossible. Think about haircuts. Some stylists charge more than $40 for a haircut, while others may charge as little as $8. While you and I might argue that there is no difference between a $40 haircut and an $8 one, this would be our opinion, not a fact. Obviously, some people think that a $40 haircut is better than an $8 haircut or they would not spend the extra money.

Unfortunately our standard economic statistics have no way of measuring the difference between them. To government statisticians they are all just haircuts. As a result, if more people start to get more expensive haircuts, government statisticians may actually count this as a drop in productivity. The reason is relatively simple. When society spends more to get the same number of haircuts, then our government statisticians assume that we are experiencing haircut inflation.

However, if we asked the people who purchased the haircuts if they were more satisfied, they would say yes—otherwise they would not have spent more. So rising expenditures for haircuts may not indicate inflation at all. In fact, as society gets wealthier and consumers begin to shift toward higher-quality purchases, it may appear that prices are rising, but in fact quality and satisfaction are higher. When quality and satisfaction rise, by definition that is an increase in productivity. On the other hand, if inflation took off and the price of an $8 haircut rose to $20, then people would be spending more for the same service. This would not be an increase in satisfaction, but instead would be an increase in inflation. As you can see the key to measuring productivity depends on whether people are spending more to get better quality or whether they are spending more for the same quality. Obviously this is an impossible question to answer, so the government does the next best thing—it assumes that productivity growth in many service categories of the economy is zero and it assumes that if people are spending more for a given good or service, then inflation is occurring.

As another example of this problem, movies have more special effects in them today and as a result cost more to produce. Are higher ticket prices inflation or do they represent higher quality? The reason for asking this rhetorical question is to make a simple point. Measuring things that are going on in the economy is very difficult, especially in services, which is why it is so hard to understand the unequivocal statements made by many policymakers, private economists, journalists, and market pundits that productivity has not improved. When our government is making assumptions that productivity growth is zero in many broad categories of services, the data do not mean very much.

Despite all the problems in measuring service sector productivity, it is clearly rising rapidly. Look at some of the anecdotal evidence. For example, in a recent *Business Week* article, it was reported that in 1998 Amazon.com had $375,000 in sales per employee while Barnes & Noble had just $100,000.[22] Clearly, productivity is massively higher at Amazon.com. New Era delivery systems have increased productivity in the book delivery business by at least 50 percent per year in recent years, yet our national data completely misses this fact and economists endlessly debate about whether productivity is rising 1.5 or 1.9 percent per year. They are not doing the profession any favors and investors would be well served by ignoring these debates. If anyone attempts to tell you that the computer has not increased productivity, they are flat-out wrong.

We know that productivity has risen because the value of the network has risen. While the price of computers, cellular phones, satellite dishes, Internet connections, and phone calls plummet, their value is increasing. The reason is that the network becomes more valuable as it grows and the demand to join the network increases as the cost of joining declines. This self-reinforcing trend is in its earliest stages of development. Every day, the network is climbing in value and every day, productivity is rising as a result.

Understanding this concept is important. The world is filled with pessimistic views of this New Era. Buying into traditional economic analysis is a quick way to miss the increasing productivity and the profits that are available in the "networked world." The New Era argument is that productivity growth is accelerating and that this will boost corporate profits and individual incomes, while driving prices lower. This leads to lower interest rates and higher stock prices. If, on the other hand, the pessimists are right and productivity is not increasing, then profits will stagnate and inflation will rise. As a result, stock prices would fall and interest rates would rise. These are two completely different views of our future. Understanding the New Era and its impact on fundamental economic trends is absolutely essential for investing profitably.

Despite the profits at stake, and the overwhelming evidence of a New Era, many economists cannot break their ties with Old Era models. One of those models is the Phillips Curve, mentioned previously. In its simple form, this model states that when unemployment falls below a certain level, then wages start to rise. Wage increases then cause producers to raise prices, which increases inflation. Higher inflation forces labor to demand even higher prices. This wage-price spiral continues until the Federal Reserve raises interest rates enough to cause a recession and drive unemployment back above the magic level dictated by the Phillips Curve. Once the economy has cooled down, then growth can resume.

This model has its roots in the writings of Thomas Malthus (1766–1834), a famous economist whose view of the world was quite pessimistic. In fact, his view of the future was downright disturbing. Malthus believed that population tended to outgrow its ability to produce food. Malthus predicted that as population exceeded the food supply, disease and starvation would cause the population to shrink. When the population shrank enough to sustain itself again, the process would start all over.

In 1798, Malthus published the pamphlet, *An Essay on the Principle of Population*. In it he wrote,

> [P]opulation, when unchecked, goes on doubling itself every twenty-five years, or increases in a geometric ratio [but] the means of subsistence increase in an arithmetical ratio. . . . Take the population of the world at any number, a thousand millions, for instance, the human species would increase in the ratio of—1, 2, 4, 8, 16, 32, 64, 128, 256, 512, &c. and subsistence as—1, 2, 3, 4, 5, 6, 7, 8, 9, 10, &c. In two centuries and a quarter, the population would be to the means of subsistence as 512 to 10.[23]

Despite the fact that Malthus was proven wrong because agricultural output kept pace with both population growth and longer life spans, this dismal view of the world continues to pervade economic models. While very few modern-day economists would dare sing the praises of Malthus, many disguised versions of these very ideas sway economic and political thinking to this day.

The most prominent among them is the environmentalist movement. Although many think that the worries over our environment are a recent phenomenon, they are not. Ever since Malthus, the imagined scourge of economic growth has worried many groups. In 1972, a group named The Club of Rome published the findings of a complicated mathematical model of the world economy. Their model predicted a "sudden and uncontrollable decline in both population and industrial capacity,"[24] unless steps were taken to limit growth very soon. Specifically, their model showed that before the end of the millenium the world would run out of copper, gold, lead, mercury, natural gas, petroleum, silver, tin, and zinc.[25] In addition, their calculations predicted that the world would run out of arable land by 1999.[26] The Club of Rome, and others, based their beliefs on ". . . one simple fact— the earth is finite."[27] Unchecked economic growth would inevitably surpass earthly limits, leading to an ecological or economic collapse. They said that the world would know when this was happening, because "food prices will rise so high that some people will starve. . . . "[28] Obviously, The Club of Rome was wrong. Commodities are more plentiful, their prices are falling, and there are fewer people starving today, not more.

Because of these mistakes, today's predictions of economic problems are much more muted. Although we rarely hear such dire warnings of an earth out of balance, we do hear other limits to growth arguments. For example, Alan Greenspan, echoing the thoughts of other Federal Reserve Board members in testimony before Congress in June 1998, said, "I remain concerned that economic growth will run into constraints as the reservoir of unemployed people available to work is drawn down." He went on to say that unless the economy slowed we could witness a "buildup of pressures that could derail the current prosperity."[29] Other pessimistic warnings by economists—that the stock market is in a bubble, consumers and businesses are too leveraged, and wages are beginning to rise too fast—belong to the "limits to growth" family of economic theories. No wonder economics is called the "dismal science."

Just as Malthus and the Club of Rome were wrong, however, so are the modern-day dismal scientists. Compare the numerical views of Malthus with the network of fax machines. While modern-day dismal scientists see only a static future in which resources eventually are used up, the New Era is built on increasing returns where additions to the network create more value, not less.

Which of these views comes closer to the truth? The economy has shown no signs of having limits. In fact, standards of living, wealth, growth, and opportunity continue to rise as they have for thousands of years. Lincoln saw this and it should not be a surprise for those who believe in the "fire of genius" and the spirit of entrepreneurial capitalism. Ideas stoke the fire of growth and only by taking the freedom of having ideas away from people can the fire be doused. Today, that fire is burning brighter than it ever has in the United States and living standards are beginning to explode upward as a result. In the years ahead, the optimistic view of the world will be even easier to defend than before.

MACHINE OR LIVING ECOSYSTEM

The reason that the pessimists are wrong is that they continue to analyze the economy using models built in the industrial age. They view the economy as a machine that can overheat or that needs a tune-up every so often. To be fair, the view that the economy is a machine has its roots in U.S. history. Americans conquered a vast continent, built railroads across it, invented wonderful things, and won two world wars by organizing. As Thomas Hughes wrote in his book, *American Genesis*, "During the era of technological enthusiasm [1870–1970], the characteristic endeavor was inventing, developing, and organizing large technological systems. . . ."[30]

Our success in these endeavors led many to believe that we could manage the economy like Henry Ford managed a car plant. By moving tax rates, regulations, or government subsidies up and down or by tweaking interest rates, the government and the Federal Reserve could prevent the machine from breaking. This type of economic management has been labeled "fine-tuning." However, as the 1970s taught us, this approach to economic policy does not work. The end result of the economic fine-tuning experiment was double digit unemployment and inflation.

Fine-tuning is impossible for a simple reason. As Michael Rothschild in his book, *Bionomics*, pointed out, "The capitalist economy can best be comprehended as a living ecosystem."[31] It is not a machine. A machine's temperature can be measured and its useful life can be estimated by watching similar machines, but an economy cannot be measured effectively. As shown, if our statisticians cannot accurately measure inflation or productivity, they cannot measure growth either. Attempting to manage a system that is not measurable is a recipe for disaster.

The attempts at fine-tuning continue, however. The most prominent fine-tuners today are the economists at the Federal Reserve. In 1996 and 1997, the Fed consistently argued that the economy was close to overheating and that a preemptive tightening in monetary policy was necessary.

They argued this by making two points: Unemployment was too low, and high stock prices showed that investors were "irrationally exuberant." The Fed's models forecast that low unemployment would eventually cause wages and inflation to rise. Their models also showed that the stock market was overvalued and that a crash could hurt the economy. These facts, they argued, warranted intervention so that the stock market would not get too high and that low unemployment would not cause inflation.

These views, however, did not take into account America's technological revolution. The computer is changing every business in the world. The strength in productivity is holding prices down and driving wages up. More importantly, the boom in technology is creating incredible profit opportunities, which deserve to be valued highly in the stock market. The economy is fundamentally different today than it was 25 years ago and the models that the Fed uses to measure it are inadequate.

For example, 25 years ago, the library, door-to-door salesmen, and an occasional small bookstore were just about the only places to get books. Today, mega-bookstores, online bookstores, and virtual bookstores exist. Clearly something has changed and using old models to interpret it is a huge mistake.

When libraries were the major source for books, employment opportunities in the book delivery business were limited. As wealth rose and consumers could afford to buy books rather than wait for books to be returned to the library, bookstores began to proliferate. In the early 1980s, Crown Books, Inc. opened mega-bookstores and discounted books heavily by using the technology available at that time. Remember alphabetical listings on microfiche? While not real-time data, this technology was better and faster than any other alternative at the time.

Today, the computer has allowed the creation of even larger bookstores. Barnes and Noble and Borders stores carry upwards of 150,000+ book titles under one roof, and amazingly, because of computerized inventory systems, they know where they all are—in real time. They also sponsor book clubs and have become very much like the libraries I remember as a child. But the story does not stop there. In 1994, Jeffrey Bezos started Amazon.com and the book delivery business was changed again. But innovation continues. Virtual books can now be downloaded right from the Internet into a book-shaped computer that is designed to hold books in computer files and display them on a backlit screen.

The point is not to tell a history of the book business, but to show how technology has caused a rapid proliferation of New Era businesses in a field once dominated by Old Era libraries. In addition, this short history shows why models of the economy built in the industrial age do not work. Obviously, each one of these new businesses must hire workers and, at least initially, the old businesses continue to operate. Old Era firms and New Era firms coexist during the initial stages of the transition. This duplication causes the unemployment rate to decline even more than the strength of the recovery alone would suggest.

Traditional Keynesian-based economic models immediately assume that this drop in unemployment will increase inflation because low unemployment causes wages to rise; but the decline in unemployment caused by the invention of lower-cost delivery systems in the book business cannot cause inflation. In fact, the reason that these businesses are proliferating is they can provide the same or even better service at a lower cost.

In this case, it is clear that low unemployment is associated with falling prices, not rising prices. The Phillips Curve is completely wrong. In fact, low unemployment and the higher real wages that it causes actually signal a vibrant and growing economy that is experiencing deflation. Prices are falling because productivity is increasing as new and more efficient processes of production, distribution, and sales are proliferating. Interestingly, rising real wages will eventually hurt bookstores that do not increase productivity and lower costs. Rising real wages and an inability to raise productivity caused Crown Books to file Chapter 11 bankruptcy in 1998. Old Era technology did not stand a chance against the online model of business developed by Amazon.com. In fact, Crown Books may have been the first Old Era company to be truly "amazoned," a term used to describe how new business models based in new technology can destroy those businesses that cannot compete.

Models of the economy that treat it as a machine miss these dynamic changes and underestimate the wealth that the new economy can create. Fears of inflation or excessive economic strength are misplaced and by trying to fine-tune the economy, great harm can be done. It takes faith to believe in the market, but free markets, more than any other system, have earned that faith. In fact, the economy will automatically take care of the problems that cause many economists to worry. Old Era firms that do not increase productivity will go out of business. New Era firms that use productivity to lower price will thrive. This dynamic churning that underlies every economic system is the natural process of wealth creation. Not only is the economy self-correcting, but it also behaves like a living ecosystem.

LIMITLESS GROWTH

Although the innovations we have seen during the past two decades are impressive, they pale in comparison to the innovation we will see in the future. Every industry will feel the force of change and every industry will be the better for it. But the change will be traumatic. For example, the Commerce Department, in a report issued during June 1999, estimated that by 2006 "almost one-half of U.S. workers will be employed by industries that produce information technology or are intensive users of it."[32] "Consumer sales over the Internet were about $10 billion [in 1998] and are expected to top $100 billion by 2003. Business to business commerce over the Internet was $43 billion [in 1998] and is expected to be $1.3 trillion in 2003."[33] History shows that the growth of online sales is exponential in nature. For example, in 1998, Amazon.com was 4 years old and reported total sales of $610 million. This was nearly four times the $150 million in sales it took Wal-Mart 15 years to produce.

Egghead Software closed all its retail outlets in early 1998 and moved its business to the Web. Guess what? Its sales rose. The shift is just beginning to take place. Although retail outlets will not disappear, growth will taper off. Overnight package delivery will explode, and costs will continue to fall. As costs fall, demand will continue to rise and living standards will rise with them.

The rise in the U.S. stock market and the explosion of Internet stock prices are signs of the power of the Web. Opportunities are expanding and there are no limits to growth. In an online mall, there are no checkout lines and floor space is not limited. Information and availability are the truly valuable commodities today and the heart of innovation and growth is the network. The amount of information being shared every minute of every day dwarfs the amount of information available to people in the Middle Ages or even during the midst of the Industrial Revolution. The reason for the explosion of information is that the networked economy allows the replication of information at virtually no cost. As information plummets in cost, it proliferates rapidly. Because information is the DNA of economic innovation, its proliferation virtually guarantees more innovation and with it much more economic stability.

Imagine 500 years ago. For an Italian to learn about the Gutenberg printing press, not only would the information need to travel hundreds of miles by word of mouth, but the Italian would also need to travel in order to see it. There were no trains, planes, or automobiles; there was no telephone. As a result, travel was risky and took a long time. During the Industrial Revolution, for a European entrepreneur to learn more about U.S. production techniques, an Atlantic crossing and a long train ride were the least that was required. Once the information was gathered the trip needed to be reversed. Although the round trip likely took less than a year, and was certainly faster than a fifteenth-century trip from Rome to Vienna, the cost of information was quite high.

Today, the same information can be gleaned after a few-hour plane flight. Even faster, a phone call, teleconference, or even a perusal of web pages allows information that once took years to disseminate to be shared in minutes. Moreover, as the network expands, both the value of and the speed at which information travels will increase dramatically.

THE TECHNOLOGY EXPLOSION

One way to measure the explosion of New Era technologies is to look at the share of business magazines that are devoted to high-tech ads or reporting. In September 1977, a count of pages in *Business Week* showed just 5 percent of the pages devoted to what we would consider high technology. In September 1987, the number of pages had grown to 20 percent of the magazine. By September 1997, the number of pages had climbed to 60 percent and today that total is close to 75 percent.

The explosion in New Era technology is remaking our world in so many ways that it is impossible to know them all. Suffice it to say that our economy is going to be totally remade by the computer and the network of the future. Radio and television will be broadcast over the Internet, every automobile will have an Internet connection, and cellular telephones will be as powerful as desktop PCs in no time. Efficiency will continue to increase and costs will continue to fall. The distance between producer and consumer will virtually disappear and information will continue to rise in value relative to hard goods. Do not underestimate these changes. There is a reason that high-tech stock prices have risen to such high levels and it is not irrational exuberance.

The astute use of technology can dramatically impact production costs and we are in the infancy of its use. A good example of this is the airline industry. As long ago as 1995, United Airlines invested $10 million into computers for its San Francisco–based maintenance headquarters. These computers are the heart of United's aircraft maintenance information system (AMIS). "The newest generation of commercial jet aircraft . . . takes in data on as many as 600 parameters from tiny onboard computerized sensors. . . . Cockpit crews check diagnostics with laptop computers. Ground stations track performance, route parts and service crews where needed, and perform maintenance trend analyses that save millions of dollars in labor and parts inventory. Most important, by constantly monitoring aircraft, a tech-savvy airline staff minimizes the need for expensive, unscheduled service stops and groundings."[34] The savings from this system is as much as $200 million a year for United even though many of its planes are older and not fully integrated into the system. These savings go straight to the bottom line, allowing costs to fall and earnings to increase. Moreover, a positive feedback loop causes demand for flying to increase as schedules and safety become more reliable and prices fall.

Checkout scanners achieve the same kind of cost savings for retailers and for manufacturers. By connecting manufacturers, warehouses, and retailers, scanners and the real-time information they gather allow inventory levels to fall at all levels of the distribution chain. Just-in-time inventories only work when information is real time. The network allows that to happen; and given the increase in online shopping, it is becoming increasingly important for retailers to shave costs. Internet sales sites can keep very low inventory, bill customers immediately, and pay suppliers later. The result is huge sales per dollar of capital compared with retail outlets which pay for bricks and mortar plus inventory.

While the Internet is becoming middleman in retail, it threatens to eliminate the middleman in many other industries. For example, because of the ability of the Internet to deliver digital music to consumers, musicians are increasingly making the decision to skip the record label and move straight to the Internet. The traditional power in the music industry is slowly moving to the artist and away from the studio. After all, it is the process of creation that gives music its value, not the process of stamping CDs. If the creator of music can control its distribution too, then prices will fall dramatically while choices multiply.

THE RELENTLESS PUSH TO EFFICIENCY

The efficiency of the Internet is changing every industry worldwide. In addition to retail sales and stock trading, Internet banking is just around the corner and online education is taking off. The only thing holding us back today is bandwidth; however, we are laying thousands of miles of fiber-optic cable every year and its capacity continues to increase. The network is beginning to tap into the power of itself and the potential of sharing the computing power of all our computers is immense.

Many books have been and will be written about technology and its impact on business. This book is not one of *those* books. Instead, this book attempts to show that today's technology truly is different. The economic paradigm is changing and investors must understand this fact. The New Era of Wealth depends on many things, but without technology, it would not exist.

References

[1] Landes, David S. 1998. *The wealth and poverty of nations: Why some are so rich and some are so poor,* 1st ed. New York: W.W. Norton & Company.
[2] Ibid.
[3] Ibid.
[4] Page 191.
[5] Page 300.
[6] Page 300.
[7] Encarta CD Encyclopedia.
[8] Landes, p. 305.
[9] *Historical statistics of the U.S. 1800–1970,* Dept. of Commerce.

[10] Landes, p. 307.

[11] Gilder, George. 1989. *Microcosm: The quantum revolution in economics and technology.* New York: Simon and Schuster.

[12] Gilder, p. 40, Mead quote.

[13] Gilder quote, p. 38.

[14] Quoted by Gilder in *Microcosm*, p. 40.

[15] Gilder, ibid.

[16] Gilder, p. 106.

[17] Davis, Bob. 1999. Think big. *The Wall Street Journal*, 11 January, p. R14.

[18] Bannock, Graham, Baxter, R. E., and Davis, Evan. 1992. *The penguin dictionary of economics*, 5th ed. London: Penguin Books.

[19] Browning, John and Reiss, Spencer. *Wired Magazine*, "Encyclopedia of the New Economy - Part III." May 1998, page 105.

[20] Arthur, Brian W. 1994. *Increasing returns and path dependence in the economy*, 4th ed. Ann Arbor, MI: University of Michigan Press, p. 4.

[21] Kelly, Kevin. 1998. *New rules for the new economy.* New York: Penguin Books, p. 25.

[22] Laderman, Jeffrey M. and Smith, Geoff. 1998. Amazon.com, the wide world of commerce. *Business Week*, 14 December, pp. 106–122.

[23] Malthus, Thomas. 1798. *An essay on the principle of population*, pp. 37, 38; Patricia James, p. 62.

[24] Meadows, Donella H., Meadows, Dennis L., Raners, Jørgen and Brehrens III, William W. 1972. The limits to growth: A report for the Club of Rome Project on the predicament of mankind (a Potomas Associates book). New York: Universe Books. Graphics by Potomac Associates, p. 23.

[25] Meadows et al., pp. 56–59.

[26] Meadows et al., p. 50.

[27] Meadows et al., p. 86.

[28] Meadows et al., p. 52.

[29] Greenspan, Alan. 1998. Testimony before the Joint Economic Committee, U.S. Congress, June 10.

[30] Hughes, Thomas. 1989. *American Genesis: A history of the American genius for invention*, 10th ed. New York: Penguin Books.

[31] Rothschild, Michael. 1990. *Bionomics: The inevitability of capitalism*, 1st ed. New York: Henry Holt and Company.

[32] Page, Susan. 1999. E-world fuels U.S. economy, report says. *USA Today*, 22 June, p. 1.

[33] Wolf, Richard. 1999. Billions of dollars hang over Internet tax debate. *USA Today*, 22 June, p. 1.

[34] Tosi, Umberto. 1995. Digital air, *Forbes,* 4 December, p. 100.

2

GLOBALIZATION AND ECONOMIC EFFICIENCY

The advances of technology are making the world a smaller place. Money, information, and goods can move faster than ever before and globalization is a key trend in making certain that resources are used in the most efficient manner. As an exclamation point to these developments, my wife and I visited the Lake Louise area of Canada on a ski trip late in 1998. Our hotel had a combined Internet and game room. Whenever I walked past that room, more people were using one of the four computers than were ever playing board games. In itself, this is a sign of the times, but I tell this story to make a different point.

The fact that hotel guests were using free computers is not that surprising. What was surprising is how they were being used. The only time I ventured into that room, I sat next to a twenty-something Canadian who was day trading U.S. stocks over the hotel's computer using the Internet. During our brief conversation he asked me what I thought about DELL and told me that he felt that their quarterly earnings report would be an upside surprise.

Some will read this anecdote and sneer that it proves a "bubble" exists in financial markets. These pessimists will be reminded of the 1920s, when even shoeshine men were giving out stock tips. In addition, they will view this young trader as a threat to markets. After all, the pessimists will say his capital isn't patient and if stocks start to fall he will just add to the volatility, but this pessimistic view is wrong.

In its essence this story is quintessential New Era. Borders are collapsing, capital is moving rapidly at little cost, and the world is getting smaller but deeper, every day. Technology is opening frontiers and creating freedoms that were only dreams 20 years ago. This young Canadian is voting with his capital and the world is listening. Why? Because capital, access, and opportunity are the water of the New Era. In the past, cities and even whole countries were built around access to water. That's why Chicago was built on Lake Michigan, San Francisco was built on a bay, London evolved around its Atlantic Ocean ports, and Vienna was built on the Danube River. These waterways and ports are not only beautiful, but they also made transportation possible and allowed low-cost access to trade channels and the global economy.

Today, our young Canadian friend is freely adding to the river of capital with his hard-earned money, and one of the fastest growing lakes that this river is feeding is high-tech investment in the United States. Like water, capital always flows downhill, not uphill. "Why fight it," water and capital seem to say. Downhill for capital means that it flows to the places where it is treated best—to the places where taxes are low, regulations are minimal, and risk and return have a good balance. In addition, capital looks for opportunity. A dynamic, growing, and opportunity-filled economy always attracts the capital necessary to fulfill its potential. The United States has become such a place, and technology is the reason.

Do not take this statement the wrong way. All the Internet trading sites in the world cannot make an economy strong or guarantee wealth. After all, both Russia and Japan have easy access to great ocean ports. Nonetheless, their economies are suffering because they do not treat capital well, which is a shame in today's world where capital is readily available. The history of the last 200 years clearly shows that when countries start to do the things that capital likes, their economies prosper. This is especially true today. The speed and mobility of capital in this high-tech age have created a global economic environment very sensitive to shifting policy decisions.

Just as domestic economic models have broken down, what used to make sense in global economics is no longer appropriate. When capital was not as mobile, massive systems of redistribution and the high tax rates necessary to pay for them did not reduce competitiveness as much as they do today. As the world becomes smaller because of technology, however, capital moves more rapidly and sources of competition increasingly come from the outside. Today, an economy is punished for attempting to protect its citizens or corporations from competition. Economic efficiency is being forced on the world and protected people or companies have no incentive to increase their competitiveness.

Fed Chairman Alan Greenspan in an April 1998 speech, pointed out that in the years following World War II, "in economies not broadly subject to international trade, competition was not as punishing to the less efficient as it is today." He continued by saying that in today's world any country that has a large social safety net must choose between "shortfalls in living standards . . . or loosening the social safety net. . . ."[1] Technology has increased the speed of transactions, broken down investment borders, and allowed competition on a global scale.

Even companies that once had a monopoly in a small market or geographic niche are facing fierce competition. The reach of the networked economy is immense. For example, dental manufacturers in Germany, which have traditionally held a mini-monopoly producing for dentists within a 100-mile radius, now face competition from all over the world. Today, dentists can send pictures over the Web, or molds through overnight delivery, and then pay for products by wiring money or even using a credit card. Thus, those local dental manufacturers which thought they were immune now face global competition.

When a company must compete against foreign competitors that pay lower taxes or face less regulation, the battle is over before it starts. The initial response by many global businesses and government leaders is to use government to block the competition. Often this protection is in the form of tariffs or outright bans on imports. Another political response is to allow the competition, but then promise any worker that loses his or her job unemployment benefits. Either way, the government is not fixing the original problem (high taxes, for example) and is, in essence, preserving inefficiency. The end result is a less vibrant economy which will not attract foreign or domestic investment and will most likely run a trade surplus.

Interestingly, the super-competitive environment created by the networked economy has exposed these pressures as much more than mere theories. But they did not just build up overnight; it has taken at least 20 years. George Gilder put it this way in 1989.

> Even observers who comprehend the nature of information technology, however, often fail to understand its radical effect on international economics. The decline in the value of raw materials entails an equal decline in the value of geography. In an age when men can inscribe new worlds on a grain of sand, particular territories are fast losing economic significance.
>
> Not only are the natural resources under the ground rapidly declining in value, but the companies and capital above the ground can rapidly leave. . . . Capital is no longer manacled to machines and places, nations and jurisdictions. Capital markets are now global and on line twenty-four hours a day. People—scientists, workers, and entrepreneurs—can leave at the speed of a 747, or even a Concorde. Companies can move in weeks. . . Geography has become economically trivial. . . . It is people and ideas that matter, not places and things. . . . As most economists see international exchange, goods come first, and capital movements follow to compensate for imbalances of trade. But in the quantum era, capital markets are far more efficient than goods markets, which are hobbled with transportation cost, cultural differences, and protectionism. . . . Therefore capital movements now often come first and goods follow.[2]

These thoughts seem so clear and obvious, but many economists and opinion makers still do not understand. The trade deficit takes center stage in many models of the economy. When it goes up, this is thought to be a bad sign for an economy. When it goes down, it is thought to be a good sign. Talk show host and perennial Republican presidential candidate, Patrick Buchanan, is one of the most vocal proponents of this theory. What he is ignoring is that capital is leading the charge today and only by attracting capital is an economy able to compete. While the U.S. trade deficit rose to nearly $300 billion in 1998, it was swamped by the size of foreign securities market activities. Data for 1998 is delayed, but in 1997, foreign purchases and sales of U.S. securities climbed to $13 trillion, a 64-fold increase from 1980. The size of financial transactions far outweighs the size of trade flows. Focusing on the trade deficit misses this key point.

During the Industrial Revolution, the United States consistently ran trade deficits. In fact, for 72 of 110 years between 1790 and 1900, the United States ran a trade deficit with the rest of the world.[3] The United States was attracting investors from around the world during those years and using those resources to import goods, services, and machines. The trade deficit existed at the same time that the U.S. growth rates were vaulting ahead of the world. The same thing is happening today. The United States is leading the world in high-tech innovation and attracting capital that fuels the fire of that innovation. At the same time, U.S. manufacturing facilities are moving overseas and then exporting back home at lower prices.

Contrary to the popular belief that says U.S. jobs will be hurt by moving plants overseas, U.S. unemployment was lower in 1998 than it has been since 1969. The dollars spent importing goods into the United States are recycled back through the country as investments. This capital inflow must equal the trade deficit—after all, the accounts must balance. The capital inflow and investment creates jobs and opportunities, while cheaper imports allow incomes to stretch further.

And, as if it were not enough to worry about trade deficits, some economists stay awake at night worrying that capital inflows will stop. As with the trade deficit, this worry is unfounded. According to the *World Competitiveness Yearbook (WCY)* published by the International Institute for Management Development, a foundation based in Lausanne, Switzerland, the United States has been the most competitive nation in the world for the past 5 years.

The WCY rankings measure the success nations are having in providing "an environment that sustains the competitiveness of enterprises."[4] It uses two types of data to capture both quantifiable and qualitative information—172 different pieces of hard criteria and an 87-item questionnaire returned by 4,314 executives. The data are divided into eight categories or input factors that impact competitiveness. These factors include rankings on the domestic economy, internationalization, government, finance, infrastructure, management, science and technology, and people.

According to the WCY, while the United States has remained the most competitive nation during the past 5 years, both Germany and Japan have plummeted. Of forty-six countries, Germany has fallen from sixth in 1994 to fourteenth in 1998. Japan has fallen from third in 1994 to eighteenth in

1998.[5] Interestingly, both Japan and Germany run trade surpluses. These surpluses reflect weak domestic economies and a lack of attractive investment opportunities. The decline in competitiveness of Japan and Germany should not be a surprise.

For example, until April 1999, Japanese individual tax rates reached as high as 63 percent, while the corporate tax rate was over 50 percent. On top of these taxes, Japan also has a 5 percent value-added tax and has increased government spending by nearly $1 trillion during the past 9 years in an attempt to boost its economy. Japan is now running a budget deficit that may reach over 10 percent of GDP, even larger than the massive U.S. budget deficits of the mid-1980s. To be fair, Japan instituted large individual and corporate tax cuts in April 1999, but the value-added tax remains in place and there are some concerns that the tax cuts will not be permanent.

Germany is worse. The top marginal income tax rate in Germany is 53 percent. There is also a 5.5 percent surcharge that is paid on income taxes due in order to finance unification with East Germany. German citizens, who are members of an officially recognized church, tithe by paying a surcharge on their federal taxes of 8 or 9 percent. The government then passes this on to the church. In addition, the employee portion of the social security tax is 13.7 percent (the employer also pays 13.7 percent).[6] To top it all off, Germany also has a nationwide value-added tax that increases the price of all goods by 16 percent.[7] These high taxes combined with labor market rigidities and very generous unemployment benefits have pushed the unemployment rate in Germany to above 10 percent.

Because of the increase in global economic competition, these policies are even more painful today than they would have been 20 years ago. A recent National Bureau of Economic Research study, by Rosanne Altshuler from Rutgers and two economists with the U.S. Treasury Department, Harry Grubert and T. Scott Newlon, found that taxes play a significant role in decisions about investment abroad. According to their findings, "taxes exert a strong influence on location decisions," and "foreign investment of manufacturing firms is sensitive to differences in host country tax rates." In addition, they suggest that the investment decisions may have become "more sensitive to differences in host country taxes in recent years."[8] These findings confirm what the New Era is telling us: Competition is increasing and investment flows are influenced by taxes more than ever.

High taxes and banking problems in Japan, despite recent signs of life, have mired it in recession and its economy appears years from shaking off all of its problems. Germany and many other European countries, so too burdened by big government and high taxes, also are underperforming the United States and are witnessing capital flight. Many European countries are counting on the *euro* to help boost growth.

However, in 1998—the year of the euro—Daimler-Benz bought Chrysler and Duetsche Bank bought Bankers Trust. If growth opportunities in Europe were truly improving then why would these world-class companies choose to expand outside of Europe? Moreover, many believe that U.S. markets are overpriced, which makes these investments doubly dumb in the eyes of the pessimists. The truth is, however, these economies are not as attractive as the United States is from an investment standpoint.

Despite the attempts by many economists to dismiss the impact of taxes and regulation, the contrast between Japan and Europe on one hand and the United States on the other is crystal clear—policies matter. In these countries, bad government policy has eroded the benefits of one of the greatest technology booms in history. Obviously, the United States stands well above the rest of the world in terms of its ability to utilize capital and provide dynamic investment opportunities.

Despite bad policies in Germany, the German stock market has performed very well in recent years and the German DAX 30 stock index rose by 17 percent per year between 1993 and 1998. This was only slightly less than the 19.2 percent annual average increase in the Dow Jones Industrial Average of thirty U.S. stocks during the same period. However, these huge company stock indices do not always reflect the true underlying strength of an economy. The companies that make up the DAX 30 index in Germany are "global" firms, not German firms. In many cases, large German companies have more employees outside Germany than they do inside. The increase in stock values for these firms is a better indicator of worldwide growth than it is of German economic strength. For example, Siemens AG, one of the largest German firms, had a total workforce of 438,000 on March 31, 1999. This workforce was made up of 244,000 employees outside of Germany and 194,000 in Germany. Moreover, the entire increase of 22,000 employees that Siemens reported in the 6 months between September 30, 1998, and March 31, 1999, occurred outside of Germany while the domestic workforce remained unchanged. Despite Germany's high unemployment rate (over 10 percent in early 1999), taxes and regulations drive the cost of labor so high that it pays to expand internationally rather than domestically.

Broader German stock indices that include midsize companies and better represent the economy have significantly underperformed U.S. stocks. For example, between the end of 1994 and the end of 1998, the DAX 100 index increased by 122 percent and the MDAX (mid-cap German companies) increased just 58 percent. During the same period the S&P 500 climbed 168 percent. But comparing these stock indices leaves the real weakness of the German financial system hidden.

At the end of 1998, Germany had only 741 publicly traded companies versus over 9,000 in the United States. Even more astounding is that the United States had 506 Initial Public Offerings (IPOs) between September 1997 and September 1998,[9] while Germany had just 218 IPOs during the past 10 years (1989 to 1998).[10]

In Germany, securities laws make it difficult, if not impossible, for small companies to issue public stock. This limited access to capital markets robs the fuel of the New Era economy and keeps the entrepreneurial fire burning dimly. The German and Japanese systems rely on big banks that find it difficult to lend to small entrepreneurial companies. This smothers the ability of the economy to innovate. To prosper in the New Era, banks and securities markets must learn how to lend to entrepreneurs wearing jeans, not suits. Economies that limit the ability of these entrepreneurs to find capital will pay for it through lower growth rates, higher unemployment, and a brain drain. When investing in foreign companies, stick with the large international players that are growing along with the expansion in world trade. Be careful of small companies which are often capital starved and taxed heavily.

THE DOLLAR IS KING IN
THE GLOBAL ECONOMY

The dominance of the United States in the global economy and the weakness of our competitors have led to another positive factor impacting U.S. financial markets. The dollar has become the world's currency of choice. As a sign of how strong and universal the dollar has become, even Cuba is using dollars. What is most amazing about this is that the United States has an embargo on trade with Cuba. Therefore, the only way that Cubans can establish a fair value for the dollar is by trading with other countries. If the dollar retains its value while moving through second- and third-party hands, it truly is an amazing store of value.

In 1995, 1997, 1998, and again in 1999, one after another, countries around the world saw their currencies lose up to 60 percent of their value versus the U.S. dollar. Mexico, Thailand, Malaysia, Indonesia, Russia, and Brazil have experienced a dramatic decline in the value of their currencies. There are two reasons for the devaluation of these currencies. First, the dollar has been super strong because of tight Fed policy. Second, these countries mismanaged economic policy. They printed an excess supply of money, while following fiscal policies that reduce the demand for investments in their economies. When supply exceeds demand, prices fall.

In each of these countries, the central bank printed too much money. More importantly, the International Monetary Fund asked each of them to raise taxes. Increasing, or threatening to increase, taxes lowers the demand for investments in any country. The result is inflationary pressures and capital flight. Eventually the currency must fall. The New Era global economy does not allow mistakes in policy to last for long.

For example, in early 1999, the Brazilian *real* experienced a 40 percent devaluation relative to the dollar. This devaluation was predictable. The Brazilian Central Bank had nearly doubled the supply of the *real* in the previous

2 years. Between December 1996 and December 1997, the Brazilian monetary base grew by 60 percent, followed by another increase of 22 percent in 1998. The Brazilian government then began to implement tax increases imposed by the IMF as conditions for loans. The tax increases, especially an increase in corporate taxes and one that nearly doubled a tax on banking transactions, reduced the demand for Brazilian investments, increased capital flight, and lowered potential growth in Brazil. The combination of the excess supply of money and the reduction in demand for Brazilian investments led to unstoppable downward pressures on the *real*. Despite promises from Brazil not to devalue, it was inevitable.

The devaluation was a death sentence for the Brazilian economy. Virtually overnight, the purchasing power of Brazilian citizens and the value of Brazilian companies on world markets plummeted by 40 percent. Any Brazilian who had debt in U.S. dollars, but earnings in Brazilian *reals*, saw their personal debt burden rise by 40 percent as well. The inevitable inflation and the higher interest rates that devaluation will cause guaranteed a serious recession. The combination of inflation and recession lowers living standards, drives up unemployment, reduces investment, and will lower tax receipts to the government.

Interestingly, one of the most successful investors in the world, George Soros, blames capitalism (not government mistakes) for global financial problems. As he wrote in 1998, ". . . financial markets have recently acted . . . like a wrecking ball, knocking over one economy after another."[11] Soros proposed the creation of new international institutions to control the flow of money around the world. As an analogy, he compared the global capitalist system to a "gigantic circulatory system, sucking up capital . . . at the center and then pumping it out to the periphery. . . ."[12] He then suggests that the problem with today's financial markets is that the center is no longer pumping to the periphery.

This analogy is fatally flawed, however. The global financial system has no center. It is true that most of the world's capital at some point flows through New York, Chicago, Los Angeles, London, or Tokyo, but the owners of that capital live all over the world. The periphery is the center and the center is the periphery. In the global financial system of the New Era, capital will flow to where it is treated the best. That is why capital has flowed to the United States from South America and Asia. It is flowing away from countries that make policy mistakes. The idea that more control at the center is needed is anathema to the whole process of free markets and the New Era of free-flowing capital and information. Soros, like Keynes before him, blames problems on markets, not policies.

But this is just an excuse. Bad monetary and fiscal policy, often designed by the IMF, is the real cause of global problems. The only explanation for why government leaders continue to follow these policies is that by blaming markets, they avoid blaming themselves. This is an even greater disaster in today's New Era economy. Remember, when the IMF moves into a country, investors leave, and when governments attempt to control capital, it will flee.

Interestingly, some countries are making decisions that could end much of the damage that global financial market turmoil brings to their economies. Argentina, for example, is seriously studying the impact of eliminating its own currency and using dollars instead. This would vanquish any possibility of devaluation and provide international investors with the certainty that they need to make long-term investments in Argentina.

This movement by Argentina is just another sign of the dominance of the United States in the global financial system. The dollar has become king. More transactions in Russia take place in dollars than in rubles; and in Mexico there are now two economies. The U.S. dollar–based part of the Mexican economy is performing very well, but the peso-based economy is still suffering from inflation and recession. The instability of currencies around the world can be fixed only by moving to a fixed monetary standard of some sort. Following World War II, that standard was the Bretton Woods system. Since President Nixon removed the United States from that system in the early 1970s, the costs of uncertainty, inflation, and devaluation have been immense.

The only question remaining is how a new system will evolve. Some believe that an international tribunal of experts, speaking from very large podiums, is the only way to reestablish a stable world monetary system. Others, including myself, believe that a new order can arrive spontaneously. Europe has decided on the first path. The major countries of Europe, excluding Britain, added a new layer of bureaucracy above their own governments to establish and manage a new European currency called the euro.

The second, or spontaneous, path is occurring while you read this book. Individuals worldwide are choosing to use the U.S. dollar as their currency of choice. They are doing so because they believe it will be a better store of value over time. In some cases South American citizens have had their life savings wiped out by devaluation and inflation two or three times in their lifetime and they are now sick of it.

Interestingly, if Argentina does officially switch to the dollar, other countries will be forced to do the same. By guaranteeing that currency instability will not visit Argentina, the Argentine government will create the number one most attractive and competitive economy in South America. The only way that other South American countries will be able to compete is by also moving to a dollar standard.

With South America moving toward a dollar standard, and Europe instituting the euro, many analysts believe that the world is moving toward three main currency blocks—the dollar, euro, and yen. Although this fact may be true, the dominant currency in the world remains the dollar. The reason is simple: A strong currency is only possible with a strong economy.

Because the United States has the strongest economy in the world, the dollar remains better than gold.

EVEN THE EURO WON'T COMPETE

To compete with the U.S. dollar, eleven European nations have agreed to switch to a common currency. This move to a single currency is a fabulous idea. The cost of foreign exchange trading will fall, transparency of pricing will help consumers, marketing costs will fall, and price stability will likely be maintained. However, the euro is not a panacea for European economic problems. Unemployment rates in Europe are above 10 percent, and economic growth rates have been one-half of U.S. growth rates. Moreover, recent large investments in the United States by some of Europe's largest companies reflect that the grander investment opportunities are really outside of Europe. The euro will not be a serious challenge to the dollar until Europe reforms its fiscal policies.

The savings from a shift to a single currency will not be enough to encourage more investment. The cost of foreign exchange transactions in comparison to the size of business deals is not that large—less than 1 percent of the total transactions cost. If it were larger, it would have impeded growth in world trade or foreign investment much more than it has during recent decades. For example, until the collapse of Asia in 1997, both trade and foreign investment grew faster than world GDP. With the global chaos that has spread since 1997, trade flows have slowed significantly. These trade flows have slowed because of overall economic uncertainty, not because of the cost of foreign exchange transactions. As a result, it is highly unlikely that the move to a single currency is going to bring a rush of new investment.

Unfortunately, the benefits of a single currency and the breakdown of trade barriers are being offset by a perverse set of developments. It would seem rational that when borders became open and a single currency was implemented, European countries would all move to make their tax rates equal by cutting them to the level of the country with the lowest tax rate. However, the European Community has moved in the opposite direction. For example, Ireland, the fastest growing economy in Europe, is under immense pressure to raise its low corporate tax rate because the European Community has decided that its low tax rates are "unfair competition" for the rest of the European Union. This is equivalent to Ford Motor Company asking General Motors to scrap its new high-tech machinery because it is "unfair" of GM to be so productive. Obviously, this is ridiculous. To be competitive Europe must cut its tax rates and the euro will not challenge the dollar until Europe is competitive. The dollar will continue to hold its dominant position as the world's most popular reserve currency as long as the United States remains committed to free markets, price stability, low taxes, and limited government.

In the end, a strong dollar and global demand for U.S. assets is providing a boost to U.S. asset values; however, this is a double-edged sword, not because this investment may slow or even stop in the future, but because the United States is benefiting at the expense of other countries. Capital flight from Brazil, Asia, Europe, and Canada is filling the lake of U.S. capital. While this is good for the United States in the short run, it is not good for the global economy in the long run.

Nonetheless, the New Era virtually guarantees that this will eventually turn around. The world is slowly learning what policies are needed for growth. While many countries will find it politically difficult to shift direction, eventually they will and their economies will begin to grow rapidly again. Despite fears that this will hurt the United States as investors move assets internationally, it will not. A vibrant and dynamic global economy will increase growth rates for every country. World economic growth is not a zero-sum game, nor is it an overly interconnected game. No matter what the rest of the world is doing, following the right policies will keep any economy healthy. No matter how well, or how badly, the rest of the world's economies are performing, U.S. economic strength is in our hands.

And, as will be seen in the next two chapters, the United States will continue to follow the right policies in the New Era. Thus, capital will continue to flow into the United States and global trade and investment will expand. Moreover, as other countries move toward the right policies, the world economy will benefit. This will boost opportunities for investors in new and dramatic ways.

References

[1] Greenspan, Alan. 1998. *The ascendance of market capitalism.* Speech delivered to the American Society of Newspaper Editors, Washington, D.C., April 2.

[2] Gilder, pp. 355, 356.

[3] U.S. Department of Commerce, Bureau of the Census. 1975. *Historical statistics of the United States, Colonial times to 1970.* Bicentennial edition.

[4] International Institute for Management Development. 1998. *World competitiveness yearbook.* www.imd.ch/wcy/brochure.html

[5] Ibid.

[6] Friedlich, Mark. 1998. *Individual taxes—worldwide summary 1998,* PricewaterhouseCooper LLP.

[7] Friedlich, Mark. 1998. *Corporate taxes—worldwide summary 1998,* PricewaterhouseCooper LLP.

[8] Altshuler, Rosanne, Grubert, Harry, and Newlon, T. Scott. 1998, January. *Has U.S. investment abroad become more sensitive to tax rates?* NBER Working Paper #6383.

[9] NASDAQ, 1999, at http://www.nasdaq.com/mktofmkts/62inipub.stm

[10] Data gathered from Deutsche Boerse AG historical statisitics and market data.

[11] Soros, George. 1998. *The crisis of global capitalism: open society endangered,* 2nd ed. New York: Perseus Book Group.

[12] Ibid.

3

THE END OF BIG GOVERNMENT

W e are beginning to see, the New Era of Wealth that began during the early 1980s is not just coincidence or luck. Technology and globalization have played an important role, but one of the most important reasons for the boom has been a nearly 180-degree turn in government policy beginning in the late 1970s and early 1980s. The reason for the change in direction was that the Great Society programs and fine-tuning experiments of the late 1960s and early 1970s were an absolute economic disaster. Faced with the results of big government, Americans had two choices: Either accept the horrible economic condition of the early 1980s as fate, or determine what went wrong and change it.

Thank goodness the American people supported change and thus the third trend supporting the New Era was put into place. Interestingly, while many politicians will suggest that Republicans are responsible for the turnaround in fiscal policy, this is not completely true. Believe it or not, in 1979 and 1980 the Joint Economic Committee of Congress, chaired by Democrat Senator Lloyd Bentsen, published documents in support of a new idea in economics called "supply-side economics."

In the introduction to the Joint Economic Report of 1980, titled "Plugging in the Supply Side," Senator Bentsen wrote the following:

> The 1980 annual report signals the start of a New Era of economic thinking. The past has been dominated by economists who focused almost exclusively on the demand side of the economy and who, as a result, were trapped into believing that there is an inevitable trade-off between unemployment and inflation .
> . . . The Committee's 1980 report says that steady economic growth, created by productivity gains . . . and a gradual reduction in the growth of the money supply . . . can reduce inflation significantly during the 1980's without increasing unemployment . . . . The Committee also recommends a targeted approach

to the Nation's structural economic problems and a deemphasis
of macro-economic fine tuning.[1]

As this excerpt shows, even politicians were learning that big government does not work. Government regulation, redistribution, and protectionism stymie economic innovation while taxes inhibit savings and
wealth accumulation. The United States has had two experiments with excessive government activism. The first was the New Deal of the 1930s. The
second was the Great Society programs of the 1960s and 1970s. The miserable performance of the stock markets and the economy in the 1930s and
again in the 1970s clearly show the damage that the expansion in government activism can cause. As an exclamation point, by the late 1980s, the
global experiment with communism had collapsed completely, putting to
rest the idea that governments could create wealth.

To understand why the size of government matters to economic
growth and financial markets, it is important to understand two ideas. The
first is that the history of mankind is a battle between wealth accumulation
and the redistribution of wealth. The second is Say's law: Supply creates
its own demand.

Both of these ideas, and their importance in explaining the creation of
wealth, become clear when we delve into a thought experiment I first en-
countered in Paul Zane Pilzer's book, *Unlimited Wealth*.[2] He asks us to
imagine an island with a population of ten people. Each of the inhabitants,
in order to survive, goes fishing every day and catches two fish. Therefore,
the island had a Gross Domestic Product (GDP) of twenty fish per day.

If two of the island's inhabitants risk starvation and take time out from
fishing to invent a boat and net, the island has a chance to improve its living standards. In Pilzer's example, two of the inhabitants do this and together are then able to catch twenty fish in a day, or ten each. This improvement is incredible in terms of fishing productivity. In fact, two
people now produce what it took all ten people to produce before.

This jump in productivity will shake up this island society and after
the invention the inhabitants have several different choices. Obviously, the
inhabitants can ignore the new productivity gains and continue to live on
the two fish they each catch. If this happens our two more productive inhabitants can take time off and enjoy leisure. Then again, the other residents could attempt to produce different goods (say fruits, vegetables, and
grains) or services (boat fixing or fish cleaning). They could then trade
these goods and services for the excess fish that the two entrepreneurs
catch. If the island's inhabitants take this opportunity, then the GDP of the
island will rise and wealth will increase. Each of the island's inhabitants
will now have a daily income of two fish *plus* whatever else the island
learns how to produce. The higher output of the island will allow it to store
and save, helping it to weather bad times or even allowing other residents
the chance to invent new goods and services.

This is how wealth is created. Entrepreneurs take risks and when they are successful, everyone is better off. This process of innovation destroys the idea of a zero-sum game that says when some people are successful others must suffer. Nonetheless, there are some political landmines along the way. Think about income distribution. Before the invention of the boat, each inhabitant had a daily income of two fish. After the invention of the boat, each of the entrepreneurs could produce ten fish in a day, while the other inhabitants caught their two. In other words, income distribution went from a 1:1 ratio to a 5:1 ratio. To some, this increase in the income for a few, despite the fact that income fell for none, is a bad sign. As a result, our island may decide to do things a little differently. For example, imagine that the eight people who did not invent the boat form a government and decide to tax the two entrepreneurs 80 percent of their daily catch so that it can be redistributed. Certainly, if the two inventors continue to produce twenty fish each day and pay their new taxes of sixteen fish, the other eight inhabitants will have no incentive to produce new goods or services. Obviously, by taxing the more productive entrepreneurs, the island not only eliminates the gains of new inventions, but also reduces the incentives to innovate.

Although this anecdote describes a simplified economy, it shows that the redistribution of wealth inhibits a society from experiencing the full impact of productivity increases. The economic theory behind this analysis is again Say's law. On our island, Say's law suggests that when the supply of fish increases because of a more productive technique of fishing, demand for other goods and services is created. The two inventors, because they have increased earnings, now demand more, and different, goods and services. It is their increased supply of goods that creates the new demand.

It is entrepreneurial effort and increases in productivity that cause Say's law to work. This example also explains why taxing incomes and profits reduces economic growth. The incomes and profits from supply must always equal demand; but by taxing away profits and incomes, the government reduces the demand for new products and therefore reduces growth and wealth creation.

The Pilzer anecdote also explains something else that may be even more important: when new inventions are successful, the inventors see their incomes rise dramatically relative to the status quo. In periods of innovation, such as during the Industrial Revolution or today's New Era, the gap between the rich and poor expands. Even though the poor are seeing their incomes rise, the Bill Gates's of the world are experiencing huge gains in income. However, this is a sign of progress, not of a problem. When markets are free, a widening income gap signals a strong and healthy economy; and any attempt to stop the income gap from widening by raising taxes and redistributing income will actually hurt the economy by slowing innovation and growth. This is exactly why the Soviet experiment with socialism failed. Socialism inhibits wealth creation.

Nonetheless, whenever wealth has been on the rise, the temptation to redistribute that wealth is strong. The battle between wealth creation and redistribution can be seen clearly in history as can its impact on markets. During those periods when redistribution was on the upswing and government activism was rampant, economic growth and wealth creation suffered. During those few periods when government activism was shrinking, economic growth and wealth creation accelerated.

The past 34 years are a perfect example. Between 1965 and 1982, when the Great Society was being built, growth slowed, inflation accelerated, and stock markets suffered. Since 1982, government interference has declined. While high-tech investment is the driving force behind the productivity increase of recent years, the pullback in government interference with the economy is what has allowed the wealth and growth of the United States to accumulate. The New Era boom in stocks did not start until 1982, but the fiscal policy seeds for the boom were planted back in the late 1970s.

THE GREAT SOCIETY AND MALAISE

The 1970s were a time of severe economic turmoil. Every broad economic measure of income, wealth, or productivity worsened. High tax rates to fund the Great Society smothered growth, while easy monetary policy boosted inflation. Every recovery was accompanied by increasing inflation and every time the Federal Reserve raised interest rates to combat inflation, we experienced a recession. Even President Carter described the economic times as a "malaise."

The problem was that economic policy was violating Say's law. By increasing taxes on productive effort, fiscal policy was short-circuiting the process of growth. The reason was that increases in incomes due to even small gains in productivity were taxed away. Instead of realizing that the shortfall in demand was caused by this burden on suppliers, Keynesian economists viewed the problem as a lack of demand. As a result, their prescriptions involved more government spending, bigger deficits, and lower interest rates to stimulate consumers to buy more.

When supply is being burdened and demand is being stimulated, the result is inflation. The correct policy response should have been to reduce taxes and stop the Fed from running an easy monetary policy. Although this was eventually done, the vested interests in economic fine-tuning and demand-side management had a difficult time shifting gears. For many, the bad economic environment was inevitable. In reading the economic literature of the late 1970s, the outlook was dismal indeed. Most economists fell into three camps. First, the bad times were here for good and the United States was in long-term decline. Second, the only way to fix the inflation problem was to endure a long period of economic recession or even depression. Third, the United States was being visited by bad luck and we should just hope for the best.

Obviously, with these fate-filled economic prognostications and the continued belief that many economists had in fine-tuning, it was difficult for those who believed in Lincoln's "fire of genius" to be heard. Nonetheless, a small group of economists, politicians, and journalists began to speak a different language. Starting in 1975, a group of a dozen or so people, including Robert Bartley, Robert Mundell, Arthur Laffer, Paul Craig Roberts, Norman Ture, Jack Kemp, Bruce Bartlett, and Alan Reynolds, started to openly discuss and write about a "new economics." An excellent history of these so-called "supply-siders" and the economy of the 1980s can be found in Robert L. Bartley's 1992 book, *The Seven Fat Years.*[3] In it, he describes the economic battles of the late 1970s and how difficult it was for the nation to head in a different direction.

Nonetheless, the nation headed in a different direction and thus began the New Era of Wealth. Unfortunately, the term "supply-side economics" has been discredited because of the jump in budget deficits during the 1980s. Supply-side arguments have been wrongly simplified down to a belief that tax cuts would cause revenue to grow and therefore eliminate deficits; however, this oversimplification is just not true. The supply-side arguments were centered in a belief of Say's law. The economy needed tax cuts to provide incentives for entrepreneurial effort no matter what happened to the deficit. In the late 1970s capital gains were taxed at a marginal rate as high as 50 precent, while income taxes went as high as 70 percent. Supply-siders argued that these high tax rates were inhibiting growth and wealth creation. It seems that these ideas have now been vindicated. After nearly 4 years of recession during the 13 years ending in 1982, the economy has now grown for 17 years with just one 8-month recession.

Obviously, taxes matter. The stagflation that the U.S. economy experienced in the late 1970s and early 1980s was so bad that politicians from both parties began to look for solutions. As shown, the Joint Economic Committee, which was controlled by Democrats, became a convert to the supply-side arguments. This conversion of many Democrats in Congress led to the first of many fiscal policy initiatives designed to increase incentives for investment and entrepreneurial activity.

On November 6, 1978, President Carter signed a capital gains tax cut that lowered the tax rate to 1960s levels. Representative William Steiger (R.-Wis.) originated the legislation to cut the capital gains tax in the House Ways and Means Committee, on April 20, 1978. As Bartley wrote in *The Seven Fat Years,* "This was the moment at which a decade of envy came to its close, and the search for a growth formula started in earnest."[4]

Prior to the cut in the capital gains tax rate, President Carter had appointed Alfred Kahn, a professor at Cornell University, as chairman of the Civil Aeronautics Board (CAB). Carter knew that Kahn wanted to deregulate the airlines and blessed his endeavors. The CAB had been established in 1938, amidst New Deal government activism to regulate the airline industry. As Daniel Yergin and Joseph Stanislaw write in their 1998 must-read book, *The Commanding Heights,*[5] it did not take Kahn long.

> In October 1978, airline deregulation became law: . . . Airlines were free to set fares competitively. And how did it work out? It is estimated that on average, air travelers in 1996 paid 26 percent less for trips than they would have if regulation had stayed in place.[6]

The small beginnings of the late 1970s turned into dramatic shifts in government policy as the 1980s unfolded. Ronald Reagan ran for president in 1980 and was advised by one of the original supply-siders, Jack Kemp. Reagan ran on a platform of tax cuts and smaller government.

> Immediately after delivering his inaugural address, Reagan performed his first official act as president: he signed an executive order eliminating the price controls on oil and gasoline that had been in place for a decade. The next day, Reagan abolished the Council on Wage and Price Stability. Reagan predicted that oil and gas prices would fall dramatically, and he proved to be right.[7]

To complement the deregulation, Reagan also pushed across-the-board tax cuts that he had promised in his campaign. Eventually he was successful in reducing the top marginal income tax rate to 28 percent and the capital gains tax rate to 20 percent. During Reagan's tenure as president, the breakup of AT&T was completed and a dramatic deregulation of the banking, trucking, and railroad industries was accomplished.

These revolutionary shifts in government policy were the seeds for the great boom in economic growth and wealth creation we are experiencing today. Although it is hard for many to cut through the rhetoric and partisan politics that surround any shift in government policy, there can be no doubt that deregulation increased efficiency and productivity while tax cuts encouraged the risk-taking that is so essential to innovation and invention. In addition, tax cuts allowed individuals to take their money out of tax shelters and begin to invest in productive ideas and companies.

In the early 1980s, the technology of microprocessors was just beginning to reshape the world. Fax machines, VCRs, microwave ovens, desktop computers, and cellular phones were just being born as new products and had very limited market penetration. But the tax cuts and deregulation of the early 1980s, combined with creative financing schemes invented by financiers such as Michael Miliken, allowed these technologies to bloom as everyday tools for American citizens.

Without the nearly 180-degree shift in government policies from the 1970s to the 1980s, the technology boom would not have unfolded in the United States as it has. The spectacular gains in U.S. stock prices and the magnificent increases we have seen in living standards would not have occurred either. The proof of this is all around us. Just ask yourself, why is the United States the center of the high-tech information age? Why didn't Germany and Japan become the center of the boom? There are many that thought they would be. During the late 1980s, the budget and trade deficits were supposed to kill the U.S. economy. Japan or Germany, according to the academic elite, were the next great economic powers and many of Reagan's enemies argued that Reaganomics was sure to ruin the country.

But this was never in the cards. Just when the cries were loudest that the United States was falling behind, it sprinted ahead. While the United States has moved toward freer markets and a tax and regulatory structure that fuels "the fire of genius," the rest of the world has not kept pace. Germany and Japan have raised taxes, been slow to deregulate and privatize, and have not figured out how to slim down government spending. This is the reason why the information age has blossomed in the United States and not anywhere else.

The fiscal policy changes pushing the New Era forward did not end with Ronald Reagan. They have continued, fitfully, under President Bush and President Clinton. President Bush completed negotiations on the North American Free Trade Agreement (NAFTA) and signed the Energy Policy Act of 1992—the first stage of electricity deregulation. President Clinton pushed through the General Agreement on Tariffs and Trade (GATT), signed legislation to end agricultural price supports, and also ended welfare, as we knew it. These changes allowed government spending to slow, reduced tariffs on global trade, and most important, gave incentives to many U.S. citizens to become productive members of society. Slower spending growth and higher tax revenues from rapid economic growth have finally balanced the budget as well.

Obviously, the Republican Congress, elected in 1994, was the political force behind a balanced budget and welfare reform; but, whereas the political affiliation of those behind the change may matter in politics, it does not matter to markets. What we have witnessed since the mid-1970s is nothing but a miraculous shift in government policy. The experiment with big government of the 1970s was a complete failure. As a result, Keynesian ideas of fine-tuning and government demand-side management have been defeated. While there are still those who believe that the Keynesian models of the economy are correct, they are more likely teaching in a university or forecasting in a back room at the Fed.

All the fiscal policy changes in the past 20 years have not been positive, but the changes that have taken place have provided fuel for the high-tech fire. Any backward drift toward more government interference in the economy would be a negative for financial markets, while further moves toward less government would be a positive.

References

[1] Joint Economic Committee. March 1980. Joint economic report 1980, Senate Report Number 96-618.

[2] Pilzer, Paul Zane. 1990. *Unlimited wealth: The theory and practice of economic alchemy.* New York: Crown Publishers Inc.

[3] Bartley, Robert L. 1992. *The seven fat years: And how to do it again,* 1st ed. New York: The Free Press.

[4] Ibid.

[5] Yergin, Daniel and Stanislaw, Joseph. 1998. *The commanding heights: The battle between government and the marketplace that is remaking the world.* New York: Simon & Schuster.

[6] Ibid.

[7] D'Souza, Dinesh. 1997. *Ronald Reagan: How an ordinary man became an extraordinary leader.* New York: The Free Press.

4

POLITICS IN THE
NEW WORLD

As the history of the past 30 years shows, the direction of government policy is a key ingredient in the accumulation of wealth. What will determine that direction in the future are the shifting sands of politics and government policy. Interestingly, two forces are at work that will continue to push government policy in the direction of more individual freedom and less government intervention. First, the information age is limiting the ability of government to manage the economy. Second, a majority of U.S. citizens now have a vested interest in the performance of financial markets that will keep the government from attacking wealth in favor of redistribution. This new investor class has become the fourth branch of government. Together these forces will move policy in the direction that supports wealth accumulation over redistribution, the fourth trend supporting the New Era.

THE IMPOTENT GOVERNMENT

In the information age, government is becoming increasingly impotent while individuals are gaining power. A belief in the marketplace is slowly replacing a widespread belief that government is the force that increases living standards and provides for wealth creation. Just as industry after industry is being dramatically altered in the New World, so is government policy. The evidence is all around us. The Social Security system is under attack for providing low returns on investment and the welfare system is now known more for its negative unintended consequences than for anything positive. The education system is battling for survival in its current form and the complicated tax code has become the butt of many jokes.

There are many reasons for the shift in the political landscape. Obviously, the failure of the Great Society to live up to its name is one reason.

Plummeting living standards and poor market performance in the 1970s were its comeuppance. But more importantly, technology allows more individual freedom, so much freedom that the government is losing its ability to enforce or regulate many different kinds of activities. For example, laws that regulate store hours (such as blue laws) are no longer enforceable when individuals can shop or bank 24 hours a day on the World Wide Web. To enforce these laws the government would have to control individuals, which is difficult to do in this high-tech age. Although the French may find it possible to raid offices and enforce a 35-hour workweek, Americans cannot. Individual freedom, as long as no harm is done to another, is a right that is hard to violate. As a result, government policy is being stymied by the rapid increase in individual power and autonomy that is an inexorable event of the high-tech era. Moreover, this trend is now firmly in place and will continue well into the future.

A vivid example of the impotence of government in today's high-tech world occurred in January 1999. Then, amidst a roaring Internet stock frenzy, the chairman of the Securities and Exchange Commission (SEC), Arthur Levitt, talked about the dangers of online investing. He spoke candidly by saying, "Online investors should remember that it is just as easy, if not more so, to lose money through the click of a button as it is to make it."[1] He was sincere in his comments, but no matter what he believed, there is little that he can do. Although government agencies have the power to regulate institutions and the SEC has the power to regulate brokers, they cannot limit the freedom of individuals to invest in any manner that they choose. Interestingly, because the information age is empowering individuals and not institutions, the regulatory authority of government agencies is diminishing rapidly. As more individuals trade stocks, bonds, mutual funds, futures, or options over the Internet, the regulatory authorities lose oversight, authority, and control. For example, financial market regulatory bodies hold brokers accountable by making them responsible for the "suitability" of their customers' investments. Like a bartender who can be held responsible for a customer who drinks too much, a broker can also be held responsible for a client's investments that are deemed "unsuitable" given the client's current financial condition.

In the new age of online stock trading, the ability to regulate is undermined. Ironically, the cost of complying with institutional regulation is one reason that brokers' commissions remain high relative to the commissions for online trading sites. Obviously there are other reasons, namely that most Internet trading sites do not offer research or advice. In addition, online trading sites remove the broker and allow the customer to assume that role. When every customer becomes his or her own broker, any increase in regulation becomes, by its very nature, highly intrusive and much more costly. In fact, as Arthur Levitt's comments show, the regulators are left with "moral suasion" as their only recourse. However, the idea of the government telling individuals where to invest is sneered at for good reason.

After all, it was the federal government that forced the S&L industry to sell all its high-yield bonds at the bottom of the market in 1989, a move that compounded the financial problems for that industry. The federal government also decided in 1979 to begin issuing 30-year government bonds to fund the deficit when long-term interest rates were at a historical peak. The United States is still paying double-digit interest rates interest on some of those bonds.

Clearly, no one has 20/20 vision about the future—neither the government nor any individual. As a result, it is hard to imagine support for more intrusive regulation of the financial markets. By definition, when you make an investment, you have already decided that it is suitable. How can the government argue with you? More importantly, if that investment goes sour on you, who is responsible? Certainly, companies that provide false and misleading information should be held accountable, but if you are your own broker, you are responsible. This increase in individual responsibility is a key to the direction of government policy in the future. The information age is empowering the individual at the expense of the institutions that have regulated trade and business for the past 100 years. Interestingly, the high cost of complying with regulation is often a catalyst for the development of systems that avoid those costs. The markets always look for the lowest cost alternative and New Era technologies are creating the mechanism to do this. Unfortunately, for those who make their living regulating markets, this shift is reducing demand for their services.

Interestingly, the markets are showing us the power of these trends. In the fourth quarter of 1998, daily online trades jumped 34 percent from the previous quarter and online trading accounted for 13.7 percent of all stock trades, up from just 9.2 percent in the fourth quarter of 1997.[2] "The numbers suggest that investors—despite complaints about poor service—are shying away from the more expensive full-service brokerages and embracing online brokers, whose fees often run less than $20 per trade."[3] While low prices are clearly the driving force behind the explosion in online trading, the proliferation of stock quotes and information is also removing the information gap between brokers and investors. The New Era drives down the cost of transactions *and* information, empowering individuals and removing the middleman in many transactions. The trend is so powerful that the market capitalization of Charles Schwab Corp. was greater than that of Merrill Lynch as of late 1998. The surge in the value of Schwab was a direct result of its ability to empower individuals—a clear sign of the value of New Era technologies. Despite its rapid growth, online stock trading is still in its infancy. As it continues to grow, the impact of regulatory authorities will diminish rapidly.

The forces that are pushing the world to more freedom did not begin with the Internet; however, the explosion of the Internet is accelerating the process. In many ways the world has come full circle in the past 100 years. The Industrial Revolution led to the "politics of big" and the dominance of systems that organized people. The 1920s saw the ascendance of Marxist thought in Russia and the 1930s were the breeding ground of Keynesian economic management and government control. The collapse of the USSR in the late 1980s and the ascendance of free markets around the world have finally laid these theories to rest. The politics of freedom and the triumph of individual responsibility are now ascending.

In January 1993, the newly elected president of the United States, William Jefferson Clinton, said in his inaugural address, "We must . . . demand responsibility from all. It is time to break the bad habit of expecting something for nothing, from our government or from each other. Let us all take more responsibility, not only for ourselves and our families but for our communities and our country." The American people were ready for these words. America had tried big government and ruled it a failure, rather than ridding the economy of risk, big government had only made things worse.

Although it was not clear at the time, the presidency of Bill Clinton would continue the process, begun under Carter and Reagan, of squeezing the final breaths out of the big government ideas of the Keynesian fine-tuners. The market was finally taking control of government policy; however, there were still some hurdles to clear. In 1993, the Clinton administration was able to push through Congress a tax increase that was called a "deficit cutting measure." Also in 1993, President Clinton proposed "an ambitious plan for the federal government to assume responsibility for the largest sector of the economy—health care—and to create a national health care system."[4] The proposal went nowhere.

Republicans, at that time a minority, mounted a highly successful counterattack. In floor debates and television advertisements they highlighted the outrageous complexities of such a program and the loss of freedom it would entail. Ultimately, this was an easy proposal to defeat, and it was important for investors. It laid the groundwork for a 1994 Republican takeover of Congress—the first time Republicans had controlled both houses of Congress in 40 years.

For many, the significance of this situation was lost; however, the markets tell the real story. The Clinton 1993 tax hike and his health care plan made the markets wonder whether big government was back. Between January 1993 and January 1995, the S&P 500 rose just 3.4 percent at an annual rate—a performance well below its historical average. Once a Republican Congress took office, however, the market was back on its record-breaking ways. Between January 1995 and January 1999, in spite of the government shutdown, the S&P 500 rose an astounding 27.1 percent per year.

The reason for this occurrence was twofold: Markets liked the Republican message and the fact that President Clinton was a "New Democrat." According to Yergin and Stanislaw, "the shutdown [of the government in 1995] and the budget debacle [that brought it about] were counted as a Democratic victory. Yet they were also a turning point for both the country and the Democratic Party. That became clear when, addressing the nation a few weeks later in his State of the Union address, Clinton said, 'The era of big government is over.' In fact, he said it twice in that speech."[5]

The markets and the economy are nonpartisan. They respond well to good policies and poorly to bad policies. Despite the tremendous rise in asset values since 1982, the road has not always been smooth. The United States has been in transition and many Americans are still not sure that free markets are the correct policy. However, it is becoming clearer every day that the markets thrive in an environment of less government and more freedom. More importantly, the direction of markets tells us the direction of the economy.

The political battles of the 1990s have been momentous. In many ways the battle lines are the same as the early 1980s, but in other ways they have moved dramatically. The government shutdown occurred because of disagreements over balancing the budget. The Republicans wanted to balance it in fewer years than the Clinton administration, but they both wanted it balanced. Republicans wanted welfare reform; Democrats did too, but in a different way than Republicans. But both welfare reform and a balanced budget were accomplished.

Welfare reform, of all the legislation passed in recent years, is the most important. According to George Will, welfare reform is the most important piece of legislation to pass since the New Deal in the 1930s. Despite dire warnings of expanding poverty and rising unemployment, the exact opposite has occurred. The 4.5 percent unemployment rate in 1998 was the lowest annual rate since 1969. Moreover, incomes for all Americans from the poorest to the wealthiest have climbed faster than inflation. This is important. When living standards are on the rise, crime rates, racial tension, and labor strife are all diminished. The evidence is clear; welfare reform has helped, not hurt.

One reason why welfare reform has been such a success is the grassroots push to make individuals more responsible for their lives. The signs are everywhere, including the Promise Keepers gathering (1997), the Million Man March held in Washington, D.C. (1995), and the Million Woman March in Philadelphia (1997). These huge gatherings of between 400,000 and 1 million people were unique for one simple reason: They were gathering not to protest some wrong but to discuss individual responsibility, reconciliation, atonement, and self-empowerment. In a PBS interview by Margaret Warner, Lekan Oguntoyinbo, a reporter for the Detroit Free Press, answered a question about what the Million Woman March focused on.

MARGARET WARNER: "And so are you saying they were more looking to themselves than to government? What were they looking—"[6]

LEKAN OGUNTOYINBO: ". . . They were clearly looking more to themselves than to government. I spoke with a woman who said, . . . The government can't give us businesses to run; the government can't teach us those old style values that black people hold so dearly, values such as cherishing the extended family, values such as religion, values such as respect, and love, and things like that that held blacks in this country together for hundreds of years through slavery and through segregation times. Those are things the government can't legislate. We need to go back to those kinds of values so they can build us up and so we can do more things for our community because there are too many problems in our community right now. The government cannot address all those problems."[7]

Clearly these events were different than others in the past. They were larger. Martin Luther King's "I Have a Dream" speech was attended by 250,000 and only Fourth of July fireworks displays, air shows, and the inauguration of Lyndon Johnson as president in 1965 were likely any larger. The press on these events focused on the controversies surrounding certain leaders, but they miss the point, because these events show that the underlying political environment supports individual responsibility, not big government.

The evidence is everywhere. Self-help and spiritual book sales are booming and church attendance is rising. Individuals are attempting to solve problems that have been typically left to the government. In other words, faith in individuals, cooperating through markets, is growing. The Internet is also pushing this trend farther and faster than many believe is possible. Because information is abundant and easily accessible, the average person can be informed on more issues than ever before. This capability provides a check not only on government, but also on business. Individual empowerment breeds a continued push for more control over our own lives.

As a result, it is relatively easy to predict a continued push toward government policies that enhance individual responsibility and the market over the next 5 to 10 years that will fundamentally change the way government and people interact. For example, in a surprise November 1998 election, Minnesota elected a new governor, Jesse "The Body" Ventura. While many have made jokes about a former professional wrestler becoming governor of Minnesota, Governor Ventura has struck a nerve with his frank talk. The following comes from the *St. Paul Pioneer Press*:

> 'Everything in your life you're personally responsible for, in some way or another. When you make a mistake in life, accept that yourself. Don't look to the government to bail you out of the mistake,' he said. 'Too much today, someone makes a mistake and the government has to come in and has to right the wrong. That ain't what government should be doing. That ain't what people should be doing, because that destroys core values.'

In a state sometimes said to have a government program for every problem, Ventura's attitude goes against the grain. But his high numbers in a recent Minnesota Poll suggest that many Minnesotans share his views. His popularity and high visibility give him a platform from which to argue his views.

'I get angry when I see these people come over with signs, welfare rights. You don't have a right to welfare. Welfare is charity, and that's done out of the goodness of people's hearts. But it is not a right. I find some of these people very selfish. They think that they have the right to take someone else's hard earned money. I couldn't live with that. I would have a hard time sleeping at night.'[8]

The popularity of Jesse Ventura is not a fluke. The nation has truly begun to shift and, as a result, the trends in government policy changes will continue to move in the direction of individual responsibility and away from government responsibility. The information age is changing all of politics.

The economy is proving itself capable of creating opportunities and taking care of problems that many felt it could not. Welfare reform did not result in a massive jump in the number of homeless people, NAFTA did not cause an outflow of jobs that Ross Perot said would sound like a "giant sucking sound," and budget surpluses did not result in a slowdown in economic growth. Free markets have worked, and slowly the New Era is dragging politicians and voters along.

A PIECE OF THE ROCK AND THE FOURTH BRANCH OF GOVERNMENT

One reason why big government does not stand a chance is that now more Americans own stocks than ever before in U.S. history. According to a February 1997 in-depth national survey released by The Nasdaq Stock Market and conducted by Peter D. Hart Research Associates, 43 percent of all American adults either own stock mutual funds or stock in individual companies—double the number who owned stocks just 7 years before. With the number of investors climbing, the body politic has become even more sensitive to policy decisions that will impact markets negatively.

As a result, protectionism, tax increases, or major government spending programs will be avoided at all costs. Conversely, policies that help markets are more likely to be followed. For example, on October 8, 1998, Congress passed legislation to keep state and local governments from taxing transactions on the Internet for 3 years. By doing this, Congress provided a big boost to the fledging market. Economist, Larry Kudlow, one of the leading proponents of New Era economic thought, has shown that the day this legislation passed the Senate, technology stocks started to rally. Any shift in this policy would be a negative for investors that hold technology stocks. More importantly, the connection between policy and market response would be obvious. It is no longer only wealthy individuals and corporations that feel the impact of policy changes. Now, average investors (and voters) are more likely than ever to understand the link between policy and market response. As a result, a fourth branch of government now rides herd over the other three, and it is not the press. When people own a piece of the rock, they want the rock kept solid.

The bottom line is that government policy will have a difficult time turning back toward big government control at any time in the future. More importantly, the odds of major changes in government policy that enhance individual responsibility and markets are very high. Pressures coming from both users and investors should lead to market-based overhauls of the health care, education, and energy markets. In addition, a partial privatization of Social Security with some sort of personal savings accounts is likely. Finally, during the next decade a complete overhaul of the tax code is likely. All these changes will continue the trend toward less government that began in the late 1970s. While vested interests will fight every step of the way, there is no power like that of individual power and eventually even the strongest vested interests will be forced to buckle to the common sense of limited government and individual responsibility. Just as this has been good for financial markets during the past 17 years, it will be good for financial markets as the New Era unfolds over the next 20 or 30 years.

References

[1] Schroeder, Michael. 1999. SEC Chairman Levitt warns of online trading risks. *Wall Street Journal*, 28 January, p. A2.

[2] Lee, Charlie. 1999. Online trades reach new highs, but e-broker problems still exist. *Wall Street Journal*, 29 January, p. C1.

[3] Ibid.

[4] Yergin, Daniel and Stanislaw, Joseph. 1998. *The commanding heights: The battle between government and the marketplace that is remaking the world.* New York: Simon & Schuster.

[5] Ibid.

[6] Public Broadcasting Corporation. 27 October, 1997. Online Newshour. *Show of strength, www.pbs.org/newshour/bb/race_relations/july-dec97/*

[7] Ibid.

[8] O'Connor, Debra. 1999. Despite fractious public exchanges Ventura sticks to gospel of self-reliance. *St. Paul (Minnesota) Pioneer Press*, 14 February, p. A1.

5

MONETARY POLICY: FORECASTING THE FED

The fifth and final trend buttressing the New Era is a drop in the rate of inflation. The high inflation of the 1970s and early 1980s destroyed wealth, while the lower inflation of the 1980s and 1990s has made a positive environment for creating wealth. One way to understand how inflation undermines wealth creation is to look at its impact on business decisions and lifestyles. A client once told me an interesting story that clearly shows its insidious nature.

The story took place in the late 1970s. At that time a Rocky Mountain-based oil company was faced with a problem. It received large checks for oil it sold, rising inflation had driven interest rates into the double-digit range, and the cost of waiting for the checks to clear (the float) was exceedingly high. To help reduce the time its checks floated, the oil company bought a small bank. How important was this to the company? It was plenty important. If it took 5 days for a $20 million check to clear and interest rates were 10 percent, the lost interest was $27,397 (nearly the cost of one employee). Every day that the company could reduce float on that $20 million check was worth $5,479 and by buying a bank they reduced float time by 2 days. Because even a small oil company has huge cash flow, high interest rates could drive the cost of float to millions of dollars per year. Buying a bank was a brilliant, and rational, strategy for cutting costs.

However, even owning a bank did not cut float time to zero and as the Fed boosted interest rates to over 20 percent to fight inflation in the early 1980s, the cost of float ballooned. To deal with this costly problem, the company decided to hand-deliver checks—even at banks as far away as Houston—to reduce float time further. To do this they flew a corporate plane around the country. Someone had actually figured out that the cost per hour to fly the plane was less than the interest foregone on the corporate cash flow.

What is amazing about this story is not the ingenuity of the oil company, but what it shows about the insidious nature of inflation. Using a corporate plane to deliver checks is a waste of resources, and this story is just one story in a million. Inflation causes a mass misallocation of resources that thwarts economic growth and wealth creation. Inflation creates cost overruns in building projects, prices people out of homes, and causes great uncertainty in any business plan.

However, the United States was not the only country to suffer a beating from inflation. In South America, during the hyperinflation of the early 1980s (which reached above 10,000 percent annually), consumers spent their entire paychecks as soon as they received them because prices were rising on a daily, or even hourly, basis. Most Brazilians owned deepfreezes so they could store excess food which they were forced to buy before prices moved higher. In noninflationary times, the only people who own deepfreezes are hunters or families with many children. Obviously people do things that they would not normally do when inflation gets out of control.

The examples are endless, but the pain of inflation and its costs to an economy is clear. When inflation spirals out of control, interest rates rise, uncertainty increases, the economic landscape of prices is distorted, effective tax rates rise, and investments are shifted into hard assets rather than financial assets. In the late 1970s, analysts were predicting $100 barrel oil and that farmland prices would continue rising. Eventually, many banks, oil investors, and farmers went bankrupt because of decisions they made that depended on ever increasing prices for raw materials and continued inflation. These decisions made no sense once the inflationary spiral stopped.

In addition, decisions made before the inflationary spurt of the 1970s also came back to haunt whole industries. For example, the S & L industry was loaded with 30-year mortgages at interest rates of 6 percent or less. This was fine when short-term interest rates hovered between 2 and 4 percent during the 1960s, but when short-term interest rates rose to double-digit levels because of the inflation of the 1970s, these institutions lost money every day. They were paying much higher interest rates to depositors than they were receiving on their investments. Despite the attacks on the character of the S&L industry, and of its executives, the vast majority of losses in the industry were the result of 1970s inflation and the high interest rates that it caused. Inflation can destroy wealth and undermine growth.

Eradicating inflation was essential to the New Era, and the decline in inflation during the 1980s and 1990s is one of the most important of the five key trends that have supported the boom in wealth. To understand inflation, however, we must understand the Federal Reserve. Contrary to popular opinion, the 1970s inflation was not caused by low unemployment, budget deficits, a falling value for the dollar, or by OPEC raising oil prices. It was also not caused by labor unions demanding higher wages and corporations giving in. All these explanations blame inflation on some outside force as if it was uncontrollable and each of them is an *effect* of inflation, not a *cause*. Inflation is caused by only one thing—bad management of monetary policy by the Fed.

As the Nobel laureate Milton Friedman said, "Inflation is everywhere and anywhere a monetary phenomenon." In other words, the Federal Reserve, because it controls the money supply, is always the cause of inflation. This is why Paul Volcker and Alan Greenspan have become household names. Over the past 20 years, starting soon after President Carter appointed Paul Volcker as chairman of the Federal Reserve, the rate of inflation has steadily declined. Today, the U.S. economy is at virtual price stability and the economy is enjoying the fruits of that long and hard process of eliminating inflation.

IT'S A JOB, NOT A RELIGION

One of the first things to grasp about monetary policy is that it is the Fed's job to keep prices stable in the economy, just like it is a pilot's job to land a plane safely. If the pilot makes a mistake bad things happen, but if that pilot lands safely very rarely do the passengers applaud. The same should be true of the Fed. If the Fed makes a mistake and creates inflation as it did in the 1970s, then the Fed should be vilified; but if the Fed does its job correctly, then the world should hardly notice. Obviously this is not reality. Alan Greenspan is lauded as one of the saviors of our economy because he has been chairman of the Fed while inflation has been virtually eradicated. One reason that he has been put on a pedestal is that managing monetary policy is a difficult job. In addition, the Fed has the power to move interest rates, a policy that immediately impacts every American citizen and many around the world.

This power to move interest rates, however, is often misunderstood. There is no magic button or lever in the boardroom at the Fed that moves interest rates up or down. To raise rates, the Fed must withdraw funds from the banking system making those funds scarce. If the Fed wants to lower interest rates it must inject funds into the banking system which makes funds plentiful. In other words, the Fed can control only one important variable of the economy, the money supply. Through the manipulation of the money supply, the Fed causes the federal funds rate (the rate at which banks loan excess reserves to each other) to move higher or lower. While moving interest rates down can stimulate borrowing, the only way people can borrow more is if the Fed actually puts the extra money into the system.

Importantly, if the Fed's main policy tool is to either print new money or to not print new money, then its power is limited. Think about that for a minute. Printing money (and lowering interest rates) cannot make an economy wealthy. If it could, counterfeiting currency would be legal. But counterfeiting is not legal because the counterfeiter gets something for nothing. The same is true for the economy. If the Fed prints too much money, we all feel wealthier for awhile; but eventually the value of money will fall. The Fed has the power to ruin a good economy, but price stability alone is not enough to create a good economy. Price stability creates an environment that is conducive to entrepreneurial innovation, but the innovation is what creates wealth, not Fed policy. Another way to think of this is that the Fed can do a great deal of harm, but it can do very little good.

Money is only a commodity. People invented money because it made life easier. At first beads or shells were used as money, then gold and silver, but eventually paper money replaced them all because of its ease of transportation and accounting. Money is a store of value that alleviates the need to barter. For example, it might be hard for me, an economist, to find a plumber that wanted economic advice. It is much more productive for me to trade my services to someone who is willing to pay money for them and then to use that money at some later date to pay for the services of a plumber. It is the services that economists, plumbers, and programmers provide that create wealth, not money. Money is just "grease in the wheels of commerce" and as long as it remains stable in value, it serves its purpose.

The value of money, like any commodity, is determined by its supply and demand. If there is a bumper crop of corn, its price falls. The same is true of money. If the Fed prints more money than the economy needs then its value falls and by definition, when the value of money falls, that is inflation. Why? Devalued money buys fewer goods. Or, in other words, the prices of goods and services, in terms of money, will rise. In simple form, this is inflation. Money loses its value.

Milton Friedman, in a recent interview, described the system like this. He asked us to imagine that the Fed controls the heating unit on a big building. If the Fed turns up the heater too much (prints too much money) then the building will become too hot (causing inflation). The opposite problem would be that the Fed turned the heater off (printing less money) and the building became cold. This would cause deflation—a decline in the price of goods and services in terms of money. Deflation means money is rising in value relative to goods and services.

The Fed's job is to keep the temperature just right. If it does that consistently, then most of us would never worry about the Fed just like we don't worry about our heaters kicking on. However, the Fed, because humans run it, makes mistakes. The mistakes in monetary policy that the Fed made in the 1970s caused a tremendous amount of damage. So far, in the past 17 years, the Fed has made fewer mistakes, which is nothing to get excited about, because the Fed is just doing its job. Nonetheless, because the Fed can always make mistakes, New Era investors must be attuned to monetary policy.

BALANCING ACT

The Fed's job is to keep the heater turned to just the right temperature. This is a hard job, however, because there is no unanimously agreed upon thermostat to read. In addition, the size of the building keeps changing, which makes it more difficult to maintain the right temperature. This analogy perfectly explains the inflationary mistakes that the Fed made in the 1970s. Then, taxes were high and rising with the top tax rate reaching 70 percent on any income over $100,000. Government spending shot from 17.2 percent of GDP in 1965 to 23.2 percent in 1982 and the regulatory burden was horrendous. *The Federal Register,* a listing of all federal regulations, rose from 16,850 pages in 1966 to 87,011 pages in 1980.[1]

In essence, these policies smothered the economy like a wet blanket and caused the building (the economy) to become smaller. Because the economy cooled down due to these policies, the Fed kept thinking that its heater was not turned up enough. Therefore the Fed kept pumping the heat in faster, which exacerbated the economic problems that already existed. It was a vicious circle. Capital gains taxes shot up because they were assessed on inflated gains and inflation pushed individuals into higher tax brackets. The slower the economy grew because of these inflated tax burdens the more the government tried to spend to get it going again and the further the Fed lowered interest rates. Eventually, the heater was on so high and the economy was taxed so heavily that very few entrepreneurs could survive.

The policy mix of burdensome government and inflationary monetary policy was guaranteed to cause higher inflation. Big government smothers the entrepreneurial spirit and reduces the supply of new goods and services. Easy monetary policy, and the low interest rates that accompany it, increases demand. Whenever supply is held back while demand is artificially stimulated, inflation is the result.

VOLCKER AND GREENSPAN TO THE RESCUE

This situation changed in 1979 when Paul Volcker became chairman of the Federal Reserve Board. He immediately turned off the heater, but fighting the inflation of the 1970s was painful. Volcker raised interest rates in 1979 *before* taxes were cut and regulatory burdens were eliminated. As a result, interest rates shot up to 20 percent and the U.S. economy suffered two severe recessions in the early 1980s.

In essence, the reverse policies of the 1970s were put into place in the 1980s. While Volcker turned the heater down, Reagan cut taxes, deregulated whole industries, and began to cut the size of government. This allowed the building to grow in size, which also helped push its temperature down. It is harder to overheat a bigger building. Looking back, the Fed could have taken it a bit slower, but while the economy may have avoided some of the acute pain of withdrawal, it would have just drawn out the process. There is no painless way to fix the problems of monetary mistakes. Business decisions had been made with high taxes and high inflation in mind, long-term wage contracts had been signed, tax and inflation shelters had been funded, excess investment in raw material production (such as farmland, oil wells, and mines) had occurred, and prices had moved upward. The process of ending inflation rips all these decisions apart.

Every time the Fed holds interest rates too low for too long, malinvestment occurs, which eventually must unwind. The economy must go through a cleansing process and it takes years, if not decades, for the economy to rebound from problems that bad policy creates. Volcker began the process of wringing inflation and inflationary expectations from the economy and today, 20 years later, the economy is finally bearing the full fruits of those efforts.

Volcker presided over the decline in the rate of increase in the Consumer Price Index (CPI), from over 14.5 percent in 1980 to a low of 1.2 percent in 1986. The process was not finished, however. The 1986 dip in inflation was due to a sharp decline in oil prices. Without energy prices, the CPI was still rising at 3.8 percent and service prices in 1986 were still rising at a 5.0 percent annual rate. The average yield on the 30-year Treasury bond during 1986 was 7.78 percent and during the next 5 years it averaged 8.55 percent. Obviously, the bond market did not yet believe that inflation was defeated, and it was right.

THE GREENSPAN ERA

The final blows against inflation were left to Alan Greenspan who was appointed chairman of the Federal Reserve in August 1987. Today, in the Greenspan era, bond investors are finally beginning to believe that the Fed has defeated inflation. In 1998, another year of falling oil prices, the CPI rose just 1.6 percent, however, after excluding energy prices, the CPI rose just 2.4 percent while service prices rose 2.5 percent, one-half of their increase in 1986. But even these low levels of inflation are overstated. According to the Boskin Commission, named after Dr. Michael Boskin, the chairman of the Council of Economic Advisors under President Bush, the CPI overstates inflation by about 1.1 percent per year.

One problem that the Boskin Commission highlighted in its 1996 report was "substitution bias." In a nutshell, this problem results when the price of one good, like chicken, rises and consumers respond by buying a less expensive substitute, like pork. Because the CPI is a "fixed-weight" index and always assumes that consumers buy the same quantities of every good each month, this causes the CPI to overstate inflation. The Bureau of Labor Statistics is in the process of fixing these problems; however, the

United States already calculates other measures of inflation in an "expenditure-weighted" index. The Commerce Department estimates inflation when it calculates the gross domestic product data and adjusts inflation, on a quarterly basis, by weighting expenditures as a share of GDP. This more accurate measure of inflation, named the implicit price deflator for the gross domestic product, increased just 0.9 percent in 1998, its slowest rate of increase since 1959.

These signals suggest that the Fed has come very near victory in its fight to end inflation. Slowly the bond market has begun to recognize that the Fed is winning the battle. In 1998, the yield on a 30-year Treasury bond averaged 5.58 percent, its lowest average yield since 1977 when the Treasury first issued the 30-year maturity. The 10-year Treasury bond fell to an average yield of 5.26 percent in 1998, its lowest annual average since 1967. While many analysts believe that yields cannot fall further and bond yields shot upward in early 1999, this is just not true. During the last period of sustained low inflation, in the 1950s and 1960s, interest rates on Treasury bonds were well below 4.0 percent. As the New Era unfolds, as long as the Fed continues to follow a monetary policy that will reduce inflation, bond yields should once again return to levels not seen in 40 years.

FORECASTING THE FED

One of the most intriguing debates of the New Era has been about monetary policy, inflation, and deflation. Cutting through the clutter is essential for making good investment decisions. To do that, however, it is important to discuss the different methods and theories that have been developed for measuring the Fed.

There are three different paradigms for assessing the current state of monetary policy: the monetarist paradigm, the demand-side or Keynesian paradigm, and the supply-side paradigm. The monetarist paradigm is the simplest. Monetarists believe that measuring and watching the money supply is all that is needed to forecast the Fed and inflation. This theory is attributed to Milton Friedman and Anna J. Schwartz, who wrote an influential book entitled *A Monetary History of the United States* in 1963. Their theory, although complicated, can be boiled down to the fact that when the Fed prints money the economy gets a boost. If the Fed prints too much money, then inflation occurs. For example, if the labor force is growing by 1.0 percent per year and productivity is increasing by 1.5 percent per year, then the economy can only expand its production by 2.5 percent per year. If the Fed prints more than 2.5 percent more money every year, say 3.5 percent, then inflation will be 1.0 percent. Of course if the Fed printed 10 percent more money every year, then inflation would be 7.5 percent. Why? Too much money would be chasing too few goods.

While this theory remains one of the greatest breakthroughs in economic history, there are a number of problems in applying it to economic forecasting. First, it is difficult to measure money. In the 1960s, when Friedman and Schwartz wrote their book, nearly all money was held in banks and, as a result, could be measured accurately. Today, money market funds, mutual funds, overseas branches of U.S. and foreign banks, and the use of the dollar worldwide make it nearly impossible to measure money. For example, it is estimated that over one-half of all U.S. currency is held outside the country. Second, estimates of productivity growth are horribly wrong. As a result, if money is immeasurable and productivity estimates have large errors, using the money supply to forecast inflation is virtually impossible.

The Keynesian or demand-side theories about monetary policy have also been proven useless in recent years. These models measure monetary policy by looking at real economic indicators rather than the money supply. For example, Keynesian analysts believe that the economy cannot grow faster than say 2.5 percent per year or that the unemployment rate cannot fall below 5 percent without creating inflation. In essence this is the same analysis as the monetarists, but they come at it from the other side. Keynesian analysts assume that any growth in the economy above their estimates of its speed limit or any drop in the unemployment rate below their estimate of its "natural" level must mean that the Fed is printing too much money. Or, in other words, the only reason that the economy is growing this fast is because the Fed is holding interest rates too low.

Bringing these two theories back into Friedman's analogy will help. If we cannot measure how much heat the heater is pushing into the building and if we cannot measure how big the building is, then managing monetary policy is nearly impossible. For example, while the money supply has been growing rapidly in recent years, the building has also been expanding. Not only have New Era technologies boosted the supply of goods and services and caused productivity to increase, but the international demand for U.S. dollars is also rising. Dollars are being used worldwide like never before. As a result, the goods and services that dollars are used to purchase (the building that the Fed is trying to heat) are expanding. If the building is expanding, then what appears to be rapid money growth is not necessarily inflationary.

This brings us to the final but simple view of the way to measure monetary policy. The supply-side view of Fed policy begins with the assumption that the money supply is nearly impossible to measure. It also assumes that the underlying rate of growth in the economy is also not known with certainty. As a result, low unemployment or fast economic growth is not necessarily inflationary, because we don't know how to measure it and we don't know how fast the economy can truly grow. Supply-siders suggest that the only way to know if the Fed is too easy or too tight is to look at sensitive indicators of monetary policy and inflation. If the heater is on too high these indicators will flash warning signals. These indicators include the price of gold and commodities, the value of the U.S dollar on world markets, the yield curve (or the spread between long- and short-term interest rates), and the level of the real federal funds rate.

THE SUPPLY-SIDE VIEW IS CORRECT

The supply-side view of monetary policy has been the best at explaining the 1990s. Between 1996 and 1999, real GDP growth averaged 4.0 percent per year, the unemployment rate was below 5.0 percent for 2 years in a row, and the money supply grew at a 6.5 percent annual rate. According to Keynesian and monetarist analysts, this should have caused inflation; however, inflation continued to fall. Because most members of the Fed believe in one of these two models of the world, they were confused. The minutes of the Fed's February 1999 Federal Open Market Committee meeting put it this way, "A number [of members] referred, however, to the experience of recent years, which suggested that the inflation process was not well understood and that inflation forecasts were subject to a wide range of uncertainty."[2] In many ways this admission was amazing. If you think about it, it was just like a group of NASA officials admitting that they did not understand how they put men on the moon.

The reason why the Fed seems so confused is that they are looking at all the wrong indicators. Because we cannot measure money and because the rate of growth in the economy is not subject to speed limits, the best thermometers of monetary policy are sensitive inflation indicators.

For example, in 1992 and 1993, the Fed was trying to boost economic growth by holding interest rates very low. In fact, the Fed added so much money to the economy that the federal funds rate fell to 3.0 percent in 1993, the same level as inflation. This meant that the real (or inflation-adjusted) federal funds rate was zero, which is too low because it essentially allows banks to borrow money for free. While the economy did not grow rapidly as a result of these policies, the price of gold and other commodities soared. Gold prices rose from under $330 an ounce in late 1992 to over $380 an ounce in late 1993. The Bridge/CRB Commodity Futures Price Index, which measures seventeen sensitive commodity prices, rose by 10.4 percent in 1993. In addition, while long-term interest rates fell in 1993, the spread between short-term interest rates and long-term interest widened significantly. The wide spread suggested that long-term investors believed short-term interest rates should move higher.

All these indicators were correct. Inflation moved higher in 1993 and 1994, the Fed raised interest rates from 3.0 percent to 6.0 percent and the 30-year government bond yield rose dramatically from under 6.0 percent in late 1993 to over 8.0 percent in late 1994, one of the worst bond market performances ever.

Real Federal Funds Rate

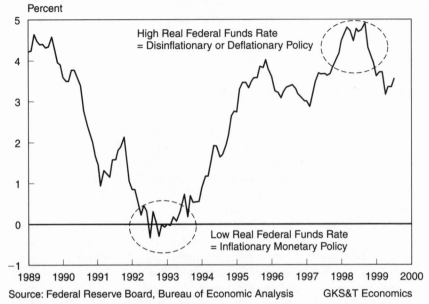

Source: Federal Reserve Board, Bureau of Economic Analysis   GKS&T Economics

Federal funds rate minus the 12-month change in the Personal Consumption Deflator

Exactly the opposite happened in 1997 and 1998. The Fed was then holding the federal funds rate at 5.5 percent, while inflation was falling toward 1.0 percent, which meant that the real federal funds rate rose dramatically (see chart). This high real federal funds rate suggested that the Fed was holding interest rates too high. The result should have been expected. Gold prices fell from over $400 an ounce in 1996 to under $300, commodity prices fell by 20 percent, and the spread between long- and short-term interest rates narrowed considerably. This meant that long-term investors thought that short-term interest rates should fall. Once again these indicators were correct. The Fed was eventually forced to lower interest rates, the rate of inflation continued to fall, and long-term interest rates set record lows.

These sensitive market indicators are the best gauges of Fed policy. They do not rely on estimates of potential growth or of some estimated lower limit to the unemployment rate. Rather than trying to estimate whether the heater is turned on or if the building is getting larger, these sensitive indicators actually measure the temperature. If gold prices and commodity prices are rising, then inflation is likely to rise. If inflation is likely to rise, then interest rates are likely to rise. If gold and commodity prices are falling, then inflation is likely to fall as will interest rates. These indicators sidestep the debate about whether the economy is growing because the Fed is too easy or whether it is growing because of a surge in innovation. They tell us what Fed policy truly is.

THE FED, INTEREST RATES, AND INFLATION

The best way to see how confusion over monetary policy can occur is to think about how the Fed views the economy. For example, during the past few years, when members of the Federal Reserve Board woke in the morning, turned on CNN or CNBC, and read their papers, they saw nothing but incredible economic growth. The unemployment rate is at record lows, the stock market has climbed to dizzying heights, and the economy has grown at a 4.0 percent annual rate. When Fed members see this amazingly strong economic activity they must make a decision. They must decide if the economy is strong because entrepreneurial spirit and high-tech investment have boosted potential growth or because they are holding interest rates too low.

This is an important decision. If the Fed thinks that the economy is growing rapidly because interest rates are too low, and therefore it is pushing too much money into the economy in order to hold rates down, then the Fed will fear higher inflation and be tempted to raise interest rates. If the Fed thinks that the economy is growing within the bounds of its potential given an improved productivity outlook, then the Fed will not worry about inflation and will either hold rates unchanged or possibly cut them. However, as Alan Greenspan said, "We do not now know . . . whether current developments are part of a once or twice in a century phenomenon that will carry productivity trends nationally and globally to a new higher track, or whether we are merely observing some unusual variations within the context of an otherwise generally conventional business cycle expansion. The recent improvement in productivity could be just transitory, an artifact of a temporary surge in demand and output growth."[3]

THE FED'S DILEMMA WILL CREATE DEFLATION

This confusion, admitted by Chairman Greenspan, leads us to one final conclusion about monetary policy in the New Era. Because the Fed believes that the economy cannot grow as rapidly as it is without creating inflation, it will continue to hold interest rates above the level at which it should. The impact is that the Fed will not be supplying enough dollar liquidity to the system and deflation will be the result.

In fact, during recent years and in the decade ahead, the Fed will follow exactly the opposite policy of the 1970s. Then, as was already mentioned, high taxes, regulations, and spending were holding the economy back. Instead of realizing that there was nothing they could do about it, the Fed kept lowering interest rates in an attempt to get the economy moving again. The result was inflation.

Today, lower taxes, fewer regulations, and less spending of the 1990s, combined with a technological revolution more powerful than the world has ever seen, has driven economic growth upward. Because the Fed views the world from the demand side, it mistakes the resulting strong growth and low unemployment rates for excess money creation. Therefore, its first inclination is to raise interest rates even though inflation remains at bay.

The impact of this policy will be to create deflation in the economy. In other words, as the economy produces more goods and services, but the Fed holds back on the money supply, prices will fall in dollar terms. This is already happening to a wide variety of commodities, goods, and services. As the chart below shows, gold and commodity prices have retraced much of their rise during the 1970s. As long as they continue to fall—and the current trends in monetary policy suggest that they will—deflation will be a reality. More importantly, gold prices have been a fabulous indicator of the direction of interest rates. As the next chart shows, gold prices have led the way to lower interest rates in the 1990s and they continue to point toward lower rates ahead.

Gold and Commodity Prices

Source: Commodity Research Bureau, Wall Street Journal   GKS&T Economics

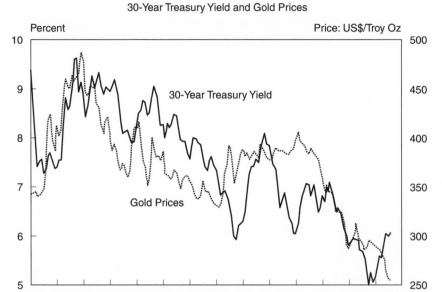

30-Year Treasury Yield and Gold Prices

Source: Federal Reserve Board, Wall Street Journal   GKS&T Economics

DEFLATION IN THE NEW ERA

Already deflation is impacting a wide variety of goods and services. The most obvious are computer prices that are falling by 30 percent or more per year. Commodity prices, especially for agricultural products, have fallen to 23- or 24-year lows in the late 1990s and industrial metals prices are 25 percent less than they were in the late 1980s. Less obvious is the price of durable goods. Automobile prices are down 1.2 percent in the past 2 years and used car prices are down almost 6 percent in the past 3 years.

Service prices, which are not very accurate, are still rising according to our government statistics; however, the costs of many services are declining dramatically. Online trading and phone call prices have plummeted, while online auction markets are clearly lowering the average cost of airline ticket prices and hotel rooms by the day.

There are two reasons for this deflation. First, New Era technology is increasing productivity rapidly. Second, the Fed continues to hold interest rates too high. These two factors should make investors much less worried about inflation in the years ahead. The sensitive inflation indicators mentioned in this chapter will help you forecast the Fed. When gold and other commodity prices are falling, the Fed rarely raises interest rates. However, if the Fed raises rates in a deflationary environment, prices will fall further and deflation will become a problem.

As long as prices are declining slowly, say at 1 percent per year, the economy will be fine. This would be much like the Industrial Revolution when prices fell an average of 0.6 percent per year for 40 years. In that case, consumers' purchasing power rises slowly from year to year and little disruption occurs in the economy. However, if the Fed drives prices down much more than 2.0 percent per year, stocks and the economy will be in trouble. Bonds, on the other hand, love deflation. Just look at Japan, where 10-year government bond yields are below 2.0 percent.

While U.S bond yields are unlikely to fall to 2.0 percent, a deflationary policy coming from the Fed will push yields down dramatically in the years ahead. In the New Era, inflation will remain low and the benefits of this will continue to push interest rates down and keep the economic environment conducive to entrepreneurial activity.

References

[1] Bianco, James. 1999. BiancoResearch, Inc., Barrington, IL. www.BiancoResearch.com.

[2] Federal Reserve Board. 1999. *Minutes of the federal open market committee,* 2–3 February, *http://www.bog.frb.fed.us*

[3] Greenspan, Alan. 1997. *Monetary policy testimony and report to the Congress,* 22 July. Washington, DC: Federal Reserve Board.

6

VIRTUOUS CIRCLE: HOW THE TRENDS WORK TOGETHER

Despite winning six NBA championships in 8 years, there never seemed to be enough credit to go around to satisfy everyone in the Chicago Bulls basketball franchise. While it is impossible to list all the reasons why the franchise became so successful, without Michael Jordan, the Bulls would not have won six titles. More importantly, Michael Jordan could not have won those titles alone. Michael's supporting cast was important. Bulls coach Phil Jackson was the glue that held the team together. Moreover, without great supporting players (many made to look like stars by playing with Jordan), the Jordan era would not have been so successful.

So it is with the U.S. economy. Despite attempts by politicians and the Federal Reserve to take credit for the New Era, technology is the Michael Jordan of wealth creation. Without New Era technology, and Lincoln's "fire of genius," the United States would not have experienced the boom of the past 17 years. Nonetheless, all by itself, technology is not enough. The economic environment must be conducive to the advancement of technology. Globalization and free trade, a shift in fiscal policy toward individual responsibility, and a stable value for our money are the essential supporting cast for the New Era of Wealth.

Unlike Michael Jordan, technology is available to everyone in the world. As a result, economic growth and wealth creation should be a worldwide phenomenon. The United States, however, seems to be garnering most of its rewards. Japan is mired in recession and Europe is stagnating, despite the promise of its new single currency, the euro. Even though Japan and Europe are experiencing low inflation, like the United States, their burdensome fiscal policies and rigid financial markets hold back entrepreneurial innovation. Other major economies, such as Brazil, Mexico, Russia, and Indonesia, continue to fight inflation *and* bad fiscal policies. Except for Britain and a few small countries such as Korea, Ireland, New Zealand, and Chile, the United States is the only economy that has been able to develop the synergies available when all five of the key trends laid out in the previous chapters work together. When they do work together, the power of these five trends is much greater than the benefits of each separately. *The trends work in a virtuous circle of wealth creation.* They build upon each other and create not just a better economy, but an increasing economic potential. This boosts the profits and stock prices of many firms and is what creates wealth for New Era investors.

THE EVIDENCE

The evidence in support of these trends is overwhelmingly positive. In October 1999, the U.S. economy entered its 103rd month of continuous economic expansion—the longest peacetime expansion in U.S. history and only three months short of the longest expansion ever. During the four years ending in June 1999, real GDP expanded by 3.8 percent at an annual rate, its fastest 4 year growth rate since 1986. Unemployment fell to 4.2 percent in early 1999, its lowest level since 1969. In addition; the Consumer Price Index (which remains overstated) rose just 1.6 percent in 1998, its smallest increase since 1967. Moreover, the implicit price deflator (a broader and more accurate measure of inflation than the CPI) rose just 0.9 percent in 1998, its smallest rise since 1959. The combination of rapid growth and low inflation boosted stock prices by more than 20 percent per year for four consecutive years.

This fabulous economic performance did not just sprout up overnight. In reality, the U.S. economy has been performing exceptionally since 1982. The previous record for the longest peacetime economic expansions, of 92 months, was set between November 1982 and July 1990. The recession that ended that recovery was one of the shortest on record. These two New Era recoveries blow away history. The average length of the twenty-six peacetime economic expansions since 1854 is just 29 months. For the United States to experience two consecutive recoveries of three times the historic average, interrupted by only one 8-month recession, is nearly miraculous. Since 1854, the U.S. economy has never experienced a period of growth as sound or as long. For a stark comparison, the period between 1969 and 1982 included four recessions that lasted a combined total of 42 months.[1]

Even more amazing is the number of potentially catastrophic economic events that could have derailed this period of prosperity, but did not. The stock market crash of 1987, the credit crunch and banking problems of the late 1980s and early 1990s, the tax increases of 1990 and 1993, and the collapse of the Japanese stock market in 1990 were all considered a threat to the New Era. The Mexican economic collapse in 1994, the 1997 Asian crisis, the 1998 Russian bond default, the implosion of the Long-term Capital Management hedge fund, the 1999 devaluation in Brazil, and only the second impeachment of a president in U.S history were also thought to be severe threats. Despite these events, the U.S. economy continued to perform spectacularly. In the fourth quarter of 1998, U.S. real GDP grew 6.0 percent at an annual rate, while the German economy contracted by 0.4 percent. Economists blamed the poor performance in Germany on Asian and Russian economic problems. Those same problems should have hurt U.S. growth, but they did not. The U.S. economy has been built on a rock and can withstand storms that would have thrown it into recession during the 1970s. More importantly, the five trends that created the boom are unlikely to dissipate any time soon. In fact, led by technology the virtuous circle can continue to push the economy higher for decades to come as long as the five trends remain intact.

THE ALL-STAR AND SUPPORTING CAST

Technology is the all-star of the New Era. Ideas and innovation are always the source of increasing wealth. Whether it is with steam shovels or satellite phone systems, by learning to make more with less, share information faster, or just invent new things, technology is the driving force behind all economic advancement. Today's technology, however, is different than that of the past. The networked economy, driven by advances in computers and telecommunications, has created astounding opportunity. Information, capital, and new ideas travel at the speed of light across fiber-optic cables and, as a result, the era of increasing returns has replaced the era of diminishing returns. Competition has become global and efficiency has become the password to the secret of business survival.

Globalization, the second trend of the New Era, is an integral part of the team. Potential markets have expanded, and capital moves freely and quickly throughout the world. By making the world smaller, technology allows the optimum allocation of resources and production facilities. As long ago as 1817, the famous economist, David Ricardo, discovered the "law of comparative costs" and how international trade increased overall economic well-being. He showed that, even if one country could produce every good on the face of the earth more efficiently than any other country, it would still benefit from trade. In essence, the international division of labor creates wealth just as the division of labor does domestically. For example, a programmer who designs new computer chips, but also has a knack for automobile mechanics, does not benefit economically by ignoring programming and fixing a car, even if the programmer is better at fixing cars than the local mechanic. The programmer is much better off, and so is the economy, as long as the programmer concentrates on what adds the most value.

International trade, by expanding the available choices and increasing competition, is good for wealth creation; however, we don't need a theory to prove this point. In the past 17 years, as trade barriers have fallen, world trade and investment have increased faster than world GDP. This would not be the case if parties on both sides of the transaction did not benefit. Technology speeds up this process and globalization speeds up the growth of technology. The law of increasing returns shows that the more members a network attracts the more the network is worth. International networks are in their infancy and will continue to add to wealth as they grow.

Another development of the interaction between technology and globalization is that the impact of government policies is amplified. As the cost of transactions falls toward zero, very small differences in tax rates or regulatory burdens can be arbitraged by businesses and individuals. As a result, those countries that keep market interference to a minimum will benefit at the expense of countries that do not. One interesting piece of anecdotal information shows the increasing sensitivity of individuals to tax rates. In 1996 the German government ordered raids on German banks, to discover whether they were helping clients move money to Luxembourg. Luxembourg has lower tax rates than Germany and rational individuals were moving their capital to the lower tax country. The concerns that led to these raids are the same concerns that have led the European Union to ask member countries to raise tax rates so that so-called "unfair competition" will not occur. This, however, is a losing battle. There is only one closed economy and that is the world economy. The European continent cannot isolate itself from the rest of the world without paying a heavy price in economic growth. Technology is breaking down barriers every day and the cost of moving capital, labor, and even production facilities is falling.

Because of its relatively low tax rates, the United States has begun to attract huge amounts of capital from all over the world. The Securities Industry Association estimates that foreign purchases and sales of U.S. securities in 1997 grew to $12.7 trillion, a 64-fold increase from 1980 and a 200 percent increase since 1990.[2] Some of this investment has been driven by the dynamic growth of the U.S. economy and the opportunity that it has created. Conversely, plummeting currencies and troubled economies abroad have also caused some of the capital inflow. Sadly, the United States benefits from the fact that other countries are not living up to their potential. This benefit is a mixed blessing. It is always better to benefit from a strong global economy with other countries fulfilling their economic potential, than it is to benefit because they are doing poorly. In fact, if the rest of the world were performing better, U.S. economic strength would be enhanced, not hurt. There are no limits to growth and the global economy is not a zero-sum game.

In the 1980s, many economists predicted that Japan and Germany would dominate the world economy and that the United States would fall behind. Today, many of those same dismal scientists are worried that hard times for these same economies will drag the United States down. Neither worry should bother investors as long as the United States follows good policy. Think about it. If your kids get sick, but you have been sleeping right, eating right, and exercising, you are unlikely to get sick. On the other hand, if you have been burning the candle at both ends, traveling too much, eating fast food, writing a book, and working too hard, you probably will not avoid catching that cold. The point is that the United States has been following the right policies. By doing so we attract capital from around the world which feeds the fire of invention and innovation to an even greater extent. As a result, productivity is up, wages are rising faster than inflation, and interest rates keep falling. In addition, the U.S. economy seems impervious to global economic calamity.

GETTING THE BEST FROM THE TEAM

The pressures just described are forcing governments and investors to look at fiscal policies in a different light. If high taxes to pay for generous welfare and unemployment benefits cause capital flight and slower growth, then an economy will suffer. In addition, data are now available to make the connection between cause and effect. In the past, the debate over the impact of government policy was much more political, esoteric, and theoretical. In the New Era, it is exposed like never before. Following the collapse of the Iron Curtain and the poor performance of the U.S. economy during the 1970s, government management of the economy has become suspect. In effect, the emperor's clothes are slowly being stripped away. Since the late 1970s, when the United States began to deregulate, shrink government as a share of GDP, and cut taxes, we have been booming.

Entrepreneurs must be allowed to reap the rewards for the risks that they take. High taxes reduce those rewards, while low tax rates increase them. Interestingly, government actually benefits from a vibrant entrepreneur. In 1998, the United States experienced its first budget surplus since 1969. The combination of two developments led to this surplus. First, tax revenues have been soaring because taxable wages and capital gains are rising much faster than inflation. Second, government spending has declined sharply as a share of GDP. While much of this decline has occurred because of cuts in defense spending, low unemployment and rising incomes have reduced the need for government services. In effect, the technology boom is helping to create an environment that is conducive to its own self-interest. Budget surpluses are now estimated to be so large that tax cuts are seriously being considered.

KEEPING THE TEAM FOCUSED

Even though the negative impact of many government policies is now widely understood, there is no guarantee that government activism will not make a comeback. After all, it was during the boom times of the 1920s and the 1960s that the Smoot-Hawley Tariff Act and the Great Society were implemented. These activist policies hurt the economy and investors a great deal. Nonetheless, politics in the New World has changed. Our Chicago Bulls analogy may help to explain why.

Of all the Chicago Bulls (and maybe of all the NBA), Dennis Rodman was the most volatile and disruptive player. Despite being the best rebounder in the league, no one knew what he might do next or how his antics might impact the team. In the 1998 season, the Bulls and Dennis worked out a contract with special incentive clauses (worth millions) for good behavior. Those good-behavior clauses kept Dennis in check during the 1998 season and he contributed much to the team's success.

Especially in the United States, the New Era is providing the same incentives for politicians and policymakers. First, at least 43 percent of, or more than 120 million, Americans own stocks. As a result, bad policies will impact many more individuals, and voters, than ever before. Good policies that help the economy and financial markets perform well will be rewarded, while bad policy ideas will be punished. The theme of the 1992 Clinton presidential campaign was "It's the economy, stupid." This was the perfect campaign strategy and the perceived weakness of the U.S. economy in 1992 led to the defeat of George Bush. More importantly, a strong economy is credited with helping President Clinton withstand the scandals that have surrounded his administration.

The same is true worldwide. Helmut Kohl lost his job as German chancellor in 1998, to Gerhard Schroeder, in large part because of a weak German economy. In early October, just 3 days after winning the election, Gerhard Schroeder was taught an important lesson in the New Era. During a speech in Paris he gave strong support to the French idea of placing greater controls on international capital flows in order to prevent the global financial problems that occurred in 1998. He said that "there needs to be better control of capital flows and of the financial system in general or it could seriously impair economies and not just emerging economies."[3]

The markets' response to Schroeder's speech was dramatic and painful. The German stock market fell to a new yearly low the next day as the German DAX index fell 5.5 percent, while a broader market, the Xetra Dax fell 7.6 percent.[4]

Chancellor-elect Schroeder learned his lesson. Eight days later, when reiterating his concerns about market speculators and capital flows, a reporter for *Dow Jones* wrote that Schroeder "didn't want to discuss any of the details of any proposed regulation."[5] This began a slow backing away from the idea. By the time he was inaugurated as chancellor in early November 1998, his speeches had become much less pointed or radical. "We do not stand for right-wing or left-wing economic policies but for modern policies of the social market economy," he said in his first major speech to the German parliament since being sworn in just 2 weeks before.[6]

Despite the shift in Gerhard Schroeder's rhetoric, his finance minister, Oskar Lafontaine, showed no sensitivity to fundamental economic forces. As a socialist, he proposed increasing taxes on the wealthy, redistribution of resources to the jobless, and a 32-hour workweek. He persisted in his beliefs, despite a disappointing stock market performance and a decline of –0.4 percent in German GDP during the fourth quarter of 1998. Eventually, the pressure became overwhelming and on March 11, 1999, Lafontaine resigned his post. The day after his resignation, the DAX stock index shot up over 5.0 percent. At one point during that trading day it was more than 7.0 percent higher—the equivalent of nearly 700 Dow Jones Industrial Average points. Sensing the mood of investors at a press conference the next day, Schroeder said, "I plan to relieve the burdens on business as well as the weak members of society who need our care."[7] While carefully crafted, this statement shows once again that Schroeder is determined to make markets happy.

This metamorphosis of Germany and specifically of Gerhard Schroeder is similar to the change that overcame President Clinton between 1993 and 1996. He moved from wanting to nationalize the U.S. health care system to claiming that big government was over. The New Era has created a new constituency of investors that react swiftly and decisively to shifts in government policy. This "fourth branch of government" has become a force that provides massive incentives that sway politicians, just like Dennis Rodman's contract forced him to alter his behavior. The global marketplace has taken away the power of politicians to deliver on promises or to manage the economy. What was once possible for politicians, in an age of less information and slower capital flows, has now become futile.

OUR MONEY

In basketball, players can always count on the ball and the hoop to be the same size no matter where a game is played. Imagine what would happen if the size of the ball or hoop differed in every stadium. The ability of players to improve through practice would disappear. What would players practice with if they never played games with the same size equipment? Thank goodness, the game is not played this way. In many ways this explains why sound money is so important. Money is the basketball of the economy. After training for years to increase our business skills and acumen, a sharp change in the value of money would make that training useless. If money changed in value dramatically every day, it would be impossible to plan for the future. When inflation is raging, as it was in the 1970s, the economy is hurt because consumers make decisions based on how the value of money is changing, not because of true underlying economic fundamentals.

When inflation is high, consumers buy things before they need them, businesses invest in new machines that they do not need, and plant managers build bigger inventories than they want because they all know the price will rise in the future. When inflation is high, interest rates are high and future earnings are worth less. Moreover, inflation increases uncertainty. Uncertainty inhibits the success of entrepreneurs who must make calculations about the future.

This is why the fifth trend, a decline in the inflation rate, is so important to the New Era. Not only has low inflation helped the economy, but the New Era economy has also helped keep inflation low. Rising productivity has allowed the economy to produce more with less; globalization and deregulation have increased competition and efficiency. Each of these has made the Fed's job—of managing monetary policy and keeping inflation low—easier.

In the 1970s, the economy was not built on a rock. As a result, even small mistakes in monetary policy could send it into a recession or an inflationary spiral. Today, the economy remains so robust that monetary policy has remained very stable. For example, between February 1995 and February 1999, the federal funds rate was held in a range between 6.0 percent and 4.75 percent—the narrowest 4-year range for the federal funds rate ever. Whereas the focus on the Fed by the press and investors has become intense, actual policy changes have been minor.

Nonetheless, because the Fed has focused on keeping inflation low, the New Era has progressed. Low inflation increases certainty of the future, allows resources to be utilized in a more efficient manner, and boosts stock values. These developments then boost investment in New Era technologies, which increase productivity. Higher productivity increases growth and lowers inflation. This virtuous cycle within a virtuous circle increases the power of each of the other four key trends. Low inflation strengthens the dollar and boosts foreign investment in the United States. Low inflation also reduces effective tax rates by pushing individuals more slowly into higher tax brackets and also by avoiding the inflation of capital investments which raised capital gains tax rates in the 1970s.

Interestingly, for a number of years, the Fed as a whole has been very worried about the potential for rising inflation. In fact, Chairman Greenspan told Congress in 1997 that the Fed was "puzzled about how an economy, operating at high levels and drawing into employment increasingly less experienced workers, can still produce subdued and by some measures, even falling, inflation rates."[8] This puzzlement, as we saw in the previous chapter, comes from the fact that the Fed believes that the economy has limits and that whenever unemployment falls below a magic rate, wages and inflation must accelerate. Because of this institutional bias toward demand-side models at the Fed, inflation is unlikely to become a problem for years to come.

The economy is likely to remain strong because of high-tech productivity growth; and as long as the Fed believes that this strong growth is inflationary, it will hold interest rates above the level to which they would fall to naturally. By doing so they are printing less money than the world truly desires and the value of the dollar will climb as inflation continues to fall. The only concern from an investor's standpoint should not be about the potential for inflation, but instead should be about the prospects for deflation. A little deflation is a good thing, but any deflation greater than 2.0 or 3.0 percent is bad. The reason is that interest rates cannot fall below zero. When deflation gets out of control it can be worse than inflation. We only need to look at what deflation did to the U.S. economy in the 1930s and to Japan in recent years. In neither case were interest rates that even fell below zero for a short period, low enough to boost economic activity.

PUTTING IT ALL TOGETHER

The five key economic trends laid out in the previous chapters are the underlying reasons for the New Era of Wealth. They are also the reason that the economy and financial markets will boom for the next 20 to 30 years. The five trends work in a virtuous circle and foster rapid growth, low inflation, and wealth creation.

Entrepreneurial activity and technology are increasing productivity and efficiency. Smaller government, fewer regulations, and lower tax rates have helped create a better environment for this innovation. In return, plentiful jobs, rising incomes, and widespread investing put even more pressure on the government to get out of the way. With over 120 million stockholders today, the political pressure on the government is to foster wealth creation, not redistribution. Technology limits the effectiveness of government regulations by allowing individuals to sidestep them. In addition, low inflation creates the necessary environment for long-term investing, which in turn makes monetary policy easier to manage.

Although unlikely, a shift in these trends could occur. This would be the only way that the New Era could come to an end. The next chapter discusses what investors should watch for when assessing the prospects for a change in these five trends. Vigilance is a virtue for investors.

References

[1] All data on expansions and contractions are decided upon by the Business Cycle Dating Committee of the National Bureau of

Economic Research. These data are then published by the U.S. Department of Commerce and published in table C-51 of the *Survey of Current Business.*

[2] The 1998 Securities Industry Factbook. 1998. New York: Securities Industry Asociation.

[3] Coleman, Brian and Kamm, Thomas. 1998. Germany's Schroeder backs controls. *Wall Street Journal,* 1 October, p. A16.

[4] Coyle, Thomas. 1998. German stocks end sharply lower: Xetra Dax tumbles 7.6%. *Dow Jones Online News,* 1 October, online.

[5] Keto, Alex. 1998. Germany's Schroeder emphasizes need for global econ rules. *Dow Jones Online News,* 9 October, online.

[6] Berlin, Andrew Mccathie. 1998. Schroeder battles poor start to German leadership. *Australian Financial Review,* 12 November, p. 17.

[7] Drozdiak, William. 1999. Schroeder faces obstacles on road to 'new center.' *Washington Post,* 13 March, p. A15.

[8] Greenspan, Alan. 1997. *Monetary policy testimony and report to the Congress,* 22 July. Washington, DC: Federal Reserve Board.

PART 2

PREPARING YOUR PORTFOLIO FOR THE COMING BOOM

7

FOUR THREATS TO
THE NEW ERA

In January 1999, the day that Michael Jordan retired from basketball for the second time, the Chicago Bulls dynasty officially came to an end. Post-Jordan basketball in Chicago is decidedly different. During the 1999 season seats were empty, national television was no longer interested, and the spark was gone. This metaphor for the life and death of all living things pervades economic and financial market thinking. It seems so natural to assume that everything good must come to an end and that boom times in the economy must give way to a bust. Pessimists argue that the end is bound to come and that there is only one question. When? This view of the economy, however, is entirely too pessimistic. The economy is not ruled by time. It cannot get too tired to perform. *What brings boom times to an end are policy mistakes.* Before moving on to the investment strategies for the New Era, it is important for investors to learn to recognize which policy mistakes can bring the boom to an end.

History is strewn with prosperous nations that either collapsed completely or suffered difficult and long-lasting economic hard times. Many analysts argue that these economies just ran out of luck. But luck plays only a very small role in the creation of wealth over time. While inventors and entrepreneurs sometimes stumble upon innovations (such as the computer) which can boost growth, the policies which government puts into place are of even greater importance. An honest look at history shows that policy mistakes are the only thing that can end the boom. Here is where the comparison between the Chicago Bulls and the U.S. economy and financial markets comes to an end. Technology—the Michael Jordan of the economy—will not retire for many decades. The benefits of technology and our networked economy are only just beginning. Thus, the supporting cast of players—globalization, fiscal policies, a shifting political culture, and low inflation—is of utmost importance.

The importance of this supporting cast can be seen globally. For example, the failure of socialism led to the collapse of Russia and Eastern

European economies. Cuba, once a booming economy, has returned to the level of a third-world country under socialist rule. Why? Socialism does not recognize individual property rights and without them the "fire of genius" behind innovation cannot exist. For example, in terms of invention, China was well ahead of Europe at the turn of the first millenium. Chinese inventors created moveable-type printing presses 400 years before Gutenberg did. However, as David Landes wrote, "for all that printing did for the preservation and diffusion of knowledge in China, it never 'exploded' as in Europe."[1] Why? China did not have free markets and a system of property rights in place to take advantage of this incredible technology. Clearly, policies can make all the difference.

Not only can policy decisions keep progress at bay, but they can also bring good times to an end. This can be clearly seen in some of history's most famous bursting bubbles—the crash of 1929 and the Great Depression, the U.S. malaise of the 1970s, and the Japanese stock market crash of 1990. Each of these market crashes or periods of economic stagnation can be traced to government policy mistakes. More importantly, from these events, history suggests four threats to the New Era that investors should watch carefully.

- Protectionism and political interference with market competition.
- Excessive government regulation and spending.
- Tax increases.
- Monetary mistakes that cause deflation or inflation.

To understand these threats, it is important to analyze past periods of rapid wealth accumulation and to study their demise. Within that analysis, a pattern emerges which will highlight for investors these threats to prosperity.

THE GREAT DEPRESSION

Like an old wives tale, the story that the stock market crash of 1929 and the Great Depression were caused by a bubble in the market lives on and on. As recently as March 1999, David Dreman, author of *Contrarian Investment Strategies* and a columnist in *Forbes*, equated the U.S. stock market in 1999 with the South Sea Bubble and the market of 1929. He wrote, "With hindsight, the market was wildly overpriced just prior to the 1929 crash, when it traded at a P/E of 22."[2] Despite this relatively popular view of the U.S. markets, it is not clear that the stock market was overvalued in 1929. In the 1920s the United States was experiencing a boom in productivity and profits much like it has in the past few years. The technology of production lines and electric motors was driving stock prices higher and the economy was roaring.

Although many may want to believe that the market fell just because it was overvalued and a bursting bubble caused the Great Depression, the true cause of the stock market crash of 1929 can be attributed to government policy mistakes. These policy mistakes then led to others that are the real cause of the Great Depression. One reason that an overvalued market and irrational investors are blamed is that policymakers instinctively shift blame for problems away from policies and decisions that they control and onto things that they cannot control. It is much easier to fault the irrational excesses of individuals or bad luck than it is to blame faulty government policy. After all, government has a vested interest in protecting its turf. As Lawrence Lindsey, former Federal Reserve Board governor wrote in his 1999 book, *Economic Puppetmasters*, "protecting the system is the reason that, during a crisis, complicity in finding a scapegoat is extraordinarily widespread."[3] The system that Lindsey is talking about is the system of government economic institutions. Shifting blame from these institutions onto an individual scapegoat or onto "irrational markets" perpetuates the problems that these institutions cause and the system is left intact to cause its mayhem all over again.

There are two problems with these institutions of the government and the Federal Reserve. First, the economic models that they use are fundamentally flawed. They view the economy as being driven by demand, not supply. In other words, rising stock prices reflect excess demand for stocks, not a fundamental shift in the future earnings prospects for many companies due to changing technology and entrepreneurial innovation. By viewing the world through the lens of demand-side models, government institutions and those who lead them tend to believe that the economy can be managed. Second, the institutions that have been developed and the political system that they support are driven by vested interests—both political and economic.

In the 1920s and 1930s, vested economic interests, and a government gullible enough to think that it could manage the economy, found an important ally in John Maynard Keynes. Keynes believed that it was the job of the government to manage the economy and that individuals would make mistakes in economic logic. In the Keynesian theoretical world, individuals would save too little, consume too much, and bid up the price of assets to irrational levels. According to Keynes, it should be the government's job to direct investment, redistribute income, and manage the level of interest rates so that the economy would operate more efficiently.

Keynes's influence gathered strength after the crash of 1929, as his ideas about managing the economy found fertile fields. In fact, during the 1920s, the Federal Reserve was already manipulating interest rates to manage the economy and after the crash, the race to find a scapegoat was on. Many believe that the reduction of the discount rate in August 1927, from 4.0 percent to 3.5 percent, engineered by Benjamin Strong, the dominate Fed chairman of the 1920s, fueled euphoria in the stock market that was bound to cause problems.[4] Following the rate cut, the stock market roared ahead and many argued that the Fed must do something to stop it. However, despite raising interest rates from 3.5 percent to 5.0 percent in 1928, the boom continued and many believed that the Fed should increase rates further to calm the speculative fever gripping Wall Street.

In mid-1998, John Cassidy, writing for *The New Yorker*, also compared the U.S. economy and stock market of the 1990s with the 1920s and argued that the Fed should raise interest rates to avoid a repeat of the 1929 crash. In his analysis of the crash of 1929 he traced the mistaken Fed policy to a meeting on February 5, 1929. On that day, George Harrison, the president of the Federal Reserve Bank of New York, visited Fed Chairman Roy Young (Strong's successor). He "asked Young to immediately raise from five to six percent the interest rate at which the Fed lends money to banks—a move that would reduce speculation by raising the cost of borrowing money."[5] According to Cassidy, "Young feared that raising interest rates might spark a stock market crash rather than prevent one. He turned down Harrison's request and didn't raise the discount rate [from 5.0% to 6.0%] until August. By then it was too late."[6]

Cassidy's view of the 1929 crash is conventional wisdom. Nonetheless, it is highly suspect. In fact, it appears that Young was right initially and that interest rate increases by the Fed in 1928 and 1929 were a key factor in causing the crash. What most pundits miss when analyzing the period of the late 1920s is that the United States was experiencing deflation. As a result, interest rate increases were the worst policy response to a rising stock market. While the price of gold was pegged in a global system of fixed exchange rates, other prices were declining. Between 1925 and 1929, the price of silver fell by 25 percent and the Consumer Price Index fell for 5 consecutive years. The reasons for these price declines were twofold: The economy was experiencing rapid productivity growth, and the Fed confused the technology-driven economy and exuberant stocks for easy monetary policy. By raising interest rates from 3.5% to 6.0%, during a time of deflation, the Fed made that deflation worse. Deflation pushed commodity prices down and squeezed corporate profits. Farmers and textile producers, rather than blaming the Fed, blamed foreign competition for falling prices and put pressure on Congress to pass protectionist legislation.

In 1929, Congress passed the Smoot-Hawley Tariff Act and in 1930, President Herbert Hoover signed it into law. The act, which raised tariffs by more than 30 percent on a vast array of goods, literally shut down world trade. Jude Wanniski, in his book, *The Way the World Works*, details the impact of the Smoot-Hawley legislation on the stock market during 1929 and 1930. In his book he carefully traces the progress of the Smoot-Hawley trade bill through Congress and shows that every time the bill made forward progress the stock market stumbled and when the bill met resistance, stocks bounced back.[7] Despite the signals that the stock market was sending, the Smoot-Hawley Tariff Act was finally signed into law.

This turned what was a deflationary policy mistake by the Fed into a massive collapse of the stock market and the economy.

Interestingly, those who blame the Fed for holding interest rates too low throughout the 1920s have not been able to explain why inflation never appeared. If the Fed was creating too much credit, the economy should have experienced inflation, not deflation. In fact, the 1930s turned into the worst deflationary spiral that the United States has ever experienced. Fed policy mistakes turned what was a gentle deflation of roughly 1.0 percent per year in the late 1920s, into a deflation of 10 percent to 15 percent per year during the early 1930s. The policy mistakes did not stop there. New Deal government spending and massive tax increases to pay for that spending held the economy down for years to come. In addition, a vast regulatory environment was built up in the 1930s as John Maynard Keynes convinced the world that market failure was the cause of economic problems, not government policy mistakes. Because of the implementation of Keynesian policy prescriptions, the economy remained stagnant and unemployment remained in the double-digit range until late in the decade.

MALAISE AND STAGNATION IN THE 1970s

The period between 1965 and 1982 was the worst 17-year period in U.S. stock market history. After adjustment for inflation, investors in U.S. stocks during that period saw negative returns. This period should show investors that stocks do not always go up. Investors would have beaten both stocks and bonds during this period by investing in short-term money market instruments.

This period of malaise was predictable. The policies followed were exactly the opposite policies that the United States has implemented during the current New Era of Wealth. Lyndon Johnson began building the Great Society in 1965 and government spending shot up from 17.2 percent of GDP in 1965 to 23.2 percent in 1982. To pay for this increase in spending, tax rates were pushed higher. In 1965, households in the 80th to 85th percentile of income earners faced a marginal income tax rate of less than 25 percent. By 1981, this same group paid a marginal income tax rate of over 35 percent.[8] Regulation also climbed during this period as the number of pages in the *Federal Register* rose by 416 percent between 1966 and 1981.[9]

The Great Society fiscal policies of redistribution, rising taxes, and burdensome regulation acted like a wet blanket on the economy, limiting productivity growth and slowing wealth creation. Slower economic growth caused the Federal Reserve to push interest rates down to keep the economy growing. Eventually, the Bretton Woods system of pegging the dollar to gold and then pegging other major currencies to the dollar became unglued as the Fed printed an excess amount of money. Foreigners began to demand gold instead of U.S. bonds and the United States responded by devaluing the dollar relative to gold. By devaluing our currency the United States went through virtually the same economic mess that Brazil, Thailand, and Malaysia have gone through in the past few years.

THE VICIOUS CIRCLE

The policies of the 1960s and 1970s resulted in a vicious circle of economic problems. High taxes limited innovation, slower productivity growth created an environment conducive to inflation, and then the Fed fueled that inflation by mistaking slow growth for tight money. High inflation increased uncertainty, pushed taxpayers into higher tax brackets, and caused interest rates to rise. The result was more uncertainty, lower P/E ratios, and falling profits for corporate America. In addition, stop-and-go monetary policies caused a series of four recessions between 1969 and 1982—one of the worst periods of U.S economic performance in history.

Interestingly, the nature of this vicious circle was lost on most economists at the time and on many economists to this day. Conventional wisdom said that the problems the economy was experiencing were just a series of bad breaks caused by OPEC and other problems outside the control of government policies. Economists who believe that the government can manage the economy refuse to admit that mistakes in government economic management caused the stagflation of the 1970s. Nonetheless, it is clear that the twin problems of double-digit unemployment and inflation ended in the early 1980s when these policies were changed. Investors who want to avoid the damage done by bad policies should heed the evidence of the 1970s.

LEARNING FROM JAPAN

Another famous market crash that caused tremors throughout the financial community was the 1990 collapse of the Japanese stock market and the malaise that has befallen this once powerful economy. In the mid-1980s, the Japanese economy was considered the dominant economy in the world and by 1989, the Nikkei stock index had climbed to near 40,000. Then the problems began. The Nikkei average plummeted to under 16,000 by 1992. Today, Japanese government debt has ballooned to over 100 percent of GDP, Japanese banks have over $1 trillion in bad loans on their books, unemployment has risen to an all-time record, and the economy is in the midst of at least a 2-year long recession.

Again many economists missed the smoking gun. Conventional wisdom suggests that the stock market was in a bubble along with real estate and that when that bubble burst, the good times ended. Like other economic disasters, however, this theory ignores government policy mistakes. In April 1989, Japan implemented a nationwide value-added-tax of 3 percent. In January 1990, Japan pushed the capital gains tax rate from zero to 20 percent. The increase in taxes on consumption and investment caused the end of the Japanese miracle. In addition to raising taxes, the Japanese central bank also boosted short-term interest rates from under 4.0 percent to 6.5 percent between March and December 1989 despite the fact that inflation was just 1 percent before the increase in the value-added-tax in April. As a result, the Japanese economy has experienced deflation and stagnation simultaneously. While the Japanese stock market was most likely overvalued in 1989, these policy mistakes, which are similar to our policy mistakes of the 1920s, turned a market correction into an economic collapse.

Since then, the Japanese have tried the same Keynesian economic prescriptions that world history shows do not work. Japan has tried to spend its way out of its malaise by pushing through between $700 billion and $1 trillion in public works spending projects in the past 7 years. In addition, they have lowered short-term interest rates to 0.1 percent. However, the Japanese economy continues to be mired in recession. Although this short history of Japan's current problems leaves much unsaid, it covers the high points. Japan must learn to have faith in the entrepreneurial process and stop trying to manage its economy. Japan must cut taxes and regulation in order to grow again. Entrepreneurial effort is the only way to create wealth, especially in the New Era. As this book was being written, Japan was beginning to do the right things. Corporate and Individual tax rate reductions that took place in April 1999 may be just the medicine that the Japanese economy needs. Time will tell.

THE FOUR THREATS

The quick review presented here shows that government policy has *not* been a neutral factor in economic history. In fact, each of the four threats to the New Era was somehow involved in all of these market crashes. By understanding this idea, investors can protect themselves if these mistakes by policymakers begin to occur again. Protectionism, tax increases, government expansion, and bad monetary policy are detrimental to the stock market. For the bond market, these policies are not all bad. Deflation brings interest rates down, while inflation pushes interest rates up.

THE MARKETS AS TASK MASTER

While history clearly shows the damage that bad policy can do, politicians will always be tempted to use their power to protect certain constituents and to manage the economy; however, the markets no longer allow mistakes to go very far.

For example, in the late summer of 1998 stock markets in the United States fell over 20 percent from July to September. The Starr Report and economic problems with Russia, Asia, and Latin America at the margin were clearly creating uncertainty. However, the most important reason for the decline was that the Fed was holding interest rates too high.

The reaction of the stock market to a July 21, 1998, speech by Fed Chairman Alan Greenspan shows the sensitivity of markets to the Fed. The NASDAQ stock index peaked at an all-time high on July 20, 1998, at over 2,000 and began its slide on July 21, the day that Greenspan gave testimony to Congress. Why? Greenspan said that the Fed was still thinking about raising interest rates when the market expected a rate cut. At that time, virtually every Treasury market interest rate was below the federal funds rate (an invented yield curve). The markets were telling the Fed to cut rates, so news that they were still thinking about raising rates was very damaging.

Within 6 weeks after the NASDAQ had fallen by 20 percent, the Federal Reserve shifted gears. On September 4, 1998, when Greenspan gave a speech in California that suggested that the Fed was now thinking about cutting interest rates, the stock market had one of its biggest 1-day rallys ever. The Fed's about-face shows the power that markets now have over policymakers, but this has not always been so. In the New Era, markets will help prevent policymakers from making mistakes. After all, what Fed, Congress, or president wants to go down in history as causing a crash in the markets?

STORM CLOUDS

As this book was being written, clouds were appearing on the horizon. The Japanese, Russian, and Asian economies were in virtual chaos, Brazil had devalued, the U.S. trade deficit was ballooning, and protectionist pressures were increasing. In fact, the U.S. Commerce Department had instituted tariffs against dozens of European exports because of what it called unfair trade practices regarding the importation of bananas. In addition, tariffs and quotas against steel producers from Japan and Brazil were being seriously threatened. On the antitrust front, Microsoft was under attack by the Justice Department and the Federal Trade Commission was scrutinizing Intel. Moreover, the Fed was holding interest rates too high, threatening to raise them further and creating deflationary pressures. These developments create uncertainty, but the world has changed and it is unlikely that the mistakes of the past will be repeated. New Era trends suggest that both policymakers and investors are shifting their perspectives about which policies work and which do not. Nonetheless, the four threats to the New Era are real and investors must watch policymakers carefully.

It would be nice to know exactly how to tell when the threats to prosperity are high enough to warrant a shift in investment strategy, but there are no hard and fast rules. For example, tax rates are higher today than they were during the Industrial Revolution, but the economy is performing exceptionally. One reason is that other countries have tax rates and policy environments that are much worse than the United States and therefore capital flows to our shores. What matters most is the direction of policy. In 1993, the momentum in policy was toward tax hikes and a government takeover of the health care system, and investors paid the price of higher interest rates and a lethargic stock market. Since then, the momentum has been toward less government interference and tax cuts. As long as the momentum does not shift back again the New Era will continue.

References

[1] Landes, David S. 1998. *The wealth and poverty of nations: Why some are so rich and some are so poor,* 1st ed. New York: W.W. Norton & Company.

[2] Dreman, David. 1999. The contrarian: Bubble psychology. *Forbes,* 8 March, p. 148.

[3] Lindsey, Lawrence. 1999. *Economic puppetmasters: Lessons from the halls of power,* 1st ed. Washington, DC: The AEI Press.

[4] Brooks, John. 1969. *Once in Golconda: A true drama of Wall Street 1920–1938.* New York: Allsworth Press, pp. 90–94.

[5] Cassidy, John. 1998. Annals of finance; Pricking the bubble. *The New Yorker,* 17 August, pp. 37–41.

[6] Ibid.

[7] Wanniski, Jude, 1978, "The Way the World Works", Morristown, New Jersey, 1989 3rd edition. Polyeconomics, Inc.

[8] Genetski, Robert J. 1986. *Taking the voodoo out of economics.* Chicago: Regnery Gateway, Inc.

[9] Bianco, James. BiancoResearch, Inc.

8

SHIFTING PERCEPTIONS

Although the odds of government policy mistakes that could bring the New Era to an end are limited, they are not zero because many of our most influential policymakers are reluctant to believe in the New Era. Despite the fact that manufacturing productivity is soaring, economic growth has averaged nearly 4 percent per year since 1996, and inflation has remained virtually nonexistent, these economists refuse to believe that the underlying structure of the economy has changed. Like those who thought planets revolved around the earth, they are using the wrong models. They view the world through Keynesian-based, demand-side, Phillips Curve models that worship diminishing returns. In this view of the world, economic growth cannot exceed 2.5 percent and unemployment cannot fall below 5 percent without causing inflation. In addition, they believe that irrational investors, not government policy mistakes, cause market problems. These analysts conclude that the Fed should react to strong growth by raising interest rates. They also believe that any tax cut now would stimulate the economy too much and cause inflation. In their models, the economy is doing the impossible—growing rapidly without inflation.

As Federal Reserve Board Governor Laurence Meyer said in June 1998, " . . . I sometimes hear from those who insist that the old paradigm of limits has been replaced by the new era paradigm, in which global competition and productivity improvement on demand guarantee that any level of utilization rates and any level of growth can be sustained with low stable inflation. Needless to say, I reject this vision. Old limits may give way to new limits, but if the new limits are not respected, there will be a price to pay."[1]

Alan Blinder, a Princeton professor, former economic advisor to President Clinton, and current economic advisor to presidential aspirant Al Gore, wrote in late 1997 that, "growth optimists do not want harsh realities to ruin their dreams. But the evidence shows long-term growth is in the 2 percent to 2.5 percent range." He added that, "a productivity miracle based upon the computer may be just around the corner. Perhaps. But, if so, it is around the *next* corner, not the *last* one." He even described New

Era thoughts as "poppycock."[2] In his denial of the New Era, Blinder actually suggests that the computer has harmed productivity growth. He wrote, "don't be taken in by the hyper-hype. Sure, I now can surf the Net, send and receive e-mail in seconds, and have more computing power on my desk than ever before. But has any of this made me produce more GDP per hour of work?"[3] Part of his explanation for believing that the computer has not raised productivity is that, "the human brain has not advanced apace with the microprocessor."[4] Because Blinder does not believe in the productivity revolution or the New Era, he has explained the current economic environment as a bunch of "lucky breaks"[5] caused by falling import, computer, and energy prices; however, as has been shown in the previous chapters, the New Era is not just luck.

Nonetheless, Blinder and Meyer are not alone. In December 1997, Paul Krugman, an unapologetic Keynesian economist wrote that "the reason I can't buy into the New Economy is actually very simple: Despite all the incentives, I can't bring myself to endorse a doctrine that I know to be just plain dumb."[6] Krugman, who teaches economics at MIT, went further in 1999 when he wrote, "The problems of the 1990s have distinct similarities with the problems of the 1930s; so do the solutions. We had better all start relearning our Depression economics."[7]

Krugman is convinced that the problems the world economy experienced in 1998—Russian meltdown, Asian collapse, and the spread of these problems to Latin America—signal the need for more government control and higher inflation. He wrote that "the world became vulnerable to its current travails not because economic policies had not been reformed, but because they had."[8] He saw problems with the very reforms that brought the New Era prosperity back to the United States. In particular, he complains about four reforms that exhibit the "virtues of old-fashioned capitalism": (1) the "liberalization of international transactions," (2) the "liberalization of domestic financial markets," (3) the "reestablishment of price stability," and (4) the "restoration of fiscal discipline." He claims that these reforms have made the world more "vulnerable" to "instability and sustained economic slumps." His proposed solution is to limit capital flows, reregulate financial markets, run bigger budget deficits, and seek low inflation, not price stability.

This pessimistic assessment of the New Era is both a reaction and an overreaction. Like most good thinkers, Keynesians are stuck in the model of the world that they grew up learning and teaching. Despite its flaws, the model forces its adherents to react to every bump in the road with calls for a government fix of one sort or another—even though the evidence suggests that government policy mistakes cause the bumps in the road.

The collapse of Asia and Russia are directly related to bad government policy. Asia's banking sector was politically influenced into making many bad loans while Russia lacks the "rule of law." In addition, the central banks of Asia, Russia, and Brazil forced devaluation by printing too much currency. Their monetary policies were never focused on price stability, so blaming price stability for their problems is nonsense. These countries are experiencing massive inflation which robs them of economic potential. In addition, international bailouts do not help. Implicit IMF bailout guarantees act like insurance and cause many international investors to invest more than they would without the potential bailout. As a result, market forces are not allowed to work and the IMF causes many more problems than it ever solves.

Despite these mistakes in policy, many Keynesians tend to overreact by calling for capital controls and more government regulation. As Chancellor Schroeder learned in Germany, however, markets do not like capital controls. The freedom to move investments is the freedom to protect investments. Capitals controls, by limiting investor freedom, increase the risk of investment and therefore diminish its value. Capital controls would reduce worldwide investment, not increase it. Capital controls would make financial markets less stable, not more. True stability comes from allowing capital markets to grow deep and diversified, and the only way that can happen is for markets to remain free.

For example, one benefit of owning an automobile is the freedom of movement that it provides. If the government were to somehow limit your use of that automobile, say letting you drive it on every other Tuesday, then its value would fall precipitously and the demand for autos would drop. Sure the roads would be less crowded, but the economy would grow more slowly. On the other hand, many government policies regarding automobiles increase their value. Road signs, driving laws, and good roads increase the value of all vehicles. Private insurance helps too. People drive more carefully because they know that their insurance premiums will go up if they get in an accident. The result has been that consumers have demanded safer cars and higher speed limits. What happened? The United States has had fewer auto-related fatalities, not more.

The same truths carry over to international investing. If capital flows are hindered by rules that allow only long-term investing and that limit the amount or type of investment, international investment will decline as will world growth. In that same vein, the enforcement of property rights and contracts increases the value of an investment. Countries such as Russia, who default on debt payments, reduce the demand for potential future investment in their nation. Moreover, investors who learn not to count on bailouts will demand safer investments that are protected by the rule of law.

In the New Era, markets will force efficiency on both government and corporate entities around the world. Government interference in this movement would be a huge mistake. This fact is slowly dawning on policymakers. Japanese politicians have instituted tax cuts in an attempt to boost their economy and also lowered interest rates to near zero in the recognition that deflation has harmed economic activity. And while there will always be naysayers, the transformation in policy has begun.

THE THREE STAGES OF DENIAL

In his book, *On Liberty,* the philosopher John Stuart Mill wrote that new ideas, which challenge the status quo, travel through three distinct phases of denial or acceptance. First, they are called untrue, naïve, or wrong. Second, they are blasphemy, against religion or threatening to civilization. Finally, they become received opinion or common sense and within anyone's reach.[9]

Today, debate about the New Era has reached such an emotional level that we seem firmly planted in the second phase. Nonetheless, investors who believe in the New Era and ignore the arguments of Meyer, Blinder, Krugman, and Soros stand to benefit a great deal. Eventually, the New Era will become common sense and the excess profits will be gone.

The transformation of one of the most well-known economists of the twentieth century provides an excellent example of how the evidence of a New Era is beginning to shift perceptions of the economy and even impact policy. In February 1997, Federal Board Chairman Alan Greenspan said, "Is it possible that there is something fundamentally new about this current period that would warrant such complacency? Yes, it is possible. Markets may have become more efficient, competition is more global, and information technology has doubtless enhanced the stability of business operations. But, regrettably, history is strewn with visions of such 'new eras' that, in the end, have proven to be a mirage. In short, history counsels caution."[10] At that time Greenspan did not believe.

Just 5 months later Greenspan seemed to warm to the idea of the New Era. In July 1997, he said, "We do not now know, nor do I suspect can anyone know, whether current developments are part of a once or twice in a century phenomenon that will carry productivity trends nationally and globally to a new higher track, or whether we are merely observing some unusual variations within the context of an otherwise generally conventional business cycle expansion."[11]

Then in September 1998, he finally gave the New Era thinkers some credibility; however, he was not convinced that old ideas should be thrown out completely. In essence, he was saying it is against religion to believe too fervently. He put it this way, "Some of those who advocate a 'new economy' attribute it generally to technological innovations and breakthroughs in globalization that raise productivity and proffer new capacity on demand and that have, accordingly, removed pricing power from the world's producers on a more lasting basis. There is, clearly, an element of truth in this proposition. But, although there doubtless have been profound changes...there is one important caveat to the notion that we live in a new economy, and that is human psychology."[12]

Despite this small doubt, the transformation of Alan Greenspan now seems to be complete. In March 1999, Greenspan said, "A remarkable element in our recent prosperity has been the rapid acceleration in the application of computer and telecommunications technologies, which have engendered a significant increase in productivity in this expansion." He added that he never ceases to be "amazed at the ability of our flexible and innovative economic system to take advantage of emerging technologies in ways that raise our productive capacity and generate higher asset values."[13]

INDIVIDUALS KNOW, POLICYMAKERS WILL FOLLOW

The transformation of Alan Greenspan is important. As chairman of the Fed he is in a unique position to push policy and economic thinking in the right direction. He does not always win these debates, however, nor has he remained absolutely convinced about the true nature of our prosperity. In mid-1999, Greenspan relapsed into his Phillips Curve past and the Fed raised interest rates twice from 4.75 perent to 5.0 percent and then to 5.25 percent. Nonetheless, New Era stocks are exploding, a record setting number of IPOs are occurring, and more investors than ever own stocks. Moreover, commodity prices are falling and wages are rising faster than inflation. Individuals understand what is happening. Despite the constant drumbeat of pessimism in the background, they are investing as if they know something that policymakers do not. Eventually this optimism and the overwhelming evidence of the New Era will win more resolute converts among policymakers and will ensure that the New Era continues.

Interestingly, the very nature of the transformation to New Era thinking holds within it the pressure for it to gain momentum. Those who continue to believe in government control of the economy are forced to offer either little ideas or very big ideas. For example, Krugman believes that an international agreement to control capital flows is necessary, but he has little support for this draconian step among politicians or other economists. Capital controls are just too invasive. Others call for a trillion dollar international Marshall Plan to build up suffering economies, but this would take a huge amount of political will that just does not exist. On the other hand, in early 1999, Vice President Al Gore focused much attention on airline passenger rights and helping commuters avoid traffic congestion. These little ideas are just small ripples in the swirling sea of a global economy and they highlight the impotence of the government in the New Era economy. Individual responsibility is taking root and the direction of government policy will be inexorably pulled in the direction of less government, not more.

IGNORING THE NOISE—BE OPTIMISTIC

The inexorable pull of the New Era is not as clear as many investors wish. In 1998, the stock market started to slide after global financial market turmoil convinced the pessimists that it was over. "Is it Armageddon or October 1987 revisited?" screamed the cover of the September 21, 1998, *Forbes* magazine. The temptation to be the first to call the end to the bull market of the 1980s and 1990s is strong. *Forbes* was not the only business publication to highlight the pessimistic view. Nonetheless, the NASDAQ stock index was in the process of bottoming out and on October 8 it hit 1,419.12 only to roar to 2,652.05 by April 26, 1999, a gain of 87 percent in less than seven months. Instead of ending, the New Era gained momentum. The 1998 "wall of worry" will not be the last the New Era must climb. This boom should last for the next 20 or 30 years and those that ignore the noise emanating from the pessimists will be the true beneficiaries.

Now is the best time that the world has seen since the Industrial Revolution to start a business, invest in a business, or expand a business. Entrepreneurial talent and creative thinking are rewarded like never before in the history of the world. Education pays off, risk is tied to reward, and change is the name of the game. Competition can come from anywhere and that means that you can sneak up on anyone just as easily as they can sneak up on you.

We must position our careers, businesses, and investment strategies to take advantage of the New Era of Wealth. After all, by the time the intellectuals finish fighting over who was right, the New Era will be common sense. And remember, when something becomes common sense, all the profits are gone.

References

[1] Meyer, Laurence. 1998. *Economic forecasting.* Speech delivered before the Downtown Economics Club 50th Anniversary Dinner, New York, June 3.

[2] Blinder, Alan S. 1997. The speed limit: Fact and fancy in the growth debate. *The American Prospect no. 34* (September-October 1997), p. 57–62.

[3] Ibid.

[4] Ibid.

[5] Blinder, Alan. 1999. Stated on *Wall street week with Louis Rukeyser,* January 22.

[6] Krugman, Paul. 1997. *Speed trap: The fuzzy logic of the "New Economy." Slate Online Magazine,* 18 December, http://www.slate.com/Dismal/97-12-18/Dismal.asp

[7] Krugman, Paul. 1999. The return of depression economics. *Foreign Affairs,* January/February, p. 56.

[8] Ibid.

[9] Mill, John Stuart. 1859. *On liberty.* Published 1986, Amherst, NY: Prometheus Books

[10] Greenspan, Alan. 1997. *The Federal Reserve's semiannual monetary policy report before the U.S. Senate.* Federal Reserve Board of Governors, February 26.

[11] Ibid, July 22.

[12] Greenspan, Alan. 1998. *Question: Is there a new economy?* Speech delivered at the Haas Annual Business Faculty research Dialogue, University of California, Berkeley, September 4.

[13] Greenspan, Alan. 1999. *Changes in small business finance.* Speech delivered at the Federal Reserve System Research Conference on Business Access to Capital and Credit, Arlington, VA, March 9.

9

STRATEGIES FOR CREATING PERSONAL WEALTH

In 1859, John Stuart Mill wrote, "Persons of genius, it is true, are, and are always likely to be, a small minority; but in order to have them, it is necessary to preserve the soil in which they grow. Genius can only breathe freely in an atmosphere of freedom."[1] Even though he did not know it at the time, his focus on genius and freedom was quintessential New Era. The backbone of all wealth creation and the continuation of the New Era depend on the fact that the United States remains a nurturing place for entrepreneurs. Over the past 17 years, the five key trends of the New Era of Wealth have been good for investors, business owners, and employees. Profits are rising, inflation is low, the economy is stable, and wages are up; but no matter how good things become we can always benefit by making the right investment decisions.

Although you and I will most likely never be as wealthy as the geniuses of the New Era, the choices we make today determine our future standard of living. Decisions we make today about what to invest in, which companies to work for, how much to save, whether to invest in our own business, and how much education we need will all have a huge impact on our lifestyle. Retirees must make choices with a finite set of resources, while the rest of us must invest the money we earn by putting our skills to work.

Fortunately, the underlying trends of the New Era suggest that we can all retire wealthy. What's more, we don't have to get lucky to do it. Sure we could retire rich by picking the right company, buying its stock, and avoiding every inclination to sell along the way. After all, $1,000 invested in Dell Computer Corp. (DELL) at the end of 1988 was worth $351,356 by the end of 1998—a 79.7 percent average annual return over a 10-year period.

Unfortunately, not every stock has performed this spectacularly, but the stock market as a whole has performed exceptionally well. On average, large company stocks, including dividends, have returned 18.2 percent per year since 1981,[2] and by investing in stocks, becoming a millionaire was well within reach for even an average family. For example, a family with an annual income of $50,000 that saved 10 percent of that income ($5,000) each year starting in 1981 and invested it in large company stocks, would have accumulated over $529,730 by the end of 1998. If this family had continued to save 10 percent of each year's income and their income rose 4 percent per year, their nest egg would have climbed to $642,829. Moreover, if stocks continue to rise in the future as they have in the past, our hypothetical family will surpass $1 million before the end of 2001.

A more conservative approach of buying intermediate-term government bonds would have given the family a nest egg of $305,429 at the end of 1998. If bonds continue to perform as they have in the past 17 years, our hypothetical family would become millionaires at the end of 2008.

All it takes to become a millionaire in the New Era is a disciplined approach to savings and some patience. Genius is not required and can sometimes even get in the way. Optimism is helpful, but an ability to ignore the pessimists will do. There will be many times when the experts suggest that the bubble is about to burst, that inflation is coming back and interest rates will rise. But they have been wrong in the past and, unless government policy shifts, they will be wrong in the future. The New Era has been pronounced dead numerous times, but it is resilient. Not only *can* it continue for decades into the future, it *will.* So the first strategy for gaining wealth is to remain patient and avoid trying to time the market. It will go up and it will go down, but over time the trends suggest that the New Era will be friendly to stocks.

THE FOUR TESTS—NEW ERA RESILIENCE

In its simple form, this book highlights the two main factors that will create wealth in the future—technology and the absence of bad government policy. Together these two factors will virtually guarantee that over the next 20 or 30 years the world will experience the greatest expansion in wealth that it has ever seen. The technology of computers and telecommunications has created a networked economy where productivity will increase rapidly and, with it, standards of living. Increasing returns will result in low inflation and rapid growth and in that environment, interest rates will remain low and stocks will continue to climb. However, just as the past has been filled with doubts, so will the future. There will always be something to worry about and the economy will continue to suffer shocks and seemingly insurmountable odds.

In the past 17 years the New Era economy has been declared dead at least four times. The first was in October 1987 when the stock market fell over 20 percent in 1 day. Many economists thought that a recession was inevitable, but the economy barely skipped a beat. In fact, as 1988 unfolded, the next worry became that the economy was overheating. At that same time, there was wide agreement that the United States was losing its competitiveness to Japan and Europe, but this pessimism proved unfounded as well.

The second test was during the recession of 1990 and 1991. The recession felt horrible. It ended what was the longest peacetime economic expansion in U.S. history from November 1982 through July 1990. Newspaper headlines proclaimed the end of the bull market in stocks and economists fretted about consumer debt and budget deficits. Ravi Batra's best-selling book, *Surviving the Great Depression of 1990*, first published in 1985, went through at least three different printings, with worrisome subtitles such as *Protect Your Assets and Investments and Come out on Top*.[3] To add even further to the gloom, the S & L debacle and the credit crunch were supposed to limit growth in the United States and make recovery difficult for decades to come. Nonetheless, the U.S. economy came to life again. Despite tax increases in 1991 and 1993, the wealth creation miracle of technology, free trade, and low inflation fueled the fire of growth.

The third test came in 1994. The Fed pushed the federal funds rate up from 3 percent in February 1994 to 6 percent in February 1995. Bond yields shot up with the 30-year Treasury yield rising to above 8 percent in late 1994 from under 6 percent in late 1993, one of the worst bond market performances in over 50 years. The stock market stagnated, inflation was on the rise, and later in 1994 Mexico devalued its currency by 60 percent versus the U.S. dollar. Despite all this, the U.S. stock market shot ahead in 1995 and the economy rebounded fully by 1996. The third test was passed with flying colors; even a rapid tightening in monetary policy and the collapse of Mexico could not knock the New Era economy down.

The fourth test was in 1998. We all remember it very well. The numerous apocalyptic headlines and magazine covers are highlighted elsewhere in this book. But even the collapse of Russia, Asia, Brazil, and Long-term Capital Management could not slow the U.S. economy. In fact, the U.S. economy accelerated following the global crisis of 1998. Real GDP shot ahead by 6.1 percent at an annual rate in the fourth quarter of 1998 and 4.3 percent in the first quarter of 1999 finishing off one of the strongest 3-year growth periods in history. Moreover, the stock market, after falling 20 percent from its highs in mid-1998, shot ahead late in 1998 for its fourth consecutive annual gain of greater than 20 percent.

These four tests show the resilience of the New Era economy. The virtuous circle of the five key trends work together to create a vibrant and dynamic economy capable of withstanding shocks to the system. The key is strong productivity growth. Since 1982, as productivity has accelerated the U.S. economy has experienced just one recession of only 8 months in length. In contrast, between 1969 and 1982, when productivity was much weaker the economy experienced four recessions that lasted a total of 49 months.

WEALTH ON THE RISE

The shift in the economy that began in the early 1980s has created a whole new investment strategy. Whereas buying into defensive investments such as real estate or other tangible assets protected wealth in the inflationary 1970s, investing in financial assets such as stocks and bonds is what creates wealth in the New Era. More importantly, very little wealth was created in the 1970s, but fabulous amounts of wealth are being created in the New Era. When taxes are cut, regulations are minimized, government spending is held in check, and inflation is low, then wealth creation accelerates.

Data from the Federal Reserve shows just how successful the U.S. economy has been at creating wealth in the New Era and where that wealth creation has occurred. In 1998 alone, household assets grew by $3.9 trillion or 10 percent. This incredible growth capped off what has been 17 fantastic years. From the end of 1981 to the end of 1998, U.S. household assets grew by $31.2 trillion to a total $43.0 trillion, a gain of 263 percent. During that same 17-year period, household assets held in stocks rose from $1.0 trillion to $10.8 trillion, a gain of 970 percent. But, household assets held in real estate have not fared as well. They rose from $3.3 trillion in 1981 to $9.2 trillion in 1998, a gain of just 180 percent. Assets held in Treasury, municipal, and corporate bonds rose faster than those in real estate, from $443.7 billion to $1.74 trillion, a gain of 291 percent.[4] For comparison, the Consumer Price Index rose 79.4 percent. In other words, total U.S. household assets rose by 4.4 percent per year after adjustment for inflation. At a 4.4 percent growth rate, every 16 years inflation-adjusted household assets will double.

This is in sharp contrast to the period between 1965 and 1981. Then, inflation-adjusted household assets rose just 2.5 percent per year, meaning that it took 28 years to double household assets rather than just 16 years. In addition, there has been a dramatic shift in where household assets are held. In 1965, at the peak of the post-war boom, households held 25.9 percent of their net worth in stocks and just 24 percent of their net worth in real estate. This changed dramatically during the next 16 years. By 1981, in the midst of stagflation, households held just 9.8 percent of their net worth in stocks, but 32 percent in real estate. Investors reacted in a rational manner to the inflation of the 1970s by investing more in real estate and less in stocks.

However, the New Era has changed this once again. In 1997, household stock investments surpassed real estate investments for the first time since 1968. In 1998, stocks made up 29.3 percent of household net worth, while real estate had fallen to 25.1 percent of total net worth. (See chart at top of next page.)

This shift in the balance of household assets fits perfectly with New Era themes. Idea-based assets are increasing in value relative to physical assets. Stocks, which represent ownership in businesses, are benefiting as

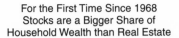

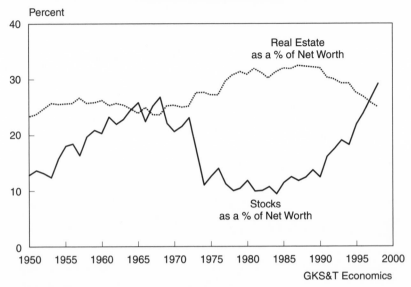

Source: Board of Governors of the Federal Reserve.

the technology boom raises productivity and profits. Physical resources, such as real estate, commodities and durable goods, are declining in value relative to the rest of the economy. The eradication of inflation has undermined one of the biggest reasons for rising real estate values during the 1970s.

When policies are focused on creating the best possible environment for creativity, genius, and entrepreneurial activity, financial assets outperform tangible assets. Given the gains in productivity that the U.S. economy is now experiencing, wealth creation will continue to astound the pessimists. There is no reason that per capita wealth cannot triple, or even quadruple, in the average working life of any American. The question for investors is how to position portfolios and careers to take full advantage of the New Era of Wealth.

Both the nature of the New Era and history give us some guidance in this effort. The virtuous circle created by our five key trends increases productivity and decreases risk, and thus holds inflation down and raises profits. In addition, the "fire of genius" creates opportunity by increasing the number of jobs, boosting incomes, and making education more valuable. This favors financial assets such as stocks and bonds and investment in education and ideas, over tangible assets such as real estate and commodities. As a result, there are four key strategies or ideas which will help create wealth in the New Era.

THE RISKS OF INVESTING IN STOCKS WILL DECLINE IN THE NEW ERA

Stock price-to-earnings (P/E) ratios have soared. When compared with earnings from the previous 12 months, the S&P 500 P/E ratio has grown from under 8 in 1981 to over 32 in early 1999. That means that investors are paying $32 for every dollar of earnings made by the companies in the S&P 500. Obviously, past earnings mean nothing to someone who buys a portion of a company today. As we know so well, companies that exist today may not be here tomorrow. So why are investors paying so much? The only answer can be that they expect future earnings to grow. While this optimism may bother some analysts, evidence that the economy has entered a New Era makes this exuberance rational, not irrational.

The economy is resilient, productivity is up, and what Joseph Schumpeter called "gale[s] of creative destruction"[5] are reinventing the economy as you read this book. This situation creates a number of very positive forces that reduce risk and therefore lead to higher P/E ratios. First, high-tech investment is raising productivity and boosting the potential economic growth rate. As a result, the economy is more robust and less prone to damage from the global shocks that have occurred over the past few years and could occur again. Secondly, inflation and interest rates are down for good, so investment horizons are lengthening and future earnings are worth more. When inflation is nonexistent, the value of future earnings will not be ripped away by a force that has nothing to do with corporate management. Inflation introduces a risk that forces investors to lower the value of future earnings. Price stability erases that risk. Finally, information is more available today than ever before which means mispriced markets cannot last for long.

For these reasons, the risks of investing in stocks in the New Era have declined. Earnings growth will stabilize, recessions will be fewer and farther between, and P/E ratios will remain high. As a result, the New Era forecast is for the Dow Jones Industrial Average to climb to 60,000 or higher by 2020. For a more detailed explanation of why the New Era will be so good for stocks and how you can benefit from it, see Chapters 10 and 11.

EVEN LOW-YIELD BONDS WILL PROVIDE A VERY HIGH REAL INTEREST RATE

In recent years, interest rates have fallen to lows not seen since the 1960s. Many investors express dismay, even shock, at how low they have fallen. However, investors must remember two things. First, today's interest rates are not an aberration. As can be seen in the following chart, for nearly a

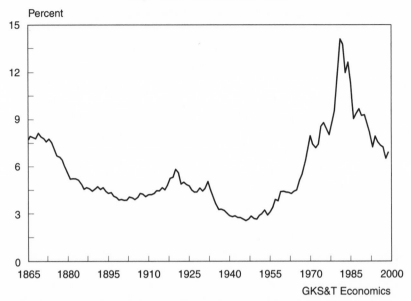

Source: Historical Statistics of the United States and *Moody's* Railroad Bonds 1865–1930, *Moody's* AAA Corporate Bonds 1931–1998.

century prior to 1970, interest rates were well below current levels. The high levels of interest rates in the past 25 years are the aberration. Current yields still remain above the levels that have existed for most of history and should fall significantly in the years ahead.

Secondly, inflation is the most important determinate for bond yields. When inflation moves up, interest rates virtually always rise and when inflation falls, interest rates virtually always fall. Between 1980 and 1999, inflation has come down from over 14 percent to under 1.5 percent. Bond investors, on the other hand, have not allowed this decline in inflation to bring interest rates as low as they should have. For example, the 10-year Treasury bond yield declined from 12 percent in 1980 to under 6 percent today.

Because interest rates have not fallen as much as inflation, real—or inflation-adjusted—bond yields are actually higher today than they were in 1980. In 1980, the 10-year bond yield was below inflation; today it is well above. Bond investors are receiving a higher return today, even at lower yields. This situation is unlikely to change in the years ahead. In the New Era, deflation is more likely than inflation. As a result, what appears to be a low bond yield is still a very solid and profitable investment. For a more detailed explanation of how to use the bond market for profit and stability, see Chapter 12.

SAVE YOUR MONEY AND STAY OUT OF DEBT

While deflation is good for bondholders, it is bad for debtors. In the 1970s, when inflation was accelerating, going into debt and buying in advance was a good financial strategy for two reasons. First, inflation drove up the prices of consumer goods. As a result, consumers had an incentive to buy early to avoid higher prices which were sure to come. Second, inflation was boosting wage rates rapidly, which reduced the burden of outstanding debt by allowing it to be repaid with inflated dollars.

In the New Era, deflationary pressures have caused many consumer prices to fall and have reduced the average annual increase in wages (even though they are rising faster than inflation). It now pays to wait before buying goods because prices are falling. In addition, deflation causes debtors to repay loans with very costly dollars. The rise in bankruptcies in recent years has been partly caused by this phenomenon.

In the New Era, saving money and reducing debt are even more important than in the past. Prices will be lower tomorrow and debt will be a drag on wealth creation. The New Era will reward good financial management. Those who are seeing their wealth rise in the New Era are spending less than they earn and investing in assets of the New Era.

Between 1995 and 1999, wages have climbed faster than inflation. It has been a long time (over 30 years) since workers have seen their inflation-adjusted wages rise for this long of a period. This increase in living standards makes it tempting to buy more expensive cars, homes, and appliances, especially when some of their prices are falling. However, the cost of borrowing to do this is excessive and is creating a great deal of pain for those families who have built up a lot of debt.

For example, in 1976 and 1977, the price of new vehicles rose by an average of 5.8 percent per year, while used vehicle prices rose by an average of 11.8 percent. The average bank-lending rate on new car loans in 1976 and 1977 was 11.0 percent. Thus, the interest rate consumers paid on car loans was less than the increase in used car prices and just 5.2 percent above new car price increases. Because car prices were rising rapidly, borrowing to buy a car was less painful than it seemed.

Today it has become much more expensive to borrow even though interest rates are lower. In 1997 and 1998, new vehicle prices fell by 0.1 percent per year and in early 1999 prices were falling at a 1.25 percent annual rate. Used vehicle prices fell 3.8 percent in 1997 and another 0.3 percent in 1998 for an average decline of 2.0 percent per year. The average interest rate on new car loans in 1997 and 1998 was 8.9 percent at commercial banks. This meant that the "real" or price-adjusted interest rate on new car loans was two or three times higher than it was in 1976 and 1977. Then, borrowers were paying 11.0 percent to finance an investment that was rising in value by 11.8 percent a year; today borrowers are paying 8.9 percent to finance an investment that is *falling* in value by 2.0 percent per year.

Obviously, there are tremendous manufacturers' rebates and special financing options available to buyers who are willing to wait. However, given the deflation that is so prevalent in the New Era, buying assets on credit has become very expensive. It is easy to see that when you borrow to buy goods that are falling in price every year, you can erode your gains in wealth significantly. Assuming an 8.0 percent interest rate and a decline in car prices of 1.5 percent, by waiting 1 year to buy a $20,000 car a consumer could save at least $1,900, or almost 10 percent. This can be the difference between beating the average national increase in wealth or falling behind.

Deflation benefits savers over debtors, while inflation benefits debtors over savers. To truly participate in the New Era, keep your debt down and your savings high. New Era entrepreneurs need capital to implement the designs that they have on the future and savers are the ones who provide it to them. Truly participating in the New Era means investing in it, not wallowing in it.

A DYNAMIC MARKET INCREASES OPPORTUNITY—TRUST SERENDIPITY

Between the 1930s and the late 1970s, many individuals learned that the best way to increase their individual wealth was to count on the static safety of governments, unions, or corporate lifetime employment. However, the New Era has changed this. Governments, unions, and many companies have failed at creating nirvana. Today, lifetime learning and career changes are rewarded. Nonetheless, there is a fine line between loyalty to a company and your best interests.

While some view this dynamism and uncertainty as a negative, it is not. Free markets are all about finding the best jobs and most satisfaction for everyone. Finding your calling will be easier than ever, and putting your talents to work in the best possible place is a surefire way to increase your earnings. After all, Michael Jordan made a lousy baseball player, but a great basketball player. Serendipity definitely plays a role, but a dynamic economy and job market makes finding the best and most rewarding career for you a distinct possiblitiy.

For many, the most profitable career may be starting a business. The dynamic economy of the New Era has created one of the best environments in U.S. history to start, own, or buy a piece of a business. Today, the difference between consumers and producers is diminishing rapidly and anyone can compete in just about any business.

In the past, large firms were often at a great advantage. They could advertise more efficiently and their large organizations could benefit from economies of scale. But today, anyone with a modem or fax can advertise worldwide. In addition, plummeting costs for more powerful computers and telecommunications equipment have virtually erased the benefits of size.

Overnight mail, wire transfers, credit cards, and jet travel have allowed even the smallest of firms to compete anywhere in the world. Ideas and nimbleness matter more than fixed assets and bureaucratic structures. Starting your own business and investing in yourself may be more profitable than owning stocks, bonds, or real estate.

INVESTING IN THE NEW ERA

What should be obvious by now is that investment strategies should change as the economic environment changes. In the 1970s, owning stocks was not a good idea. The best investment strategy for the 1970s would have been to invest in real estate, commodities, or short-term money market funds. Despite the data that show stocks have always had a positive return over a 20-year period and have only had two periods of loss over 10-year periods (both in the Great Depression), these data are not adjusted for inflation. For the 17-year period from 1965 to 1982, after adjustment for inflation, stock prices for large corporations went down, not up. On the other hand, investors in real estate, commodities, and short-term money market funds saw the value of their assets increase.

In the New Era, this has changed completely. Stocks and bonds have outperformed real estate and commodities. The five key trends of the New Era tell us that the same should be true in the future. Good policies will continue and financial assets will remain the best investments. As John Stuart Mill wrote, "The real advantage which truth has, consists in this, that when an opinion is true, it may be extinguished once, twice, or many times, but in the course of ages there will generally be found persons to rediscover it, until some one of its reappearances falls on a time when from favourable circumstances it escapes persecution until it has made such headway as to withstand all subsequent attempts to suppress it."[6]

This is the case with the New Era. The United States and a majority of its citizens understand that free markets are the best way to create wealth over time. As a result, the odds of returning to the stagflation of the 1970s and early 1980s are minimal. The implications of this and a full description of the appropriate investment strategy are spelled out in the final chapters of this book.

References

[1] Mill, John Stuart. 1859. *On liberty.* Published 1986, Amherst, NY: Prometheus Books.

[2] Ibbotson Associates. 1999. *Stocks, bonds, bills and inflation, 1998 Yearbook and 1999 Supplement.*

[3] Batra, Dr. Ravi. 1988. *Surviving the great depression of 1990: Protect your assets and investments and come out on top.* New York: Simon and Schuster.

[4] Federal Reserve Board. 12 March 1999. *Flow of funds data: Balance sheet of households and nonprofit organizations,* tables B.100 and B.100.e, Washington, DC.

[5] Schumpeter, Joseph A. 1942. *Capitalism, socialism and democracy.* New York: Harper & Row Publishers, p. 84.

[6] Mill, ibid.

PART 3

INVESTMENT IMPLICATIONS FOR THE NEW ERA OF WEALTH

10

PICKING STOCKS FOR THE FUTURE—THE TOP-DOWN APPROACH

In his 1935 book, *The General Theory of Employment, Interest, and Money,* John Maynard Keynes wrote this about the stock market, "When the capital development of a country becomes a by-product of the activities of a casino, the job is likely to be ill-done."[1]

His derogatory statements, comparing the stock market to a casino, must be understood by realizing that Keynes blamed the Great Depression on the inherent instability of capitalism. He thought that this instability was a characteristic of human nature and that government ought to work toward stabilizing the "animal spirits"[2] that created it.

The past 20 years should have erased any credibility from Keynes's theory about the role of government in financial markets. Government's role is to enforce contracts and the Rule of Law and to keep the value of money stable. As long as the government limits its actions to these roles, free and open capital markets will guarantee successful wealth creation. In the United States, this has been accomplished and more than 9,000 publicly traded companies and millions of privately held companies could not exist without a mechanism for distributing capital to its most profitable use.

Without the information that financial markets provide to both investors and corporations, economic growth would end. More importantly, without the markets to put investors and ideas together, corporations could not expand their business, build facilities, or do research and development. In addition, without free capital markets, many entrepreneurs could not bring their ideas to fruition. Businesses need capital and they find it in three well-defined markets—the stock market, the bond market, and the banking sector. These markets are not casinos; rather they are asset allocation mechanisms. Each of them serves a specific purpose and each of them provides opportunities for investors. Every other form of financing, such as venture capital or partnerships, is based on one or more

119

of these three markets. Investors share in profits or earn interest when they finance a company.

RISK VERSUS REWARD

In periods of prosperity, stocks almost always return more to investors than any other investment. The reason is that stock investors take a greater risk than other investors do. For example, during a bankruptcy it is generally true that suppliers and employees are paid first, banks and other lenders are repaid after that, bondholders are repaid next, and common stockholders are paid last. Thus, stockholders receive a risk premium that other investors do not. Stockholders are owners and they share in profits or losses. All other investors are financiers who, unless there is a bankruptcy, are paid interest on their loans. The reward for stockholders is that they receive a share of the profits after all other lenders are paid for providing financing.

What moves profits?

Corporate profits clearly come from good corporate management. If a company provides an attractively priced good or service that customers desire and the company can build or provide that product at a cost less than the consumer pays, then profits will result. Cutting costs and satisfying customers is a solid recipe for corporate success and happy shareholders.

No matter how good a corporate management team is, however, if the economic or political environment turns sour, then profit growth will be influenced. In a recession, unemployment and falling incomes reduce the purchasing power of consumers and, in turn, limit revenue growth. Inflation or deflation can cause price changes that affect the value of inventories or input costs in ways that hurt corporate profits as well. In addition, tax increases or a complete shift in the regulatory environment could foil even the best management.

As a result, it is just as important for investors to assess the earnings prospects for the stock market from the bottom up (analyzing individual corporate strategy and markets) as it is from the top down (analyzing the overall economic environment).

THE ROLE OF PRICE-TO-EARNINGS RATIOS

Despite the focus on earnings, even if they are currently stagnant, stock prices can move higher, if investors increase the value they associate with current earnings or if they expect earnings in the future to rise. Conversely, if investors value earnings less and have uncertainty about future earnings, then stocks can stagnate even if current earnings are rising. For example, between the end of 1965 and the end of 1981, the S&P 500 rose only 1.9 percent per year, from 92.4 to 122.5, even though after-tax earnings for S&P 500 corporations rose 7.0 percent per year, from $5.19 per share to $15.36 per share. Because stock prices rose at a slower pace than earnings, the S&P 500 price-to-earnings (P/E) ratio (based on 12-month trailing earnings) fell from 17.7 to 8.0.[3]

How could this have happened? Why did investors ignore the rise in earnings per share? There are three reasons and their impact on stock investors is discussed at length in the rest of this chapter. First, inflation rose at an annual average rate of 6.8 percent between 1965 and 1981, meaning that real (or inflation- adjusted) earnings for the S&P 500 rose an average of just 0.2 percent per year. Second, interest rates were on the rise, decreasing the attractiveness of stocks. Third, because the economy was in recession virtually one-fourth of the time between 1965 and 1981, the future of earnings was always in doubt. Because inflation and interest rates were high and the economy was unstable, stocks became even more risky than normal. Investors were correct in valuing earnings at such low levels.

In contrast, between the end of 1981 and the end of 1998, S & P 500 operating earnings rose 6.5 percent per year, but inflation averaged just 3.5 percent annually and interest rates declined significantly. As a result, the S&P 500 climbed from 122.5 to 1,229 by December 31, 1998, a gain of 14.5 percent per year. Stocks have climbed faster than earnings because investor's value earnings today much more than they did in the 1970s. The proof is that the P/E ratio for the S&P 500 climbed from 8 in 1981, to over 30 by the end of 1998.

More importantly, P/E ratios are likely to increase even more in the years ahead. In the New Era, profits, incomes, and wealth will explode upward while inflation and interest rates will remain low. In addition, the economy will be less likely to experience recession. As a result, the U.S. stock market will have a tremendous top-down environment. While 20+ percent gains each year should not be expected, gains averaging near 7 percent to 10 percent per year are a very real possibility. This could push the DOW to 35,000 by 2012 and 60,000 by 2020.

KEY STOCK MARKET PRINCIPLES FOR THE NEW MILLENNIUM

The tremendous boom in stock prices will attract doubters every step of the way; however, the New Era is for real. To remain optimistic and successful in the stock market, investors must keep in mind four key top-down principles of stock investing for the new millenium.

- P/E ratios will be sustained above historical norms. Recessions will be shallower and shorter than in the past, growth in profits will remain strong, and inflation and interest rates will stay low. Together, these factors will hold P/E ratios above levels history suggests are sustainable. High P/E ratios will elicit constant warnings that the stock market is overvalued; however, unless government policies change, the stock market will continue to rise.
- Value will be found in ideas, not machines. Brains will beat brawn. In the New Era, conceptual ideas are replacing physical resources as the producer of profits. Because ideas are easily and cheaply reproducible, potential profits are infinite. Invest in New Era firms that benefit from increasing returns and the networked economy, not Old Era firms that rely on increased demand for resources.
- The New Era will eradicate waste. Tremendous profits will be made in industries previously dominated by government. These include education, health care, and electric power.
- Rising wealth will increase the demand for leisure activities such as pro-sports attendance, entertainment, travel, and even flying lessons. In addition, more expensive tastes in clothing, furniture, food, and coffee too will cause phenomenal growth for firms that fill these needs. Discretionary spending on "quality of life" products will also increase. Education, health care, and information industries will continue to experience above average revenue growth.

WHY THE NEW ERA WILL BOOST P/E RATIOS

The best way to show how stock prices are affected by changing economic conditions is by using the simple model below. It shows how the value of a corporate stock is a function of the probability of prosperity and the probability of recession. For example, if a stock is worth $60 in the midst of prosperity and just $20 in recession, and each has a probability of 50 percent, then the stock is worth $40.

Stock Price = (Price in Prosperity * odds of prosperity)
+ (Price in Recession * odds of recession)

No matter what happens to earnings in the current year, stock prices will typically rise as the probability of prosperity rises and fall as the probability of recession increases. During the past 17 years, the United States has experienced just one 8-month recession (from July 1990 to March 1991). This is in sharp contrast to the period from 1969 to 1982 when the United States experienced four recessions in 13 years. These recessions lasted for a total of 49 months, averaging 12 months in length.[4]

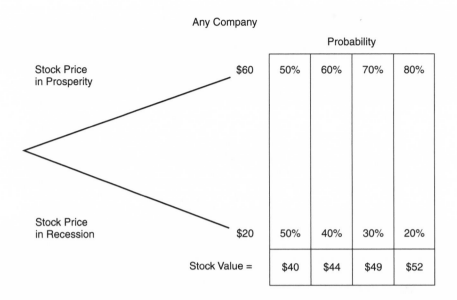

Any Company

		Probability			
Stock Price in Prosperity	$60	50%	60%	70%	80%
Stock Price in Recession	$20	50%	40%	30%	20%
Stock Value =		$40	$44	$49	$52

Longer and more frequent recessions always reduce the value of assets in an economy because they increase the risk associated with forecasts of future earnings. Therefore, the fact that the economy will be more stable and resilient in the New Era will increase the probability of prosperity and reduce risk. This will keep P/E ratios at levels that will continue to worry the pessimists. As can be seen in the chart above, as the probability of recession falls from 50 percent to 20 percent, the stock price of our hypothetical company will rise from $40 a share to $52 a share even though current profits are the same. If the company in the example will earn $2 per share during the coming year, then its P/E ratio will rise from 20 to 26 just because the odds of a recession have fallen. Conversely, if the odds of recession rise, the stock price will fall without regard to earnings.

This simple model works because profits emerge only in expanding economies. The low and falling P/E ratios of the 1970s provide a perfect example of this phenomenon. While there were many reasons for low P/E ratios in the 1970s, the most important was that the economy could not get out of its vicious circle. Government policy created an overall economic environment of stagflation and uncertainty. Growth would accelerate because of easy monetary policy, the Fed would tighten, and then the economy would go into recession. The recession would force the Fed to ease again before inflation was eradicated, setting the economy up for the next recession. No matter how good corporate management was, the overall economic environment was horrible. Over 4 years of recession out of 13 years, between 1969 and 1982, increased the uncertainty of future corporate profits and even when profits went up, stockholders were not rewarded because the risk of recession drove P/E ratios down.

The past 17 years have essentially been the exact opposite of the 1970s. Only 8 months of recession out of 17 years between 1982 and 1999 have finally caused uncertainty about future profits to diminish. As a result of this decline in perceived risk, P/E ratios are on the rise. As long as policies continue to move in the right direction P/E ratios can move to even higher levels.

P/E RATIOS AND INFLATION

While the stability of the economy is one of the most important reasons for movements in the P/E ratio, inflation plays a very important role. Inflation erodes the value of future earnings and boosts interest rates. Inflation also increases the effective tax rate on earnings. Each of these works to lower P/E ratios. On the other hand, low inflation reduces interest rates and effective tax rates, while increasing the value of future earnings. Each of these works to raise P/E ratios.

The most important of these factors is the inflation-adjusted value of future earnings. Imagine a company that will generate earnings of $1 per share every year for the next 10 years. If there were no inflation, then the present value of those future earnings would be $10. In a zero inflation environment a dollar next year, or even 10 years from now, is worth the same amount as a dollar today.

If inflation averaged 1 percent over the next 10 years, then the present value of the future earnings of the company described above would be $9.56. If inflation averaged 5 percent over the next 10 years, the present value of those earnings would drop to $8.11. Finally, if inflation averages 10 percent per year, the present value falls to $6.76. The higher the rate of inflation, the less a dollar in the future is worth.

Because of this relationship between inflation and the present value of future earnings, the current price of a stock can rise even though current earnings or expectations of future earnings do not rise. Falling inflation rates are reflected in higher price-to-earnings (P/E) ratios. In the chart at the top of the next page, the inverse relationship can be seen clearly. As inflation rose in the 1970s, P/E ratios fell. In the 1980s and 1990s, as inflation fell, P/E ratios rose.

Currently, inflation is still roughly 1 percent per year; however, as has been argued in this book, inflation is likely to decline even further in the years ahead. In fact, slight deflation is likely. Deflation would cause $1 of future earnings to have a value of more than $1 today. This bodes well for P/E ratios. More importantly, because investors and economists continue to believe that inflation is not dead, the decline in inflation we have seen in recent years has not been fully priced into markets. For example, the Congressional Budget Office forecasts inflation of 2.6 percent over the next 5 years, while the Clinton administration's Office of Management and Budget forecasts inflation of 2.3 percent.[5] In addition, a survey of inflation expectations by the

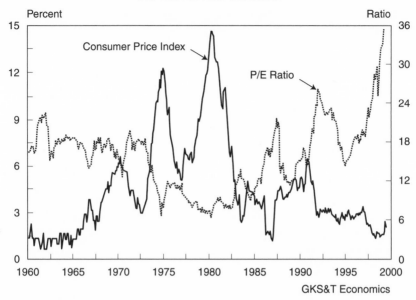

S&P 500 P/E Ratio vs. Inflation

Source: S&P and Bureau of Labor Statistics

Philadelphia Federal Reserve Bank shows that professional forecasters still believe inflation will rise by 2.5 percent per year over the next 10 years. These forecasts of higher inflation persist even though inflation has fallen to lows not seen since the late 1950s. There is still room for higher P/E ratios as New Era disinflation and even deflation become accepted as reality.

INFLATION AND TAXES

Inflation also impacts stock prices and other asset values through the tax system. Because capital gains taxes are not indexed for inflation, effective tax rates can be much higher than actual tax rates. For example, let's say that you buy $10,000 worth of one stock and that stock then rises 6 percent a year for 5 years. At the end of 5 years you sell and collect $13,382. However, because inflation was 5 percent per year during the time that you held that stock, the $10,000 investment must be worth at least $12,763 just to break even against inflation. In this example your inflation-adjusted gain is only $620. However, you owe capital gains taxes on the entire gain of $3,382 and at a 20% tax rate your tax liability is $676. This means that the taxes owed on the trade ($676) are greater than the inflation-adjusted gain ($620). After taxes, you have less purchasing power than you did prior to making the investment—an effective tax rate of over 100 percent.

When inflation falls, the effective tax rate falls as well. In the previous example, a 2 percent inflation rate means that you need just $11,041 to break even versus inflation. Because your 6 percent annual gain leaves you with $13,382, you have beat inflation by $2,341. Your taxes, at 20 percent, are the same—$676—so the effective tax rate falls to 28.8 percent ($676 tax / $2,341 inflation-adjusted gain). If inflation falls to 1 percent, then your effective tax rate falls to 23.5 percent. Of course, with zero inflation, your effective capital gains tax rate falls to 20 percent, the same as the actual tax rate. If the economy entered into deflation, then effective tax rates could actually fall below 20 percent.

In the late 1970s, the highest capital gains tax rate was over 40 percent and inflation was over 10 percent. The combination of high inflation and high tax rates caused effective tax rates to be well over 100 percent. Today, with capital gains tax rates at 20 percent and inflation virtually eradicated, effective capital gains tax rates have plummeted. The impact of tax cuts and falling inflation has been very positive for stock prices and is also reflected in higher P/E ratios.

P/E RATIOS AND INTEREST RATES

While falling inflation directly impacts stock values by increasing the present value of future earnings and by lowering the effective tax rate on capital, it indirectly impacts P/E ratios through interest rates. In fact, interest rates are the best possible comparison to stock values over time because stocks and bonds compete for investor dollars. Interest rates typically incorporate a "real" return beyond the rate of inflation. That real return exists because markets always balance themselves between alternative investments. Over time, the only difference in returns between alternative investments should be due to risk.

As a result, by comparing the 10-year Treasury bond yield (which is virtually risk free) to stock earnings we can judge alternative returns. For example, if interest rates are 10 percent, then a $100 bond will throw off $10 in interest every year. To equal that return, a $100 stock should have $10 in earnings each year. This would give this hypothetical stock a P/E ratio of 10 ($100 share price / $10 in earnings). If our bond yield fell to 5 percent, then a $100 stock would need only $5 in earnings to equal the bond yield— a P/E ratio of 20. When interest rates fall, P/E ratios rise and when interest rates rise, P/E ratios fall.

Another way to think about this relationship between interest rates and stock prices is to compare stocks' "earnings yield" to interest rates. For example, in aggregate, S&P 500 companies earned $37.70 per share after taxes during 1998. On December 31, 1997, the S&P 500 stock index stood at 970.43. As a result, the actual earnings yield for the S&P 500 during 1998 was 3.88 percent ($37.70 earnings / 970.43). If corporations paid out their entire 1998 earnings, as a dividend to investors, those who bought stocks would have received a 3.88 percent return on their initial investment.

As a comparison, an investor could have bought a 10-year Treasury bond on December 31, 1997, at a yield of 5.75 percent. Simple models that compare the 10-year Treasury bond yield to the earnings yield on stocks would suggest that on December 31, 1997, even with perfect knowledge of 1998 earnings, the stock market was overvalued because a 10-year bond would return more than the earnings of stocks. In fact, the model that compares 10-year yields to stock earnings suggests that the stock market was 48 percent overvalued. Why? With earnings of $37.70 per share, the S&P 500 should have sold at 655.62 (48 percent less than 970.43) on December 31, 1997, in order for the earnings yield on stocks to equal the 5.75 percent yield available on a 10-year Treasury bond.

Obviously, stock investors ignored this model and the S&P 500 rose 26.7 percent during 1998. There are a number of reasons for this. First, 10-year Treasury yields fell to less than 5.0 percent during 1998, lowering the earnings yield needed to equal bonds. Second, earnings estimates at the end of 1997 were much higher than the actual earnings turned out to be. According to a survey of analysts produced by I/B/E/S, a New York-based information service, 1998 S&P 500 earnings were estimated to be $50.15. Given that earnings were expected to be much higher than they turned out to be, the S&P 500 was not as overvalued as it seemed at the end of 1997. Third, corporate earnings are likely to grow, while a 10-year bond will continue to earn the same yield at which an investor bought it. In addition, the disappearance of inflation makes current earnings much less important than future earnings. In fact, even relatively slow earnings growth in a zero inflation environment will push stock earnings above bond earnings over time. Fourth, taxes on interest earnings are at individual income tax levels, while taxes on capital gains are at just 20 percent. If companies pay fewer dividends (which are also taxed as income) and instead use their profits to buy back stock, then individuals will receive corporate earnings as capital gains, not income. This tax advantage is significant.

For these reasons, the simple model that compares the earnings yield on stocks to 10-year Treasury yields has consistently shown that the stock market is overvalued during the 1980s and 1990s. As can be seen in the chart on the next page, since 1982 the earnings-price ratio, based on the past 12-month earnings, has almost always been below the 10-year Treasury yield. This implies that the market is overvalued because the yield on a Treasury bond is greater than the earnings yield for stocks. On the other hand, the model shows that stocks were undervalued for most of the 1970s.

This apparent undervaluation in the 1970s and the overvaluation during the 1980s and 1990s is not an accident. In the 1970s, the economy was in horrible shape and the risk of bad economic events was high, but in the New Era the economy has been spectacular and the risk of investing has fallen. The five key trends of the New Era have created an economy that is resilient, less inflation prone, and more likely to grow without recession.

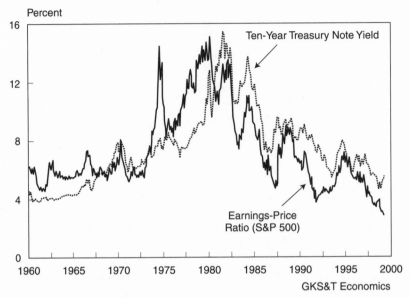

Equity Valuation and Long-Term Interest Rate

Source: S&P and Federal Reserve Board
Note: Earnings-price ratio is based on four quarter trailing earnings.

Therefore, stock investors have been rational, not irrational, when bidding up the value of stocks. In fact, as the next 20 years unfold, stock valuations are likely to remain above those suggested by this simple model. What the stock market has been telling us is that *the New Era has reduced the risk of owning stocks.* Consistent earnings growth, less risk of rising taxes, low inflation, and low interest rates mean that stocks are a much safer investment than in the past. Moreover, they will remain that way for at least the next 20 to 30 years.

TAXES AND STOCKS

Other factors also impact the valuation of stocks versus bonds. One of those issues is taxes. Because capital gains are taxed at just 20 percent and interest income is taxed at regular personal income tax rates, bond yields should be higher than stock yields to have the same after-tax return. For example, if your interest income is taxed at 36 percent, the December 31, 1997, 10-year Treasury bond yield of 5.75 percent was reduced by 2.1 percent because of taxes (36 percent of 5.75 percent). In other words the after-tax take-home yield is just 3.65 percent. Conversely, the 3.88 percent actual earnings yield on stocks during 1998 would be taxed at 20 percent— a total tax of 0.8 percent (20 percent of 3.88 percent). This means that your after-tax take-home earnings yield on stocks was actually 3.08 percent. Inputting these after-tax yields into the simple model just described shows that stocks were overvalued by only 18% on December 31, 1997, not 48 percent.

This scenario, however, is misleading. Because S&P 500 earnings in 1998 were expected to be much higher, the S&P 500 was actually undervalued on December 31, 1997. That is why stock prices shot ahead by nearly 28 percent. Models used to show that stocks are undervalued or overvalued should be handled carefully. Most of them are over-simplified. They are only guideposts that show theoretical values and are not measures of actual valuation.

Much more important than these overly simplified models are threats to prosperity. If policy mistakes are made, the market could return to the comparative valuation levels of the 1970s and P/E ratios could head back toward single digits again. Although trade protectionism is a threat today, it is not the only threat. The Federal Reserve, as a whole, is cause for concern. Many members believe that Fed policies have driven the stock market to unsustainable heights. As a result, some believe that raising interest rates to prick the market bubble is a prudent course of action; however, as we have shown above, this analysis of current stock market valuations is wrong. Low inflation, tax cuts, lower interest rates, and economic stability are the reason stocks are up, not because the Fed is pumping too much money into the economy. In fact, the Fed has helped boost stock prices by working toward price stability. To view their success as a reason to tighten would be a mistake. Eventually this realization will override the Fed's temptation to raise rates. As is argued in the preceding chapters, the New Era has built-in mechanisms for keeping itself on track. This will result in lower risks for stocks and an era of sustained and high P/E ratios.

FIND VALUE IN IDEAS, NOT RESOURCES

There are many fundamental reasons for the high P/E ratios we have seen during recent years, but one of the most important has nothing to do with interest rates, inflation, or recession. New Era companies are growing fast and the increasing returns of the networked economy have created nearly unlimited profits for companies that harness the potential of New Era technologies. As the U.S. economy becomes increasingly knowledge and service-based, more and more industries operate under the laws of "increasing returns" rather than "diminishing returns."

Because the winning companies in the New Era retain patents and copyrights on their products, huge profits and market dominance can come their way. Those companies on the cutting edge of new technologies demand high valuations. Although it is never clear which of the new companies will become the standard in any given industry, the market must value them highly even in the initial stages of development. Sure this is speculation, but it is rational not irrational.

At first, many New Era companies have no profits or, sometimes, revenue. But eventually, the winners end up with huge markets. There will always be more losers than winners in specific market niches as hundreds of entrepreneurs race to be the first. However, the winners will win big, making up for the losses of those who do not become the standard. More importantly, the competition in each industry will make the whole economy a winner because the technologies that rise above the rest will be the most efficient and productive. It is not always a pretty picture. Competition can be messy, but by its very nature, competition is the process of selecting the products that give consumers the most value.

Beta videocassettes lost to VHS video because consumers wanted longer playing videos despite what some said was the superior technology of the Beta recorder. Because VHS was able to gather an early market lead, more tapes were distributed for use in VHS videocassettes, which increased the value of VHS over Beta. This market edge was all that it took. Another example is Microsoft and MS-DOS. To this day, there are many who believe MS-DOS is an inferior product; however, because the more popular software was developed to work with MS-DOS, Microsoft grew to dominate the market for operating software and create massive returns for investors.

DOES HISTORY SUGGEST CAUTION?

New Era technologies all operate on increasing returns. As a result, their profits build exponentially over time and their stock prices will often move well ahead of those expected earnings. This results in sky-high P/E ratios that cause tremors throughout the ranks of those who believe in diminishing returns. These pessimists then resort to reminding investors of historical booms that ended in busts. One of those comparisons is the radio industry during the 1920s. Revenues for the new industry exploded from $60 million in 1922 to $850 million in 1929 and shares of Radio Corp. of America (RCA) stock rose from $5 to $500.[6] A *U.S. News* article comparing the Internet craze to the radio craze points out that in the crash of 1929, RCA investors "lost almost everything" and "three decades passed before RCA's stock got back to its pre-crash high."[7] The point of the article is that Internet stocks exhibit the same exuberance, and a similar catastrophe may befall not only these stocks but also the market as a whole.

Another gloomy article appeared in *The Wall Street Journal*. Written by David Wessel, this article discussed a surge and then collapse in London electricity stocks during 1882. Wessel wrote that the history of electricity stocks in London is "a tale whose inception has eerie similarities to today's huge run-ups in Internet stocks and might be considered cautionary: The English electric-light boom wasn't only brief, but was followed by a bust that set back the widespread use of electricity in Britain for decades."[8] The story goes like this. In the early 1880s, gas was the most popular source of lighting; however, a number of entrepreneurs thought that electric lighting should replace gas. One of the companies, Anglo-American Brush Electric Light Corp., caught investor eyes. In 1882, investor exuberance pushed its stock from roughly £8 in March to £31 by mid-May only to see it collapse by the end of the year to £6. It then took years before electric lighting prospered in London.

Both the collapse of RCA and the collapse of electric lighting shares in London are used to show the dangers of investing in high-flying stocks and to portray exuberant markets (which are called speculative) as a danger to the economy. However, these comparisons have a fatal flaw. Instead of showing that markets are to blame, history shows that the impact of bad policy decisions are the real culprit behind these stock busts. In the case of RCA, it was not the height of the stock price that caused its crash, but bad monetary, trade, and tax policies that caused the Great Depression and, with it, the collapse of the entire stock market, including RCA. In the case of the electric lighting boom in London, it was an act of Parliament that caused the bubble to burst.

As it turns out, Parliament bowed to pressure from the politically powerful gas companies and passed the Electric Light Act (ELA) in April 1882. This act gave municipal authorities the right to buy their local electric company after 21 years at very favorable terms to the municipality. The ELA included the "scrap iron" clause, which set the municipalities' purchase price for the electric companies at the "value, as isolated elements, of dynamos, wire, brick, mortar, and other components. . . ."[9] This meant that company management, knowledgeable employees, and the customer base would be valued at zero. This was a very harsh set of terms. How many people would invest in Yahoo! (YHOO), or any New Era company, if the government could buy it for the cost of its computers, office buildings, and phone lines? Such onerous terms dried up investment dollars and collapsed stock prices in lighting shares. As Thomas Hughes, an economic historian, wrote in his 1983 book, *Networks of Power*, ". . . prudent investors realized that a Parliament that could pass a constraining act in 1882 had the authority and possibly the will to frustrate development."[10]

Not only did this act of Parliament hurt technology, but it also locked London into an inferior product. Eventually the act was amended and investors and capital began to flow back into electric lighting companies; but it took 6 long years and the damage had already been done. Other cities around the world were well ahead of London in using electricity and it would take decades to catch up. By 1913, Chicago's per capita electricity usage was 310 kilowatt hours, versus 170 kwh in Berlin and just 110 kwh in London.[11]

Despite the belief that electricity stock speculation was overdone, and that many electric companies were just scams, profits began to surge at successful operations by the mid-1880s. The Edison Electric Light Company (EELC) of New York gave away electricity for free in 1882 and lost $12,000 in the first two quarters of 1883. In 1885, EELC reported a net income of $49,500 (6 percent on its capital investment of $828,000) and declared a 4 percent dividend. In 1888, while London was still dickering over the shape of electricity legislation, EELC reported earnings of $116,235 and by 1890 earnings had jumped to $229,078, a 362 percent increase from 1885. Moreover, the number of customers in its New York operations rose from 710 in 1888 to 1,698 in 1890, while the number of lamps used jumped from 16,377 to 64,174.[12] This explosive growth was exactly what investors in London during 1882 expected. They were right, but because of the Electric Light Act, it did not happen when and where they had hoped.

While the pessimists claim that the collapse of RCA and the electric light industry prove that these markets were bubbles, the real culprit was not excessive speculation, but government policy that either tilted the playing field against a new technology or caused the entire economy to collapse. Bubbles only appear in retrospect and they are often used to shift blame from bad government policy on to "irrational investors." As we move into the New Era we cannot fool ourselves into believing that these same dark forces will not come into play. Because stock prices have begun to reflect a lower risk environment, the potential for bad policy to hit them hard is very real. However, today's technology, because it empowers individuals, is uniquely suited to stymie attempts to stop it. In other words, the new high-tech arena is not as vulnerable to policy changes as the electric lighting industry was.

We can see examples of this almost every day. Just recently, in Texas, a judge made a ruling that could ban Quicken Family Lawyer (a do-it-yourself legal software package) from retail shelves. Daniel Fisher, in the March 8, 1999, issue of Forbes, wrote that the software "helps users craft a customized [legal] document by posing questions such as how many children they have and what state they live in."[13] Asking these specific questions, according to Fisher, "was enough to push Quicken Family Lawyer across the line into the illegal practice of law"[14] according to the legal community in Texas. Lawyers argued that in order to ask these questions a law degree was required, so they are fighting the proliferation of these types of software packages. They are afraid, as they should be, that as software packages become more capable and individuals become more comfortable using them, their businesses will suffer.

Although the ruling in Texas is a potential setback for Quicken, it cannot stop individuals from getting the software. The program is easily accessible by downloading from its publisher's (Mattel's Parsons Technology division) website at *www.parsonstech.com*. It is hard to imagine a Texas judge breaking into personal computers to see if someone has downloaded software from the Internet. In the New Era, vested interests, no matter how well connected, will find it harder and harder to use the power of government to fight competition. Thus, the odds of having government policy cause a major bear market in stocks are small.

In addition to the difficulty of stopping new forms of competition, the pressure of the fourth branch of government keeps politicians away as well. This was evident in 1998, when on October 8, the U.S. Senate by a vote of 96 to 2 passed legislation that would ban new taxes on the Internet for 3 years. The House had earlier passed similar legislation and the president said he would sign it. The markets cheered the passage of this bill and the NASDAQ, which had fallen 40 percent in the previous 3 months, bottomed on October 8 and then shot ahead by 60 percent over the next 6 months.

The New Era thrives when it is left alone to multiply. Taxing transactions on the Internet would slow its progress. Moreover, taxing transactions on the Internet is a complicated and controversial proposition. For example, as artists sell their music directly over the Internet for downloading onto disks or tapes, is a sales tax appropriate? The artists will already pay taxes on the income they receive from selling the music. Without the retail outlet in the middle, it is hard to justify an additional layer of taxes that would increase the complexity of Internet sales just to raise revenue.

To some, the answer to this dilemma is clear; for many others, the answers must come slowly and with much thought. With certainty it can be said that the Internet is changing the world rapidly. By boosting productivity and increasing choice it has a positive impact on economic growth and freedom. Inhibiting its proliferation would be a mistake in policy that would harm the markets and the economy. We are living in a unique period. While the economy is always evolving, it is doing so more rapidly than ever in the New Era. For investors, this means that we must focus on the New and avoid the Old.

PRODUCTIVITY BOOM—NEW VERSUS OLD

"Not only do the costs of producing high-technology products fall as a company makes more of them, but the benefits of using them increase,"[15] wrote Brian Arthur in 1994. By definition, this phenomenon of "increasing returns" raises productivity, but New Era technology has a much broader impact than most imagine. Distribution systems are more efficient, production facilities hold fewer inventories, farmers are increasing production levels by mapping farmland using GPS systems, biotechnology is increasing crop yields, cars do not need tune-ups, computer architectural design allows buildings to be made with fewer resources, and even services are becoming more productive. Less waste and more efficiency boost profits, decrease losses, and lower prices. Moreover, more information limits surprises.

Today, value-added is emanating more from conceptual products than from physical resources. Investors must realize that returns will be much greater in industries that operate under the laws of increasing returns rather than the laws of diminishing returns. Investing in the New Era requires a thoughtful approach to deciding which industries will prosper and which will whither. It is clear that information technology and communications are growing much faster than other sectors of the economy. As can be seen in the following table, business purchases of computers and telecommunications equipment as a share of real GDP rose from 0.7 percent in 1978, to 1.8 percent in 1988, and surged to 5.1 percent in 1998. Medical care, furniture, clothing, and transportation are also growing faster than the economy. While motor vehicle expenditures are essentially flat, spending on food takes up less of the family's budget, housing has declined from 10.1 percent of real GDP to just 9.7 percent, and nonresidential structures (warehouses, malls, and factories) have fallen from 3.6 percent to just 2.7 percent of real GDP.

The shifts we are seeing in the composition of our economy are bigger than at any time since the Industrial Revolution. Then, it was agriculture giving way to manufacturing. Today, it is agriculture *and* manufacturing giving way to the information age. These industries remain highly active

	20-year % change	Share of Real GDP		
		1978	1988	1998
Real GDP	67.7%			
			Rising	
Business investment in computers & telecommunications	1,123.3%	0.7%	1.8%	5.1%⇑
Furniture & Appliances	283.6%	2.0%	2.7%	4.6%⇑
Clothing & Shoes	121.7%	3.1%	3.6%	4.1%⇑
Medial Care	87.5%	8.6%	9.6%	9.6%⇑
Transportation	86.8%	2.6%	2.7%	2.9%⇑
			Falling	
Motor Vehicles	63.5%	3.5%	3.9%	3.4%⇓
Housing	61.7%	10.1%	10.2%	9.7%⇓
Food	31.6%	12.1%	10.9%	9.5%⇓
Structures (Non Res)	25.1%	3.6%	3.4%	2.7%⇓

and profitable but are slipping as a share of our total economic activity, which means that their share of total profits will also decline. As an industry declines as a share of GDP, profits are harder to attain. As a result, only those firms that utilize new technology to boost productivity will survive.

There are no hard and fast rules for picking the right companies in which to invest; however, the trends of the past 20 years can help in assessing the direction of the future. Physical resources, such as oil, minerals, and agricultural products, and consumer goods, such as automobiles and housing, will continue to take a smaller share of the economy. These changes are not new, but they are accelerating. The process can be seen in the table on the following pages which shows the members of the Dow Jones Industrial Average in 1972 when it first touched 1,000, in 1982 when it crossed 1,000 for good, and then in 1999 when it surpassed 10,000. As can be seen, only 13 of the original 1972 Dow members are still part of the index.

The companies that have been dropped from the Dow since 1972 include Anaconda Copper Mining Company, Bethlehem Steel, General Foods Corp., and International Nickel Co. The new companies include computer makers Hewlett-Packard Co. (HWP) and International Business Machines Corp. (IBM); telephone giant AT & T Corp. (T); distribution genius Wal-Mart Stores Inc. (WMT); and banking giants Citigroup Inc. (C), JP Morgan & Co. (JPM), and American Express (AXP). Interestingly, Citigroup Inc. now has the same New York Stock Exchange symbol that Chrysler used before Daimler Benz bought it.

As should be expected, the S&P 500 has experienced a similar evolution in its makeup over the past decades. In 1964, utilities comprised 19.4 percent of the total market capitalization of the S&P 500. Energy was second with 17.8 percent of the total market cap, basic materials was third with 16.5 percent. Today, technology is the number one market cap industry in the S&P 500, with 19 percent of the index. Finance is second with 14.8 percent of the total, consumer services are third at 12.6 percent.[16] However, these broad changes hide an amazing evolution within the categories, especially technology.

One clear way to see both the transformation of the economy and within industries is to follow *Investors' Business Daily's (IBD's)* price-weighted industry groupings for U.S. stocks. IBD breaks the stock market up into 197 industry groups and continuously creates new groups and revises its list. In 1991, IBD divided the computer and semiconductor industries into seven different subgroups. Since then, the sector has exploded and in 1999 IBD splits these industries into 18 subgroups. Many of the companies that make up these new subgroups did not exist in 1991. The IBD industry groups help in the analysis of the economy and the stock market by showing which industries are growing and which are declining.

The fastest growing category within the computer industry groupings has been the computer-software Internet group. In addition, a new telecommunications group was added for cellular companies. The whole

Dow 30 Stocks: 1999 (10,000) 1982 (1000+), 1972 (1000)				
DJIA 1999		DJIA 1982 In 1999 DJIA		DJIA 1972 In 1999 DJIA
1 AlliedSignal Inc (ALD)	1	Allied Corp	1	Allied Chemical
2 Aluminum Co of America (AA)	2	Aluminum Co of America	2	Aluminum Co of America
3 AT & T Corp (T)	3	American Telephone & Telegraph Co	3	American Telephone & Telegraph Co
4 DuPont Co (DD)	4	El Du Pont de Nemours & Co	4	El Du Pont de Nemours & Co
5 Eastman Kodak Co (EK)	5	Eastman Kodak Co	5	Eastman Kodak Co
6 Exxon Corp (XON)	6	Exxon Corp	6	Exxon Corp
7 General Electric Co (GE)	7	General Electric Co	7	General Electric Co
8 General Motors Corp (GM)	8	General Motors Corp	8	General Motors Corp
9 Goodyear Tire & Rubber Co (GT)	9	Goodyear Tire & Rubber Co	9	Goodyear Tire & Rubber Co
10 International Paper Co (IP)	10	International Paper Co (Common)	10	International Paper Co (Common)
11 Procter & Gamble Co (PG)	11	Procter & Gamble Co	11	Procter & Gamble Co
12 Sears, Roebuck & Co (S)	12	Sears, Roebuck & Co	12	Sears, Roebuck & Co
13 Union Carbide Corp (UK)	13	Union Carbide Corp	13	Union Carbide Corp
14 American Express Co (AXP)	14	American Express Co		No Longer in 1999 DOW
15 International Business Machines Corp (IBM)	15	International Business Machines Corp	14	American Brands, Inc
16 Merck & Co (MRK)	16	Merck & Co	15	American Can Co
17 Minnesota Mining & Manufacturing Co (MMM)	17	Minnesota Mining & Manufacturing Co	16	Bethlehem Steel Corp
18 United Technologies Corp (UTX)	18	United Technologies Corp	17	FW Woolworth Co
19 Boeing Co (BA)		No Longer in 1999 DOW	18	General Foods Corp
20 Caterpillar Inc (CAT)	19	American Brands, Inc	19	International Harvester Co

21	Chevron Corp (CHV)	20	American Can Co	20	Owens-Illinois Glass Co
22	Citigroup Inc (C)	21	Bethlehem Steel Corp	21	Standard Oil Co Of California
23	Coca-Cola Co (KO)	22	FW Woolworth Co	22	Texaco Inc
24	Hewlett-Packard Co (HWP)	23	General Foods Corp	23	US Steel Corp (Common)
25	JP Morgan & Co (JPM)	24	International Harvester Co	24	Westinghouse Electric Corp
26	Johnson & Johnson (JNJ)	25	Owens-Illinois Glass Co	25	Anaconda Copper Mining Co
27	McDonald's Corp (MCD)	26	Standard Oil Co Of California	26	Chrysler Corp
28	Philip Morris Cos (MO)	27	Texaco Inc	27	International Nickel Co
29	Wal-Mart Stores Inc (WMT)	28	US Steel Corp (Common)	28	Johns-Manville Corp
30	Walt Disney Co (DIS)	29	Westinghouse Electric Corp	29	Swift & Co
		30	Inco Ltd	30	United Aircraft

world is becoming connected. Internet portals, cellular phones, wireless communications devices, online shopping, and instant information are the drivers of the New Era. The growth rates are astronomical.

THE BOOMING NETWORK

- In March 1999, there were 158 million people worldwide connected to the Internet, up from less than 40 million in 1996. Americans using the Internet jumped from under 5 million in 1993 to 79.4 million as of March 1999.[17, 18, 19]
- At the end of 1998, 50.3 percent of U.S. households owned a PC and in the prior year 6 million U.S. homes purchased a computer.[20] As prices fall, the market penetration of computers will continue to rise.
- The number of Internet hosts (computers connected to the Internet with IP addresses) has grown from 80,000 in January 1989 to 43.23 million in January 1999.[21]
- In 1985, the U.S. cellular telephone industry had 203,600 subscribers. In 1988, subscribers had leapt to 1,608,697, an increase of 690 percent. By 1998, there were 60,831,431 subscribers, a 3,681 percent increase from 1988.[22] With prices now plummeting for digital cellular services and battery life lengthening, growth in the next 10 years is likely to be rapid. In fact, the cellular phone system may eventually replace the current copper wire system, especially as the capabilities of handheld computers and phones begin to mirror those of the desktop computer.
- America Online (AOL) had $21.4 million in sales during 1991 from 181,000 subscribers. By 1999, its sales had jumped to $2.94 billion and its subscriber base was 15 million.[23]
- Amazon.com (AMZN), the first online bookstore, sold less than $16 million in 1996. By 1997, sales had risen to $148 million and in 1998 sales reached $610 million, a 3,700 percent increase over 2 years.[24]
- Cisco Systems (CSCO) sales over the Internet have exploded. In 1996 Cisco sold slightly more than $100 million in merchandise over the Internet.[25] During its fiscal year ended July 1998, Cisco sold $5.4 billion worth of merchandise over the Internet, a 5,300 percent increase.[26]

These explosive numbers show the power of the Internet and the networked economy to change the face of the economy. The speed of the change is breathtaking. UUNet, the Internet services division of MCI Worldcom Inc. (WCOM), estimates that Internet traffic is doubling every 100 days as more voice, data, audio, and video fill the world's communication system.[27] Radio and voice traffic is being delivered over the Internet, thus dropping its cost tremendously. Consumer purchases are taking off and their exponential growth will leave no industry untouched. Do not underestimate the power of the digital revolution.

What starts out small can get big in a hurry. For example, an unknown 30-year-old in Southern California started a web page with no frills 2 years ago. His name is Matt Drudge and his specialty is getting news about news. Matt broke the story that Bob Dole would pick Jack Kemp as his running mate in 1996. He also scooped the national press by publishing news about the president and Monica Lewinsky. The mainstream press has been extremely tough on Matt, claiming that he is not a real journalist. Nonetheless, the mainstream cannot control the masses. Matt has the power of the network at his fingertips, he moves stories fast, and he is willing to write things that others may not want to. For these and other reasons his web page has exploded in popularity. In the month ending March 1999 his web page received over 18 million visitors, more than the websites of CNN, MSNBC, ESPN, *The Washington Post*, *The New York Times*, *The Los Angeles Times*, and *The Wall Street Journal* combined.[28]

There will be a day when you will listen to your car radio over a wireless Internet connection and be able to listen to the same station anywhere in the country. You will not need to put a video player in the back seat to keep your kids occupied on long trips because you will be able to download any movie they want to watch from Disney's website and show it on your flat panel pop-up screen. When you get lost, the Internet and your GPS unit will get you back on track. When you finally walk into the store (if you ever leave the house to shop anymore) you will scan the bar code of any piece of merchandise into your handheld computer which will then search the Web for the best price anywhere. If this sounds like science fiction you haven't been listening to the technology. The changes are just a few years away. They will not stop because we don't want them; they will continue until they have run their course over the next 20 to 30 years. Just a few short years ago, most people had never heard of the Internet. Today, many are using it as if it had been around forever. It will grow so fast and spread so quickly that investors cannot ignore it. It is not a bubble; it is the real thing.

Abraham Lincoln, in 1859, summed it up very well. He said, "We have all heard of Young America. He is the most *current* youth of his age. Some think him conceited, and arrogant; but has he not reason to entertain a rather extensive opinion of himself? Is he not the inventor and owner of the *present*, and sole hope of the *future*? . . . He owns a large part of the world, by right of possessing it; and all the rest by right of *wanting* it, and *intending* to have it. As Plato had for the immortality of the soul, so Young America has 'a pleasing hope—a fond desire—a longing after' territory. He has a great passion—a perfect rage—for the '*new*' . . . He is a great friend of humanity; and his desire for land is not selfish, but merely an impulse to extend the area of freedom. . . . His horror is for all that is old, particularly 'Old Fogy'; and if there is anything old which he can endure, it is only old whiskey and old tobacco."[29]

DISRUPTIVE TECHNOLOGIES
AND THE NEW ERA

As the New Era unfolds, young citizens of the world and new technology will alter the economic landscape and destroy business model after business model. Already the words of Jeff Bezos, founder of Amazon.com, are more closely listened to than the chairman of Ford Motor Company. Part of the reason for this is that Amazon.com has created a new business model while Ford remains the same.

In his 1997 book, *The Innovator's Dilemma,* Clayton Christensen discussed in very lucid terms two types of technologies, "sustaining" and "disruptive." Sustaining technologies "improve the performance of established products, along the dimensions of performance that mainstream customers in major markets have historically valued."[30] Adding cup holders or airbags to new cars is an example. This type of product improvement is a typical and low-key way of increasing value.

Less typical are disruptive technologies which "result in *worse* product performance, at least in the near-term,"[31] but eventually become dominant in their marketplace. For example, steel minimills when first invented could only compete in very low quality markets, but now compete even in high-end markets. These technologies are so new that competitors pay little attention because they believe they will not amount to much. Flying beneath the radar screen, disruptive technologies gain knowledge and power only to blow away the existing technology with a whole new approach. Investors must pay attention to this phenomenon; it explains much of what is happening today.

The reason Christensen wrote his book was to show how great firms are especially vulnerable to "disruptive technologies." Because they do everything right they are less likely to adopt a disruptive technology early enough to be a force in the industry. By listening to their customers and investors, these firms will shy away from new technologies that result in worse performance initially because the customers want a better version of what they are already using. Christensen says that rational managers "can rarely build a cogent case for entering small, poorly defined low-end markets that offer only lower profitability."[32] A perfect example is online trading. The major brokerage houses refused to believe that online trading was a good market for them to enter only to capitulate after losing almost 25 percent of their market by early 1999. And now that they have capitulated, the price wars will begin.

As the New Era unfolds, "disruptive technologies" are everywhere. Digital cameras, with their lower quality, are not a threat to high-quality camera makers yet, but they are improving fast. And what can Nikon do? Its customers want high quality and by producing a low-quality camera they may dilute their good name. In the meantime, the digital camera makers are getting better at what they do and are moving up the learning curve and down the price curve of a brand new market that could be huge in just a few short years.

Another disruptive technology is wireless Internet and network access. Today the technology remains new and the market small, but it will most likely be the next great wave of communication. Internet banking is the same. Trust and comfort are low, but the day is coming when a huge surge of people will be moving to online banking transactions, just as they have to online trading. The list is endless, and both investors and business owners must think about the "innovator's dilemma." While a business is servicing its existing customers, someone is offering an inferior product that looks as if it will never compete, let alone be profitable. Then like magic it becomes the dominant player.

Interestingly, while we have all been told to look for profits when investing, when a technology is disruptive, profits can actually be a negative. Profits at a New Era firm can mean that the firm is sacrificing long-term growth for near-term profitability. Amazon.com is a perfect example. Amazon's chief finance officer, Joy Covey, puts it this way, "We've always said we would sacrifice short-term profits to generate long-term value for our customers. I think investors will punish us if we stray from that."[33] And by watching the stock prices of Internet companies this is exactly how those investors behave. In the early stages of a huge productivity boom, investors must provide the financing for the new technologies.

Not every New Era company will be successful, however. More than likely less than 20 percent of them will make it without being bought or going bankrupt. Microsoft, DELL, and Cisco are the aberrations, not the norm, and there is no crystal ball that can tell you which to buy. It is important to remember this as you invest in the New Era. "The rising tide of economic growth does not lift all corporate boats," wrote Loren Fleckenstein, a reporter with IBD, "it lifts some, swamps a few and sinks others."[34] What is interesting is that most analysts focus on the fact that not all the New Era companies will survive, when there is an even more important question to ask. Which of the Old Era companies will survive? Disruptive technologies both create and destroy profits. Look for these technologies and invest in the New not the Old.

LOOK FOR MISUSED RESOURCES— DEREGULATION CREATES OPPORTUNITIES

As if technology did not provide enough excitement or challenge for investors in the New Era, deregulation is also playing a huge role. Industries that have been highly regulated become bloated and inefficient. As a result, they stand to make huge strides once deregulation frees them to be entrepreneurial again. The phone system is a perfect example. AT&T was always a solid investment, but the total value of it and its spin-offs (such as Lucent Technologies) dwarf its value before deregulation. While there are no other national monopolies except for Amtrak, the highly regulated industries such as health care, electricity, finance, and education are all poised for explosion as their markets open up.

Clearly banking and finance are on their way to full deregulation, and electrical power deregulation has momentum. The story is different for health care and education. They both are beginning to change at the edges, but wholesale deregulation is still a ways off. Nonetheless, there are opportunities in each of these areas as the role of government continues to diminish in the New Era.

The trend toward deregulation is one of the most interesting developments of the New Era. Individuals are showing a great deal of disappointment with sectors of the world that do not perform well. Customer service has become the definition of a good business and consumers have more power today than they ever have. And as we all know, customer service is often the last thing we normally get from our health care and education institutions. Interestingly, they are also the last great battleground of big government. As President Clinton's attempt at nationalizing the health care sector of the economy in 1993 showed, more government control is not what the majority of U.S. citizens want.

Unfortunately, the road ahead is not so clear. It appears that voters are reluctant to push wholesale change. As a result, it will be private sector initiatives that reshape these industries. New Era technologies are pushing costs down for alternative methods of education and creating new medical procedures which may cost more initially, but save immense amounts of resources over time. These sectors of the economy are likely to provide excellent opportunities for investment in the future as private sector innovations such as online education and lifetime learning tools replace and support the stodgy and bureaucratic systems in place today.

PROFIT FROM LEISURE TIME AND INCREASED WEALTH

As history shows, the more wealth an economy creates the greater the share of resources that can be devoted to entertainment, leisure, and quality of life. Starbucks coffee shops would have never made it in the 1970s, but today they thrive. Wealth is a funny thing. Because an economy only gains in wealth at the rate of 3 percent to 4 percent a year, it sneaks up on us. But there is no denying it, the United States is becoming more sophisticated and more leisure oriented. No, this does not mean that our stress level is down, instead it means we have more choices to pick from when we want to relieve our stress.

For example:

- NBA basketball attendance more than doubled to 21.8 million in the 1997/98 season, from 10.36 million in the 1982/83 season.[35]
- The Women's NBA (WNBA) finally got off the ground in 1997 and drew 1.6 million fans during the 1998 season.[36]
- Baseball attendance rose to over 70 million in 1998, auto racing attendance has climbed to nearly 20 million per year, professional wrestling attracts huge audiences, and professional golf is exploding on three fronts—women, men, and senior tours.
- The number of nonprofit symphonies founded since 1980 is 110, bringing the U.S. total to over 800. Moreover, these symphonies are not all in what we would typically call large metropolitan areas.[37]
- Theater is exploding in popularity with 27 million attending theatrical shows during 1997/98. Book sales reached over 2.1 billion in 1995 and have climbed a great deal since then.

These trends will continue into the new millenium. Wealth is rising rapidly and with it, expenditures are shifting. The shift is happening in many more ways than discussed here; however, the list shows its power. As wealth increases, demand for flight schools, language classes, music classes, movies, and vacations will grow. Businesses that once focused on just the wealthy will now have an ability to market to the majority. Airlines will fly fuller planes, cruise ships will have fuller manifests, people will ride busses less, and more Americans will own their own homes, boats, and a second car or vacation spot. What we would have called "conspicuous consumption" only 10 years ago is now normal.

These trends are important for investors—listen to them and not the pundits. How many times have you heard that eventually people will stop paying over $1 for a cup of coffee? Well, they haven't, and Starbucks stock outperformed the market for years. The New Era of Wealth will continue to create a boom in consumer goods of high quality and a boost to those companies that provide leisure and entertainment.

THE BOTTOM LINE

Stocks have been a fabulous investment in the New Era. As long as the United States avoids stumbling down the path of the government policy mistakes, as it did in the 1930s and 1970s, the stock market will remain a fabulous investment. The top-down investment analysis presented in this chapter suggests that the New Era will continue to avoid big policy mistakes and that the bubble that many pessimists think they see is nothing but the reflection of wealth creation in the market.

Listing every company, or even industry, that will profit from the New Era is impossible. However, the key trends suggest that technology (computer, biotech, and telecommunications) is the most important exposure for your portfolio. Second are companies that are using technology to enhance their profitability. Third are companies ready to throw off the shackles of government regulation, and fourth are entertainment and leisure activities. Focus in these New Era areas and you will enhance your investment returns. Despite the fact that investments in these areas of the economy have high P/E ratios, fear not. They are valued highly by the market because they have tremendous potential. Remain optimistic, the New Era is truly here.

References

[1] Keynes, John Maynard. 1935. *The general theory of employment, interest, and money.* New York; Harcourt, Brace & Company, 1964, p. 159.

[2] Keynes, p. 161.

[3] Data taken from Haver Analytics database. P/E ratios are based on four-quarter trailing earnings. Stock prices and earnings are for fourth quarter averages for 1965 and 1981.

[4] U.S. Department of Commerce, *Survey of current business,* October 1994, table C-51.

[5] Office of Management and Budget, Clinton Administration, 2000 Budget, January 1999.

[6] Lardner, James. 1999. Ask radio historians about the Internet: But if you're an investor, don't ask. *U.S. News and World Report,* 25 January, pp. 48-52.

[7] Ibid.

[8] Wessel, David. 1999. An illuminating tale for web fans. *The Wall Street Journal,* 8 January.

[9] Hughes, Thomas P. 1983. *Networks of power: electrification in western society 1880–1930,* 1st ed. Baltimore: Johns Hopkins University Press, p. 60.

[10] Hughes, p. 65.

[11] Hughes, p. 225.

[12] Hughes, pp. 45, 46.

[13] Fisher, Daniel, 1999. Arrest that software. *Forbes,* 8 March, p. 94.

[14] Ibid.

[15] Arthur, Brian W. 1994. *Increasing returns and path dependence in the economy,* 4th ed. Ann Arbor, MI: University of Michigan Press, p. 4.

[16] No author. 1999. Start up: Why it's called the information age. *Forbes ASAP,* 5 April, p.16.

[17] Nua Internet Surveys. March 1999. How many online? *www.nua.net/surveys/how_many_online/index.html*

[18] Margherio, Lynn. 1998. The emerging digital economy. U.S. Department of Commerce *http://www.ecommerce.gov*

[19] Intelliquest Company Press Release. 1999. Intelliquest Internet study shows 100 million adults online by 2000. 3 March. *http://www.intelliquest.com/press/release72.asp*

[20] March 19, 1999. *San Jose Mercury News.* Over half of US Households now own PCs.

[21] Lottor, Mark K. 1999. Network wizards, internet domain survey: Number of Internet Hosts. *http://www.nw.com.*

[22] CTIA's Annualized Wireless Industry data Survey Results. 1998. Cellular Telephone Industry Association, *http://www.wow-com.com/images/veiw_98datasurvey2.gif*

[23] Graham, Jed and Gondo, Nancy. 1999. Technology unites best stocks of 1990s. *Investors' Business Daily,* 19 January, p. A1.

[24] Margherio, Lynn. 1998. The emerging digital economy. U.S. Department of Commerce *http://www.ecommerce.gov*

[25] Ibid.

[26] Cisco Systems. 1998. Annual Report. *http://www.cisco.com*

[27] Inktomi Corporation White Paper. 1997. *http://www.inktomi.com/Tech/EconOfLargeScaleCache,html*

[28] Lyons, Daniel, 1999. Desperate.com. *Forbes,* 22 March, p.94.

[29] Lincoln, Abraham. 1859. *Second lecture on discoveries and inventions.* New Brunswick, NJ: Rutgers University Press, 1953.

[30] Christensen, Clayton M. 1997. *The innovators dilemma: when new technologies cause great firms to fail,* 5th ed. Boston, Harvard Business School Press.

[31] Ibid., page xv.

[32] Ibid., page 77.

[33] Koselka, Rita. 1999. A real Amazon. *Forbes,* 8 April, pp. 50–52.

[34] Fleckenstein, Loren. 1999. Dow stocks haven't kept up with index. *Investors' Business Daily,* 19 January, p. A5.

[35] National Basketball Association. 1999. *http://www.nba.com/history/attendance_list.html*

[36] Women's National Basketball Association. 1998. *http://www.wnba.com*

[37] Blackmon, Douglas A. 1998. From small towns to big cities, America is becoming cultured. *The Wall Street Journal,* 17 September.

11

PICKING THE RIGHT STOCKS AND MUTUAL FUNDS

The investment approach, detailed in the previous chapter, suggests that every investor should own stocks in the New Era. However, this does not mean that every stock will do well and it definitely does not mean that you should invest 100% of your assets in stocks. Even though stocks have outperformed almost every other category of investment in recent years, stocks remain risky and a steady and disciplined investment approach is the key. Only in hindsight is there a no-risk strategy for getting rich.

There are four decisions that you must make when deciding how to position your stock investment portfolio.

- What percentage of your assets will you invest in stocks?
- In what socks or industries will you invest?
- Will you manage your portfolio yourself or will you hire others to do this for you?
- How will taxes impact your decisions?

HOW MUCH SHOULD YOU INVEST?— THE RULE OF 110

How much to invest is the easiest decision of all. A simple rule of thumb I learned long ago seems to be the soundest approach to determining the percent of your portfolio that should be invested in stocks. Just subtract your age from 110 and that will give you your percentage. If you are 30 years old, 80 percent of your assets should be in stocks, if 50, then 60 percent. Even if you are 90 years old, you should still invest 20 percent of your assets in stocks.

Once you have determined the appropriate percentage of assets that should be invested in stocks using this rule, it is time to adjust the numbers. If you are uncomfortable with the results of the formula, don't follow it. Sleeping at night is much more important than following someone else's rule of thumb. But do not be scared of the stock market. Back off from the formula until you can sleep and are not tempted to look at the value of your holdings every day. There is more to life than watching stock prices move. On the other hand, if you have saved diligently and have enough resources to comfortably exceed the formula, then do it. In the New Era, as long as the Four Threats to Prosperity remain at bay, risks to investing in stocks will be low.

Another factor in your decision is some special circumstance that could change your investment strategy. If you have commitments in the near future such as tuition, a down payment on a new or second home, or health care bills, stocks are not the right choice for holding that money. They are too volatile. For example, stocks fell between 20 percent and 40 percent during mid-1998. If you needed that money in October, when stocks hit bottom, you would have much less than you thought you would. Bonds and short-term money market instruments are much better suited for holding funds that will be needed in the near term. Another special factor is the need for income. As you age, or if you are forced to take a lower paying job, you will want more income from your investments. This would also push you toward more bonds and less stocks over time.

WHAT STOCKS DO I BUY?

It is impossible to pick all the right stocks. Just look at how poorly most mutual fund managers have performed. During recent years, returns for the market as a whole have consistently outpaced the returns of mutual funds. Early in 1999, a headline in the *Washington Post* read "Index Funds Outpace the Experts."[1] "Hot market leaves most funds cold,"[2] said a *Wall Street Journal* headline. These headlines were in reference to the underperformance of managed mutual funds during the first quarter of 1999; however, this is not a new phenomenon. According to Burton G. Malkiel, author of *A Random Walk Down Wall Street*, "In most years, a Standard & Poor's 500 index fund has a rate of return about two percentage points better than the average [fund] manager's; for the 10 years ending in 1998, the index outperformed the average manager by 3.5 percentage points, and did better than more than nine out of 10 active managers."[3] This leaves individual investors with a problem. If professional fund managers, who get paid big bucks to manage these funds, cannot beat the market, what chance does an individual investor have?

As it turns out, the mutual fund managers that have beaten the market have one thing in common: They have invested in areas of the economy, which benefit from New Era trends. During the 10 years ending on March 31, 1999, including reinvested dividends, health and biotechnology funds rose 20.98 percent at an annual rate, science and technology funds were up 24.59 percent, telecommunications funds rose 20.64 percent, and financial services were up 20.72 percent. In contrast, the S & P 500 returned just 18.97% percent annually.

The rapid growth in stock values in these sectors of the economy shows that the New Era is for real. More importantly, this growth is likely to continue for years into the future. With more than 5 billion people in the world, and less than 200 million connected to the Internet, the potential for growth is massive. More importantly, the "law of increasing returns" shows that as the network expands, its value will increase faster than the number of consumers who join it. As a result, these industries and sectors are likely to experience exponential growth in the years ahead.

VALUE VERSUS GROWTH

One of the biggest debates in the investment world today is over the strategy of investing in value stocks (those selling at lower P/E ratios than the market as a whole) or growth stocks (those companies selling at high P/E ratios, but growing rapidly). In the 1990s, growth stocks have outperformed value stocks. Historically, any discrepancy between growth and value has eventually righted itself, but in the New Era this should not be the case. The combination of an economy growing more rapidly than its historical averages and the exponential growth rates of New Era technology give growth stocks a valuable advantage over value stocks. For example, value stock investors would have never bought Microsoft (MSFT) or General Electric (GE) because their stocks always sold at P/E ratios that made them look expensive relative to the market. The same thing is true of America Online (AOL).

Obviously, not all high P/E stocks will outperform the market like these three companies have. The key to finding companies that will is to look for those at the leading edge of paradigm shifting ideas. This is where we come back to Clayton Christensen and his idea about "disruptive technologies." By isolating New Era companies that will change the paradigm or model of doing business we can find and ride a wave of growth to riches. This book was not written to give you the names of new companies that will change the business landscape, but instead to give you an underlying faith in the New Era and to point you in the general direction in which it is headed. Today we can say with virtual certainty that a number of growth-oriented sectors of the economy will continue to outperform. Six New Era sectors of the economy are listed in the pages that follow. This list is not exhaustive, but instead highlights the industries and sectors of the economy that are ripe for a paradigm shift and have the potential to produce massive profits for investors who fund those companies that will push new technologies to their fullest potential. In addition, many sectors of the economy will benefit from the wealth that is created in the New Era.

- **Biotechnology and healthcare** companies are at the forefront of the next great wave of technology. DNA research will produce drugs to combat health-related problems once thought incurable. Where machinery once was the key to increased agricultural efficiency, biotech advances will quadruple or quintuple farm output in the next 10 to 20 years. The value of this research will be immense as gene mapping and DNA sequencing advance. Laser eye surgery is correcting many vision problems and allowing a growing number of individuals to throw away their eyeglasses. Clearly the New Era concepts and the companies that successfully produce and market new products in these widely divergent industries will reap huge benefits. New Era investors should have exposure in this area.
- **Telecommunication** advances are the key to moving the Internet forward in its anticipated role as the driver of voice, data, and video transmission. Fiber-optic networks are beginning to circle the globe and radio technology is advancing at a rapid clip. Companies that market switching and routing equipment are riding sky-high P/E ratios because the avalanche of broadband traffic has pushed their growth at triple-digit rates. Digital cellular networks are exploding and a worldwide standard for digital cellular communications has been established by Qualcomm (QCOM) and Ericsson (ERICY). Satellite systems, such as Globalstar (GSTRF) and Hughes' Direct PC (GMH), are bringing the whole world into the network, leapfrogging the antiquated and inadequate telephone systems of the third world. No longer will individuals need to wait for government officials or state-owned systems to provide for their needs. They will soon be able to tap into a world-class phone system at costs which will continue to fall toward pennies a minute, or even an hour. Personal communicators will allow you to take the Internet on the road with you without hooking up to a fixed phone jack. As voice, data, and video traffic increases, the owners of the new telecommunications networks will benefit incredibly and so will investors who believe in this trend.
- **Financial services** are exploding along with the increased wealth of the New Era. As worldwide trade and investment flows increase faster than worldwide economic growth and as the costs of communication plummet, the financial backbone of this new system will grow and change rapidly. Internet banking and e-money will follow the path of online trading and grow exponentially. The way money is managed, the way bills are paid, how credit is processed, the way life insurance is purchased, and even the way IPOs are marketed will be changed by the networked economy. The potential growth is nearly limitless. As

the world becomes one great interconnected financial village, resources will be directed to the very best possible use. The financial service companies that integrate themselves into this structure will not only boost economic growth, but will also profit handsomely. For example, Citigroup (C) already offers savings and checking accounts in Japan for depositors in any currency they want and monthly statements reflect the value of those deposits in multiple currencies. This is another area where investors should look to for high returns.

- **Internet commerce** will expand exponentially in the next decade as the costs of transactions and communications fall. Both business-to-business and retail e-commerce will invade every area of the economy. The 3,700 percent increase in revenues at Amazon and the 5,300 percent increase in online sales by Cisco Systems between 1996 to 1998 will be repeated in industry after industry. Online house hunting, car buying, grocery shopping, video and CD delivery, and travel planning will increasingly take place on the Web. More importantly, as computers become even more portable and the Internet moves to the airwaves, your office will travel with you. Your calendar, e-mail, stock quotes, yellow pages, maps, weather forecast, plane schedule, and phone list will go with you in a handheld personal communicator. Computer prices will continue to fall and communications speeds will increase. The high P/E ratios in this area are justified by the potential growth rates that many of the New Era.com companies possess. Do not underestimate the speed at which this new system will change the current distribution system for goods and services. All this business will increase demand for delivery services such as FedEx, (FDX) and UPS and the day is not far from now when the Post Office will be privatized.

- **Education** is one of the fastest growing areas of the New Era. Because so much of the education infrastructure is owned and operated by federal or state government, few true investment opportunities exist in this arena. Nonetheless, many companies are branching out into this sector of the economy and the business potential is growing rapidly. The New Era is changing the economy and individuals are realizing that lifetime learning is of paramount importance. The percent of people, 35 years of age or older, enrolled in college was 9.6 percent in 1970, but grew to 19 percent by 1995 and is estimated to be 20.5 percent in the year 2000.[4] In addition, private schools in both primary and secondary education are flourishing. Companies that will benefit from this surge in demand for education can be found in the pure education field. For example, Sylvan Learning Systems, Inc. (SLVN) is a for-profit provider of educational systems for families, schools, and industry. In the publishing industry, McGraw-Hill (MHP) (the publisher of this book) is developing new tools for lifetime learning and is also finding ways of speeding up the publishing process for textbooks. Online universities are likely to become more commonplace and students (no matter where they live) will have access to the best and the brightest teachers from all over the world.

- **Travel and leisure** services will expand rapidly in the new millennium and will become less cyclical, not more. Rising consumer wealth, a staple of the New Era, will increase demand for travel, and airline companies are equipped to take full advantage of this fact. Planes will be more fully loaded and larger, fuel use will continue to improve, and reliability will increase. While airlines have always been unstable investments because of the necessity for large capital outlays and their sensitivity to cyclical pressures, the New Era will reduce the burdens of each of these. The prices for planes will decline as more are demanded and the odds of a serious long-term recession are very limited. The same developments will benefit all entertainment and leisure activities. Professional sports teams are already fetching bids of as much as $1 billion, minor league baseball franchises are becoming more successful, arena football is taking off, and the Women's National Basketball Association has finally gained traction in the markets. Movies, plays, orchestras, bands, golf, skiing, hiking, and general travel are also growing more rapidly than the economy. When wealth is generated as rapidly as it has been in the past 17 years, consumers are faced with a whole new set of possibilities. For many individuals and families this means that the ability to spend money for travel, entertainment, and leisure will be greater than ever. For investors this means that high growth will occur in a broad array of leisure and entertainment industries and that profit opportunities will abound.

PURE GROWTH

Each of these sectors of the economy either thrives on increasing returns, benefits from increasing wealth, or benefits from globalization. Already each of these sectors has been growing faster than the economy; and despite the high valuations placed on stocks in these industries, there is no question that they must be in your portfolio. Although it would be nice to buy stocks in these industries when they swoon, their swoons have been few and far between. They have remained expensive and are likely to remain so well into the future.

Doubters and dismal scientists will constantly warn us that the end is nigh and at times they may seem right. However, investors that remain patient and stick with New Era stocks in growth industries will be well rewarded. Deflation benefits New Era companies. Worldwide competition presents opportunities to new technology companies that help other companies become more competitive. That same competition cuts the pricing power out from underneath companies that compete in the hard goods manufacturing industries. Old Era companies implement advances based on "sustaining technologies," while New Era companies work on "disruptive technologies." Once disruptive technologies take off they become pure growth plays and investors would be foolish to ignore them.

HOW TO MANAGE YOUR NEW ERA INVESTMENTS

The only question remaining for investors is how to buy stocks in the New Era. Should you day trade? Should you buy individual stocks? Should you buy mutual funds? Each of these strategies has paid off for many investors, but they are not all appropriate to each of us. History shows that investors benefit by sticking to a long-term disciplined investment approach built on patience and risk diversification. The only way to do this is to save consistently and invest in at least ten different stocks.

DAY TRADING

Day trading is not the best way to build long-term wealth. It requires a commitment of time that is often counterproductive. You have spent your whole life developing a skill (such as carpentry, sales, or editing) to earn money. By focusing so much attention on trading your portfolio you are missing one of the best ways to increase your wealth—becoming more productive at or leveraging your best skill. The success stories that you hear from other day traders often sound alluring and easy, but the number of real winners at day trading is quite small.

If you are bored with your job and think that a career in day trading would be more fulfilling or exciting, my best advice to you is look for a new job or go back to school. Wealth is built by becoming better at what you do best or by investing in those who are doing the same.

MUTUAL FUNDS

For beginning investors with less than $50,000 to invest, buying multiple stocks is costly, despite low-cost online trading. With a relatively small resource base, your best investment strategy is to buy stock mutual funds.

There are two reasons for this. First, despite online commissions of less than $10, you are paying more for your stocks than the big buyers do. The hidden cost is in the spread. If you make twenty trades a year, spreads plus commissions can push transaction costs to 5 percent of your portfolio's value. Second, a mutual fund can diversify across many more stocks than you can with your relatively small nest egg. Diversification lowers risk and also allows you to invest in a much broader array of companies.

These benefits come at a cost. Mutual funds take a management fee and sometimes charge front-end or back-end loads (a one-time fee for investors when buying or selling a fund). However, many fabulous mutual funds have no loads and also charge a management fee of less than 1.5 percent. These are the funds you should look for. The overall cost, for new investors, with less than $50,000, will be lower than buying and managing a portfolio of individual stocks.

At times, even large investors should buy mutual funds. The opportunity cost, in time and energy, of researching investment decisions is tremendous. Every minute you take away from your family or your chosen profession has a cost associated with it. This cost is impossible to quantify, but do not fool yourself into thinking that every time you trade a stock for $8, you are benefiting. The luxury of having someone else pick stocks and manage your money can be worth much more than the management fee charged by mutual funds.

WHAT MUTUAL FUNDS ARE GOOD FOR THE NEW ERA?

The first thing to remember is that not all mutual fund managers believe in the New Era. As a result, you could invest in a mutual fund that goes against everything in this book without even knowing it. There are two ways to avoid this pitfall. First, invest in the market as a whole—in either indexed funds or a total market fund. Second, buy stock mutual funds that invest in New Era sectors of the economy.

Because broad indices, such as the S&P 500 or the Wilshire 5000 (and the index funds which mimic them), contain stocks that represent the economy as a whole, by investing in them you will benefit from the New Era shifts that are taking place. Productivity increases, emanating from New Era technologies, have increased profits to a very high level of GDP and the economy is benefiting. When the economy benefits, the entire stock market benefits. This is one reason why mutual fund managers have had such a poor track record in recent years. Most managers chase good stocks and are therefore always behind the market as a whole, while index funds are already invested in those stocks. Another reason is that many strategists and economists have completely missed the development of the

New Era. They believe that P/E ratios are too high and the undervalued sectors are the safest place to invest. However, there is a reason that the value stocks have fallen behind; these companies benefit less from the trends of the New Era. Investing in indexed funds or the total market allows investors to avoid the pitfalls of value investing and market chasing. More importantly, some index funds charge fees of less than 0.2 percent of assets. No individual investor could manage a portfolio for less.

New Era investments in the sectors of the economy listed above will also tend to beat most other mutual funds and the market as a whole in the decades ahead. These industries will continue to grow rapidly and profits will multiply. These sectors may not beat the market every quarter or even every year, but over time New Era companies will change the world. You must own some of that potential.

For small investors, a mutual fund is often the only safe way to invest in New Era markets. For example, no one knows which competing technology will win the battle of communication delivery. Will it be cable, telephone, satellite, or digital cellular communications systems that become the dominant force in information delivery systems? Which company will solve the riddle of diabetes? What financial services firms will integrate themselves the best into the global financial village and who will survive the online trading wars? Diversification is essential when dealing with the unbelievably rapid pace of change in these areas of the New Era. As a result, only an investor or mutual fund with much larger resources can appropriately diversify in these sectors. Therefore, small investors (and large investors who want to avoid the time-consuming nature of investing) should invest in specialized sector funds in New Era growth industries.

The low-cost resources available to investors to find and pick these funds have never been more readily available. The proliferation of information on the Internet and from nationwide brokerage firms or mutual fund analysts has been incredible. Morningstar mutual fund rankings are available through America Online, screening and comparisons are offered by online brokerages such as Schwab and Fidelity, and by perusing these reports and using the tools available you can become very knowledgeable in short order. However, there is no magic bullet to picking the right funds. Just make sure that, by reading the investment strategy of each fund, the fund truly does what you think it does.

THE 50/50 STRATEGY

The New Era forces you to be exposed to the stock market so you must develop a strategy for doing so. For small investors, a strategy that will allow you to lower your risk and increase your returns is possible. It is called the

50/50 strategy and it is very simple. Invest one-half of your allocation to stocks in indexed funds and the other half in New Era sector funds. This strategy would have beaten the market as a whole in the past 10 years and allowed you enough diversification to avoid the pitfalls of trying to pick stocks.

INVESTING IN INDIVIDUAL STOCKS

The cost of online trading is coming down rapidly and will continue to do so. As a result, investors who have more than $100,000 in assets can often build their own portfolios at less cost than most mutual funds. For example, at a commission rate of $10 per trade, a $100,000 portfolio can own twenty stocks and have a turnover ratio of 60 percent (trade twelve stocks per year) for a total transaction cost of just 0.24 percent per year. Of course, the spread will continue to be a hidden cost; however, by buying stocks in 100-share multiples that cost will be kept to a minimum. Buying stocks in less than 100-share lots often results in the investor paying a higher spread over the true market price. While smaller investors can and do buy individual stocks, the cost of transactions (both trading and spread) make this a less attractive option than mutual funds.

There are two other advantages to managing your own portfolio. The first is taxes. Mutual funds must pay out capital gains at the end of every year and investors are then subject to capital gains taxes. If you manage your own portfolio, tax strategies of taking gains and losses are much more flexible. For example, there is no reason to take gains at the end of the year, when taxes are due so quickly. Why not take gains at the very beginning of the year when taxes are not due for 15 1/2 months. The flexibility of managing your own account allows your resources to be used much more efficiently. Secondly, most mutual funds can only be traded at the closing price on any specific day, but individual stocks can be traded at any time. With the cost of trading likely to move to pennies a trade in the New Era, and trading hours at U.S. stock exchanges expanding and information on stocks becoming less expensive and more available, the value of individual control is climbing daily. Eventually, even small portfolios will find it advantageous to trade their own stocks.

HOW TO BUILD A GREAT PORTFOLIO

Despite the advantages of trading your own portfolio, the greatest cost of investing, even though you don't pay cash for it, is your time. Every minute you spend researching stocks, reading articles about stocks, watching your stocks trade, or talking about stocks is a cost to you and takes away from your other pursuits. If you are Warren Buffet this is your job, but if your job is something else then your focus on investing can be a negative and you should search for ways to minimize this cost. One way to minimize costs is to find investment analysts or newsletters that can help you make decisions. As long as you listen to their advice and stick to a disciplined approach of following it, your costs of portfolio management can drop to reasonable levels.

One of the best investment analysts in the area of technology for the New Era is George Gilder. For $295 per year, you can receive his investment letter, The Gilder Technology Report. This is a small fee to pay to receive the advice of one of the pioneers of New Era thought. His 1989 book, *Microcosm*, quoted in earlier parts of this book, shows him to be a truly innovative thinker and an insightful analyst of the New Era. He focuses on the "disruptive technologies" of the New Era and is in a unique position to understand these dynamic and profitable investments. Since August 1996, Gilder has highlighted more than thirty stocks in his monthly newsletter. The current list of his stock picks from early 1999 is printed on the next page.[5] If you invested an equal amount in each of these stocks on the day that Gilder picked them as "Gilder Paradigm" stocks, your portfolio would have climbed by 82.4 percent at an annualized rate between August 1996 and June 1999. This increase was more than twice as fast as the NASDAQ, which rose 34.0 percent at an annual rate during the same period and three times faster than the Dow Jones Industrial Average which rose 23.7 percent annually.

There are other analysts in the New Era that can help you invest in other areas of the economy. Most of them exist outside of normal Wall Street channels. Find these analysts and you will benefit incredibly while keeping the maximum flexibility in managing your portfolio. As the cost of trading plummets, our investment options will multiply. In the future, you will be able to receive a new investment strategy every month, from someone like George Gilder, in electronic form that will automatically shift your portfolio by merging with your accounts in Quicken. Quicken will then direct your online trading account to make the appropriate trades. In essence, this will happen at such low cost that you will be managing your own mutual fund as well or better than the mutual funds that are available today. Not only will you be able to save, but the benefits of tax planning and the flexibility of controlling your assets will also increase.

The New Era is providing more freedom at lower cost; managing your own mutual fund is a clear example of how the power of the information age can work toward your benefit. Other systems that are coming online as you read this book will make investing on your own more profitable even with small amounts of money. The cost of information is falling dramatically and your information will be as good as those who manage funds within years. Stay in touch with the New Era because it will offer you the information that you lack today.

	Gilder Tech Portfolio as of April 9, 1999			
#	Company	Symbol	Misc	Date of Purchase
1	At Home Corporation	ATHM		7/31/97
2	Applied Micro Circuits Corporation	AMCC		7/31/98
3	Analog Devices, Inc.	ADI		7/31/97
4	Atmel Corporation	ATML		4/3/98
5	Broadcom Corporation	BRCM		17-Apr
6	C-Cube Microsystems Inc.	CUBE		4/25/97
7	Ciena Corporation	CIEN		10/9/98
8	Conexant Systems, Inc.	CNXT		3/31/99
9	Corning Incorporation	GLW		5/1/98
10	Global Crossing Ltd.	GBLX		10/30/98
11	Globalstar Telecommunications Limited	GSTRF		8/29/96
12	Intentia International AB	Int B	Stockholm Exchange	4/3/98
13	JDS Fitel Inc.	JDS	Toronto Exchange	5/1/98
14	Level 3 Communications, Inc.	LVLT		4/3/98
15	LSI Logic Corporation	LSI		7/31/97
16	Lucent Technologies Inc.	LU		11/7/96
17	MCI WorldCom, Inc.	WCOM		8/29/97
18	National Semiconductor Corporation	NSM		7/31/97
19	NEXTLINK Communications, Inc.	NXLK		2/11/99
20	Nortel Networks Corporation	NT		11/3/97
21	P-Com, Inc.	PCMS		11/3/97
22	QUALCOMM Incorporated	QCOM		9/24/96
23	Sprint Corp. (PCS Group)	PCS		12/3/98
24	Sun Microsystems, Inc.	SUNW		8/13/96
25	Teligent, Inc.	TGNT		11/21/97
26	Terayon Communications Systems, Inc.	TERN		12/3/98
27	Texas Instruments Incorporated	TXN		11/7/96
28	Tut Systems, Inc.	TUTS		1/29/99
29	Uniphase Corporation	UNPH		6/27/97
30	Xilinx, Inc.	XLNX		10/25/96

401K AND IRA

For many investors the majority of assets will be held in tax-deferred accounts such as simple IRAs or 401k accounts. These accounts, because they compound tax free, are essential for building wealth for retirement. Most 401k plans have some sort of matching by employers. Because these payments into your account will only occur if you save first, the returns to your savings in these accounts can be impressive. However, company-run savings vehicles often have very few investment options. They typically offer a large-cap stock fund or index fund, but do not offer specialized sector funds such as were discussed earlier in this chapter. As a result, it is best to use your tax-deferred account for investing in the market as a whole.

Every individual investor, however, should hold stocks outside of their tax-deferred investments. This is essential if you want to keep 50 percent of your assets in sector investments. More importantly, taxes on distributions from IRAs or 401k plans can be horrendous. Do not use them to pay for normal lifetime expenses if you can help it. You will pay a 10 percent penalty in addition to paying your current income tax rates. In retirement, your tax rates will be lower and the 10 percent penalty for early withdrawal will not apply.

Taxes alone suggest an investment strategy of investing outside of tax-deferred investment accounts. Not only will you be forced to invest in mutual funds in your tax-deferred accounts, but you will also be unable to manage your investments in profit maximizing fashion. If you change jobs and have the opportunity to shift your 401k to a self-directed IRA you can avoid this problem. However, as long as you take advantage of the 401k account at your current employer, there will always be a certain amount of your assets with limited investment options.

THE BOTTOM LINE

New Era stock investments will perform better than the stock market as a whole; however, the indexed funds, which mirror the potential of the U.S. economy, are fabulous investments. To reduce risk, lower costs, and increase returns, invest 50 percent of your stock investment dollars (in tax-deferred accounts hopefully) in indexed funds. Invest the other 50 percent of your investment dollars in specialized sector investments if you have less than $50,000, but in individual stocks if you have more. To reduce the cost of stock picking, pay attention to an advisor whose job is to know more than you do. As the New Era unfolds, you will be able to manage a fund using the advice of a knowledgeable professional at a lower cost than the expenses of current mutual funds.

References

[1] Crenshaw, Albert B. 1999. Index funds outpace the experts. *The Washington Post*, 4 April, p. H3.

[2] Damato, Karen. 1999. Hot market leaves most funds cold. *The Wall Street Journal*, 5 April, p. R3.

[3] Malkiel, Burton G. 1999. Indexes: Why the critics are wrong. *The Wall Street Journal*, 24 May, p. A16.

[4] Department of Education. 1997. *Digest of education statistics*, chapter 3-A, table 174.

[5] Reprinted with the permission of the Gilder Technology Report, Richard Vigilante, Editor.

12

USING BONDS FOR LONG-TERM REWARD

Despite the fact that bonds seem boring, they have a place in every New Era portfolio and their returns will remain above historical averages. In the New Era, inflation will be virtually nonexistent and deflation may be the norm. As a result, bonds will provide good solid real (or after-inflation) returns. In addition, investing in bonds will enhance the stability of your portfolio while providing returns well above inflation.

When the New Era began in the early 1980s, many bond investors made a huge mistake by investing in short-term bonds just before inflation began to fall. In 1980, the average yield on 3-month Treasury bills was 14.1 percent, while the average yield on 30-year bonds was 11.3 percent. Investors said, "Why should I buy a 30-year bond when the yield on a 3-month bond is so much better?" Today, that decision looks silly. Most bond investors would love to have those 11 percent bonds in their portfolio.

Surprisingly, there are still great buys in the bond market. Fabulous opportunities exist in longer-term, noncallable municipal, corporate, agency, and government bonds. When reminiscing from the early part of the next millenium the decision to buy these bonds will look incredibly smart. Because bond investors remain widely concerned that inflation will reappear, bond yields have stayed above levels that are fundamentally justified. The result is high after-inflation yields for investors.

UNDERSTANDING BOND YIELDS

For the average investor and even accomplished ones, bonds are much more confusing than stocks. While stocks get their returns from corporate profits, interest rates are determined in an international market by a complex set of factors. The simple way to understand interest rates is to think about what they represent. Interest rates are the price for shifting consumption over time. In other words a bond yield represents the "time value of money." An entity (individual, corporation, or municipality) that wants to spend today and save tomorrow must find another entity that wants to save today and spend tomorrow. The combination of these two desires gives us the rate of interest that bond investors will receive.

Every bond yield has three components: the inflation premium, the tax premium, and the real rate of interest. Only by understanding each of these can investors truly decide whether an interest rate is low or high.

The Inflation Premium

The most important component of a bond yield is the inflation premium. Inflation erodes the value of money over time and interest rates should compensate investors for that erosion. For example, if inflation is 3 percent per year, then interest rates must be above 3 percent or investors will have less purchasing power after investing in a bond than before. The correlation between the movement of bond yields and inflation can be seen in the following chart. When the rate of inflation rises, or when fears of future inflation rise, bond yields rise. When the rate of inflation falls, or expected future inflation falls, bond yields will fall.

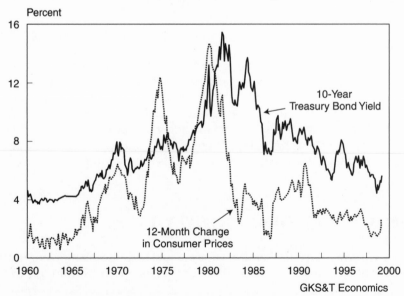

Inflation and Bond Yields Move Together

Source: Federal Reserve Board and Bureau of Labor Statistics.

This relationship to inflation is so tight that the bond market moves on every piece of economic data. This is not true of the stock market, which often seems to ignore economic data. One reason that the bond market is so sensitive is that the Federal Reserve will often change the level of short-term interest rates when inflation data heat up or if it thinks the economy is growing too fast. Because the Fed can manipulate short-term rates, it has a dramatic influence on the bond market in the shortrun. If the Fed pushes short-term rates too far in either direction, however, then long-term bond yields will react in the opposite direction.

The bond market not only moves because of the current inflation rate, but it also incorporates an expectation of inflation in the future. As a result, investors must always be cognizant of the Federal Reserve. Only the Fed has the power to cause inflation and by paying attention to the key indicators of Fed policy and the leading indicators of inflation described in Chapter 5, bond holders avoid holding bonds when inflationary pressures begin to rise. Nonetheless, in the New Era, inflation is likely to remain low and the inflation premium will continue to fall. Eventually bond investors will come to see that inflation will not reappear and bond yields will fall back to levels not seen since the mid-1960s.

The Tax Premium

The tax premium in interest rates is not well understood despite the fact that its existence is readily seen. Note the difference between municipal bond yields and Treasury bond yields. Municipal bond yields are almost always below Treasury bond yields, because municipal bond investors do not pay federal taxes on the interest they earn from municipal bonds. Another way to understand the tax premium is to realize that investors must pay taxes on corporate bond interest, while the corporation that issues the bond can deduct the interest that it pays to bond holders from its income for tax purposes. As a result, corporations pay a higher rate of interest to bond holders than municipalities do, to compensate the bondholder for this "tax premium."

The Real Rate of Interest

The real rate is the part of a bond yield that pays investors for allowing others to use their savings. The real rate of interest exists because every investor has a choice about where to invest. Investors must be enticed (paid) to buy a bond. Real rates of interest are hard to measure, but we know that bond investors want and deserve a positive return after adjusting for the expected rate of inflation and for taxes. What is left over after these adjustments is the real rate of interest.

The real rate is influenced by several factors. The first is the movement in the real economic growth rate. The rate of growth in the economy tends to be a good proxy for the returns to alternative investments. Think of it this way—investors have choices. If the average investment will yield 3 percent, then the real rate of interest will tend toward 3 percent because investors' decisions and the market for bonds will equalize returns across all investments. The second component of the real return is risk. Some investments are riskier than others and the bond market should reflect that fact. Treasury bonds are considered risk-free investments, so the real yield from them is called the "risk-free real rate of return." Every other non-Treasury bond has some risk factor that will boost its yield above the comparable Treasury bond yield. Therefore its real yield is higher than the Treasury bond real yield.

Other factors also influence the real yield for bonds, but they tend to be relatively minor when compared with the first two. They include what is called the "liquidity premium" and also a premium for the uncertainty of a payment stream. Liquidity is the ease at which bonds can be bought and sold. If the market for a bond is small, then its yield will tend to be higher than that for a similar bond whose market is big. For example, the newest issue of a Treasury bond tends to trade much more often than an older issue. Therefore, the newer issue will tend to have a lower yield because some investors value this liquidity. This situation provides an opportunity for investors, who buy older-issue bonds and hold them to maturity, because they will get that extra real yield with no increase in risk.

The uncertainty of a bond's payment stream can also boost its yield. For example, a mortgage bond faces prepayments when interest rates fall as mortgage holders refinance. Accelerated prepayments can lower the expected return and the market puts an added yield on bonds that face this potential. The same is true of a bond that is callable at some time before its actual maturity date. Because these bonds *may* have a shorter life span, investors are compensated to provide flexibility to the issuer.

Combining these different factors gives us the real yield that we expect from a bond. If we ignore taxes, the simplest way to calculate the real yield is to subtract inflation from a bond yield. In the following chart, the annual rate of change in the Consumer Price Index is subtracted from the 10-year bond yield. What remains is often called the real yield even though it still includes the tax premium. Nonetheless, it is a good proxy for the level of real returns to bond investors. As can be seen, in the 1970s real yields were often negative, because investors took a much longer view of inflation. For decades inflation had not been a problem and when it did flare up, it quickly reversed itself. Bond investors were slow to react to rising inflation in the 1970s and were hurt. In times of rising inflation investors should invest in short-term bonds (or money market mutual funds) that will adjust more quickly to the rise in inflation. During the 1965–1982 malaise, while stock holders and long-term bond holders lost money, short-term bond investors eked out small gains.

Since the 1980s, as can also be seen in the chart, real yields have been very high because investors remember the drubbing they took from infla-

Real 10-Year Treasury Bond Yield

GKS&T Economics

10-Year Treasury yield minus 12-month change in Consumer Prices
Source: Federal Reserve Board; Bureau of Labor Statistics

tion during the 1970s. Bond investors have been gun shy and have not allowed interest rates to fall as fast as inflation. As the New Era unfolds and the threat of inflation continues to fade, the risk-free real yield in the bond market will move lower. Bond investors that have faith in the New Era's ability to hold inflation down will be rewarded by buying longer-term bonds that will continue to give high returns in the future.

PUTTING THEM ALL TOGETHER AND ADDING THE FED

Putting the three building blocks together explains the current level of interest rates. When any of them change, interest rates change. The most important of these three factors for investors is the rate of inflation. The real rate and the tax premium rarely change rapidly. And even though inflation from year-to-year tends to move rather slowly, the bond market reacts very quickly to expectations of future inflation.

Expectations of future inflation are driven by many factors; however, the most important is the Federal Reserve. As was discussed in previous chapters, it is not the price of oil or the rate of growth in the economy that causes inflation, but mistakes by the Fed. When the Fed holds interest rates too low, inflation is the result. When the Fed holds interest rates too high, inflation moves lower. This situation creates a paradox in the bond market. Low short-term interest rates (artificially held down by the Fed) can actually cause rising long-term interest rates.

A perfect example can be seen in market movements during 1992 and 1993. The Fed pushed the federal funds rate down to 3 percent in an attempt to get the economy moving after the recession of 1990 to 1991. While longer-term rates came down, they remained well above short-term rates. For example, in 1993 the federal funds rate and the 3-month T-bill rate averaged 3.0 percent; however, the 30-year Treasury bond yield averaged 6.6 percent. To investors, the relatively high yields on long-term bonds, 3.6 percent above short-term bond yields, were enticing. Any investor who invested in 30-year bonds in 1993, however, lost a significant amount of money in 1994 as 30-year bond yields shot up to over 8.0 percent.

A wide spread between long-term and short-term rates suggests that investors believe short-term rates and inflation are likely to rise in the future. In 1993, investors were right. The Fed raised short-term rates from 3.0 percent to 6.0 percent between February 1994 and February 1995. This experience is exactly the opposite of bond investors in the early 1980s when short-term bond yields were higher than long-term bond yields. Then, as was pointed out earlier in this chapter, investors should have invested in longer-term bond even though short-term bond yields were higher.

The reason for this paradoxical relationship is simple. When the Fed holds short-term rates too low, inflation is the result. The signs of inflation will appear slowly. Gold prices and other commodity prices will rise, the value of the dollar on foreign exchange markets will begin to fall, and the spread between long-term and short-term rates will widen. When the Fed holds rates too high, gold prices and other commodity prices will fall, the dollar will strengthen, and the spread between long-term and short-term rates will narrow or even invert as it did in the early 1980s.

By comparing the level of short-term interest rates with inflation we can tell when the Fed is holding rates too high or too low. As can be seen in the following chart, during 1992 and 1993, the Fed pushed the federal funds rate down below the rate of inflation. In other words, real (or inflation-adjusted) short-term interest rates were negative. This signaled that the Fed was creating an inflationary environment for the economy and in 1994 bond yields shot up. In recent years, because the Fed has been worried by the strength of the economy, they have held real short-term rates high. This signals that inflation is unlikely to accelerate and that bond yields should continue to head lower.

Real Federal Funds Rate

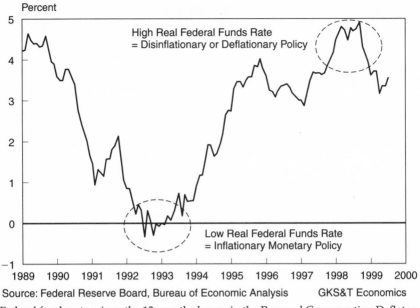

Source: Federal Reserve Board, Bureau of Economic Analysis   GKS&T Economics
Federal funds rate minus the 12-month change in the Personal Consumption Deflator

THE OLD WIVES TALE OF THE BOND MARKET

An old wives tale says that the stock market is the optimistic market and the bond market is the pessimistic market. The stock market loves strong economic growth while the bond market hates it. Bonds are considered defensive investments, while stocks are considered offensive investments. This whole view, however, is highly suspect. Both the bond market and the stock market performed horribly in the 1970s, but they have both performed well in the 1980s and 1990s. Interest rates shot up during the stagflation of the 1970s, but have trended down ever since. Despite the strong economic growth and rising stock markets of the New Era, bond yields have consistently come down and bond investors have experienced solid performance even though the economy has been strong.

There are still profit opportunities for bond investors in the New Era. While it may seem that interest rates are very low, they are still well above historical averages. The chart on page 111 shows corporate bond yields back to 1865. The data are a combination of railroad bond yields through the early 1930s and then high-grade corporate bond yields (triple A rated). As the chart shows, while interest rates today are very low when compared with rates since the late 1960s, they remain quite high when compared with the rates that existed from the late 1800s to the mid-1960s. The most important reason for relatively high yields of recent years is that bond investors have painful memories of the inflation of the 1970s. Because taxes, regulation, and government spending moved higher and the Fed pushed down interest rates to offset the damaging effects of those burdens, inflation shot higher. In the New Era, government burdens are falling while the Fed holds rates high to combat an economy that it thinks is too strong. The combination of these policies will result in deflationary pressures that will eventually move bond yields back to the levels of the 1960s. Then, the average yield on a 10-year Treasury bond was 3.5 percent, mortgage rates were under 5 percent, high-grade corporate bond yields were 4.5 percent, and long-term municipal bond yields averaged just 3.0 percent.

THE GAINS FROM LOWER RATES

Obviously lower interest rates are not a good development for investors who depend on a fixed stream of investment income in retirement. However, even low rates will provide a solid return when compared with the prices of goods and services. If inflation is zero, a 4.0 percent bond yield is better than an 8 percent bond yield when inflation is 5.0 percent. If, as is highly likely in the New Era, deflation of 0.5 percent to 1.0 percent per year occurs, then investors will achieve higher than historical average real returns even if interest rates fall to 3.5 percent. More importantly, as interest rates fall, the appreciation in bond prices accelerates. A decline in bond yields from 12.0 percent to 11.0 percent causes the price of a 30-year Treasury bond to appreciate by 8.7 percent. However, a drop from 6.0 percent to 5.0 percent boosts the price of the bond by 15.4 percent. In simple terms, a 1.0 percent drop in rates when yields are 12.0 percent is just a 1/12 decline, but when rates are at 6 percent, a 1.0 percent drop is a 1/6 decline.

While it may seem that you have already missed the big gains in the bond market, when rates fall from current levels back to the levels of the 1960s, large gains will occur. In addition, by buying bonds today with yields in the 6.0 to 7.0 percent range, your portfolio will be earning twice the market rate in the early part of the next century.

HOW TO INVEST IN BONDS

Although there are many ways to invest in the bond market, this book will focus on just three of them: buying actual bonds, buying closed-end bond mutual funds, and buying open-ended bond mutual funds. The first thing to understand is that the very best way to invest in the bond market is to buy individual bonds and hold them to maturity. However, if you plan to trade your bond portfolio then you should buy bonds in no less than $25,000 increments. Only in this way will your transaction costs be low enough to justify trading your bond investments. For small transactions, the costs are much higher in the bond market than in the stock market. The second important point to remember is that closed-end bond funds are likely to outperform open-ended bond funds in the New Era. Closed-end funds have higher returns than open-ended funds when interest rates are falling.

BUYING INDIVIDUAL BONDS

There are four types of bonds to consider when deciding which bonds to buy: municipal bonds, corporate bonds, Treasury or government-sponsored agency (GSA) bonds, and mortgage-backed bonds. Each of the four is unique, with performance that will vary in different interest rate environments.

In the early stages of the New Era, with interest rates likely to head significantly lower, mortgage-backed bonds are unlikely to perform as well as the other three. The reason is simple: As rates fall, refinancing of mortgages will cause these bonds to pay principal back earlier than investors expect. When interest rates settle into the lower levels that history suggests is possible, then mortgage-backed bonds will be a good investment again, especially if you would like your bond portfolio to provide monthly income. Because mortgages are paid on a monthly basis, investors will receive a payment (of interest and principal) monthly. To get monthly interest from corporate or municipal bonds you will need to buy many different bonds which pay interest in all the different months of the year.

Municipal bonds will be great investments in the New Era. While there are some taxable municipal issues, for the most part, municipal bond investors do not pay federal income taxes on municipal bond interest payments. In addition, many states exempt municipal bond interest from state income taxes as well, which is especially beneficial in such states as Massachusetts and California where state tax rates are very high. As can be seen in the following chart, municipal bond yields are lower than Treasury bond yields. After adjusting municipal bond yields for the tax premium, however, their yields are higher than Treasury bond yields. For example, in May 1999 the 20-year Treasury bond yield was 6.08 percent while a typical AAA 20-year municipal bond yield was 5.1 percent. If you face a federal tax rate of 28 percent, then the taxable equivalent yield on a 5.1 percent municipal bond is 7.08 percent. If you pay a 36 percent tax rate, then your taxable equivalent yield will be 7.97 percent. The formula for calculating these yields is simple: Taxable Equivalent Yield = municipal bond yield / (1 − your tax rate). For example, 5.1 percent / (1 − .28) = 7.08 percent.

20-Year Municipal Bond Yield vs. 20-Year Treasury Yield

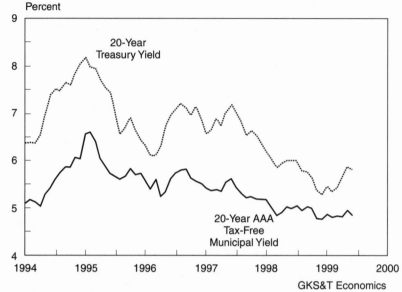

GKS&T Economics

Source: Moody's, U.S. Treasury Department

Clearly the comparable tax-adjusted yield on municipal bonds is significantly higher than the equivalent taxable Treasury bond. The generally accepted reason for the high spread is that municipal bonds face risks of default by the city or state that issued them. Historically, however, the incidence of default is rare and states and cities have never been in a better fiscal situation. In the New Era, strong economic growth will continue to reduce the spending burdens on states, while tax revenues will continue to rise. As a result, the record surpluses in state budgets will continue to grow in the New Era.

Corporate bonds will also be good investments in the New Era. However, because you already have plenty of exposure to the corporate world in your stock holdings, buying corporate bonds will exacerbate the volatility of your total investment portfolio. Nonetheless, corporate bonds, especially what are called junk bonds, can often bring high returns. Look for yields that are higher than the comparable taxable-equivalent yields you can receive from municipal bonds and invest in New Era companies. If you cannot find spreads that are wider than municipal bonds there is no reason to invest in corporate bonds.

The final two types of bonds that investors should consider are Treasury or Government Sponsored Agency (GSA) bonds. Treasury bonds are free of credit risk and are extremely liquid. As a result, they are good bonds for investors who are looking for income in retirement. GSA bonds are those that are issued by quasi-government agencies such as the Federal Home Loan Bank, Student Loan Marketing Association, or Federal National Mortgage Association. GSA bonds have the implied backing of the federal government in the case of default, but still carry higher yields than Treasury bonds. These bonds will be good solid investments and should be considered as alternatives to Treasury bonds.

THE PROBLEM WITH BOND FUNDS

Actively managed, open-ended bond funds have certain benefits for investors, but they also have negatives when compared with owning individual bonds. When you invest in an open-ended bond fund and interest rates fall, your investment is diluted when other investors deposit money in the fund. It works like this. Let's say you and 999 others invest $10,000 in a new bond fund when interest rates are at 6.0 percent. The total invested will be $10 million. If interest rates fall to 5.0 percent, the value of the bonds held in the fund will rise and you will benefit. However, if the fund is able to attract $10 million in new investment at this point because of its good performance, the fund will be forced to buy bonds that yield just 5.0 percent instead of the 6.0 percent when you originally invested. As a result, the average yield in the fund will fall near 5.5 percent and your earnings will drop. If you had purchased an individual bond when yields were 6.0 percent, then your yield would remain at 6.0 percent even after interest rates fell.

On the other hand, when interest rates rise, the bond fund will be able to invest at higher yields. If the fund can attract new investors then your yield will rise; however, when interest rates are rising and the value of a bond fund is falling, the fund has a more difficult time attracting new investors. As a result, your upside is limited no matter which way bonds move.

One way to avoid this problem is to invest in closed-end bond funds. These funds issue shares that are then traded on an exchange, such as the New York Stock exchange. The funds managers actively manage the portfolio, but the investment cannot be diluted with new investors if interest rates fall. Another type of closed-end bond fund that has been very popular with investors is a unit investment trust or defined portfolio. These trusts invest in a portfolio of bonds and then sell shares in the trust. The bonds in the trust will not be traded and will be held to maturity. As long as you do not sell there is no way that your yield can change. Both closed-end bond funds and unit investment trusts are appropriate alternatives to investing in individual bonds during the New Era, however, it still makes more sense to buy individual bonds.

IGNORE THE MYTHS AND THE PESSIMISTS

For some unexplained reason, pessimistic myths about the bond market are consistently repeated. One such myth is that because the Japanese own so many U.S. government bonds, a decision by them to sell would drive interest rates higher. The fear that the Japanese will sell their bonds makes the rounds in the bond market frequently and often creates enough concern to drive interest rates up for a short time. Do not let this fear keep you from buying bonds in the New Era. No matter what the Japanese do with their bonds, they cannot drive interest rates above fundamental levels for long.

Interest rates are determined by the three fundamental factors discussed here, not by who wants to sell or buy. If the Japanese did decide to sell all their U.S. government bonds at once, it would drive up interest rates, but rates would fall right back down to fundamental levels as investors realized that yields were climbing because of a nonfundamental factor. As long as inflation remains low, interest rates will stay down no matter who decides to sell their bonds.

This myth continues to hold sway over bond market participants because of the belief that supply and demand determines interest rates. This belief is easy to understand because the laws of supply and demand are so important in economics, but supply and demand do not determine interest rates—the three fundamental factors do. To better understand this concept, try this thought experiment. If for some reason, every 30-year Treasury bond except for one $10,000 bond was bought by the Treasury Department and retired tomorrow, would the underlying value of a 30-year bond change? Of course, if the Treasury did this all at once they would drive the 30-year bond yield lower as they enticed all the current bondholders to sell. But once this massive buyback is completed, the last bond should have the same yield as the first one bought by the Treasury. In this thought experiment there has been no change in any of the underlying fundamentals that determine bond yields. The inflation rate, the real rate, and the tax premium are still the same as they were before the Treasury Department acted.

This thought experiment shows the futility of trying to forecast interest rates by using the budget deficit or a surge of new bond issuance by municipalities, corporations, or foreign governments. Supply and demand only move interest rates in the short run, not in the long run. A recent example was the big drop in yields during 1998 as investors moved into Treasury bonds because of the uncertainty created by international financial crisis. After this "flight to quality" investment the market snapped right back and yields returned to pre-crisis levels. Despite the fact that the market always comes back to the fundamentals, supply and demand arguments are used by many to suggest either a good environment for bond yields or a bad one. Ignore these arguments. The most important factor in determining bond yields over time is inflation.

A NEW ERA FORECAST FOR BONDS

The New Era will be a good environment for investing in bonds. Inflation will remain low for decades to come and two factors will likely generate *deflation* in the New Era—productivity growth and tight monetary policy. Productivity growth will push prices down as the economy accelerates, and because our monetary authorities have learned from the mistakes of the past, a 1970s-style inflation debacle is highly unlikely. In fact, because the Fed is still worried about repeating the 1970s they will hold monetary policy too tight.

Helping these two fundamental factors will be a continued push toward a more integrated global economy. As trade increases, production costs will fall as the competitive advantages of the world are leveraged to the maximum. In addition, deregulation and privatization will continue to reduce the costs of providing goods and services.

The bottom line is that the odds of a sharp increase in interest rates driven by a surge in inflation are very low, while the odds of further declines are very high. However, do not expect interest rates to head straight down. The bond market remains fearful of strong growth and, as a result, will find its way back to lower yields only slowly. While huge returns are possible when investing in bonds, they should be viewed as long-run stabilizers for your portfolio. Nonetheless, do not wait to invest in bonds. The yields available today are historically high. Investing in long-term non-callable bonds today will lock in those high yields for years to come.

13

REAL ESTATE AND COMMODITIES

IN THE NEW ERA, SPACE AND RESOURCES ARE INFINITE

In the 1970s, real estate and commodity investments outperformed both the stock market and the bond market. The reason was simple. Inflation drove up the value of real estate and commodities, but was bad for financial assets. However, because inflation will be virtually nonexistent in the New Era and deflation will remain a very real possibility, it will not be a friendly place for these types of defensive investments.

It is not that these areas of the economy will whither, but that average returns will remain below stocks and bonds. Conceptual ideas, not resources, are the driving force behind the New Era of Wealth. The conceptual economy will continue to find ways to use fewer resources and resource producers will continue to increase efficiency. This means that commodity prices and real estate will continue to fall in value *relative* to information and services. Investors cannot count on inflation to raise the price of hard assets. Some real estate investments will do well, but on average land and buildings will continue to lag. Therefore, investors must pick their spots carefully and reduce exposure to hard assets.

INFLATION, DEFLATION, AND RESOURCE PRICES

During the 10 years ending in 1980, the median price for a new single-family home adjusted for inflation rose 10.6 percent per year, while the median resale price for an existing home rose 10.4 percent annually. During this same period, the Dow Jones Industrial Average after adjustment for

175

inflation fell 6.1 percent at an annual rate. Real estate prices consistently beat stocks in the 1970s. In just 1 year, 1978, the median price of a single-family home in the United States jumped an astounding 13.9 percent while stocks fell 8.3 percent. Consumer prices rose 7.3 percent in 1978, meaning that "real" home prices rose 6.6 percent, but stocks fell 15.6 percent.

Inflation alone is enough to cause a shift in investment strategies. In inflationary times, hard asset prices rise with the general price level, but financial assets suffer. Inflation boosts interest rates and lowers P/E ratios, but it causes hard asset prices to rise. This does not mean that inflation is good. Despite rising asset values, inflation eroded productivity in the 1970s, unemployment rose, and the economy suffered; thus the earnings potential from every kind of investment fell. While investing in real estate proved profitable, rising real estate prices pushed rents higher and drove many small businesses into bankruptcy. They also kept many Americans from buying homes.

In the New Era, inflation has plummeted and deflation has become a very real possibility. The value of resource-based investments are thus harmed. For example, during the 10 years ending in March 1999, the median price of a new single-family home rose just 2.3 percent per year, while the resale price of an existing home rose at an annual rate of 3.9 percent (see the following chart). During the same 10-year period, the Dow Jones Industrial Average, including reinvested dividends, rose 18.8 percent per year. Obviously there are some areas of the country that have seen home prices rise by much more than 2.2 percent per year. As the saying goes, "lo-

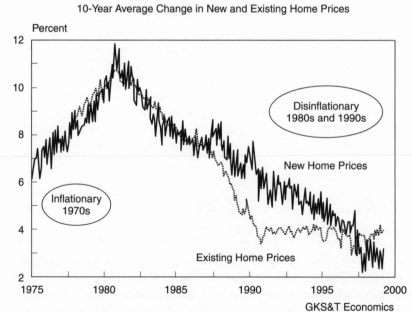

10-Year Average Change in New and Existing Home Prices

Source: New 1-Family house prices-CEN, Existing 1-Family home prices-NAR

cation, location, and location" are the three most important factors when investing in real estate. Location is becoming much less meaningful, however. The New Era will more evenly distribute people and business across the country, helping to boost values in less populated areas and slow the growth in metropolitan areas.

TECHNOLOGY AND REAL ESTATE

When you first put a teabag in hot water, the flavor and coloring swirl close to the bag. Eventually, however, the water is saturated with both flavor and color. This process of evenly distributing one thing throughout another occurs in most systems. Clearly, however, when we look around at the economy there are many things that are not evenly distributed. People, for example, tend to aggregate in big cities and then population density thins out as we move from cities to farms.

In the New Era, however, the density of our population and the distribution of business throughout the United States and the world will tend to spread out. This will take decades, or longer, but technology is already removing the cost of distance and creating an abundance of space. This process of more evenly distributing the economy will fundamentally alter the real estate landscape, creating both advantages and disadvantages for real estate investments.

For example, between 1980 and 1990, the total U.S. population in metropolitan areas grew from 177.3 million to 198.2 million, a total increase of 11.8 percent. Nonmetropolitan area population grew by just 2.6 percent, from 49.3 million to 50.5 million. Between 1990 and 1996, however, the rate of change narrowed significantly. Metropolitan areas gained 6.9 percent to 211.8 million, while nonmetropolitan area population grew by 5.9 percent to 53.5 million.[1]

It is still cheaper to locate near large metropolitan areas, but as prices for telecommunications plummet and broadband access to the Internet proliferates, the opportunity costs of living away from the city will fall. These trends have been predicted by others well before this book was written, but the actual impact of technology has taken longer than many expected. And the process will still take time. The risks of leaving a densely populated area are still high for most businesses and employees. Retailers, for example, want to serve as large an area as possible and employees want the security of multiple job opportunities. Starting a business in a small town or moving to a more rural area limits some of these possibilities.

Nonetheless, the plummeting costs of telecommunications and the ability to compete from anywhere in the world are beginning to alter the economic landscape now. Already, suburban areas of cities are growing rapidly as small business starts shoot upward. In 1965, according to Dun & Bradstreet, there were 204,000 new business incorporations in the

United States. In 1997, there were 799,000. These new business incorporations need office space as they grow. Suburban office space vacancy rates
have plummeted from 23.4 percent in 1986 to 8.9 percent in 1999 (about the
same as downtown vacancy rates) according to CB Richard Ellis. At the
same time, industrial vacancy rates have increased, from 3.7 percent in
1981 to 8.4 percent in 1998. The shift toward small businesses built around
the service economy is well underway and as it matures, the impact on real
estate investments will be tremendous. Small businesses create most new
jobs and as these businesses relocate away from cities, workers will as well.

New communications technologies mean that you no longer move
away from the best and brightest talent in the fields of education, medicine, law, and consulting when you leave an urban area. The New Era will
make anyone, anywhere, available to all.

HOUSING, REITS, AND THE NEW ERA

In order to profit from real estate investments you must carefully weigh
these shifting sands. Most individual investors have a significant investment in their own home and, as a result, should not make any additional real
estate investments; however, a second home in a prime vacation area can be
a fabulous investment. An explosion in wealth and, with it, leisure activity,
has increased the demand for vacation homes and resorts. The number of
golf courses in the United States has climbed 24 percent since 1986, from
13,353 to 16,365; and at the end of 1998, there were 1,069 courses under construction.[2] This growth highlights the increasing demand for leisure activity
in the United States. With this growth comes great real estate opportunities
for many investors. Not only will you own an investment property, but you
will also get to *use* your investment and receive tax benefits.

For most people, the investments in first and second homes represent
a huge portion of their portfolio. As a result, investing in other real estate
assets does not represent good risk management. However, some have
enough assets to begin spreading risk across different sectors of the economy by, for example, investing in real estate investment trusts (REITS).
Typically, REITS are divided into four categories—industrial, retail, office,
and apartments. While many of these investments may seem tempting,
real estate values will remain subdued in the New Era.

The value added in the New Era will be inside the building and in cy-
berspace, not in the asset that houses the ideas and people. A computer is
only as valuable as the software and information inside of it—the box
alone is not worth much. The same is true of land and buildings. They are
only valuable when they have something on or in them. In today's world,
the ideas and people who create value can move in a moment and tying
up assets in immovable objects is limiting. More and more companies are

selling buildings and leasing them back because they realize that corporate assets can be used more efficiently in other areas. Return on assets is what matters and real estate has a lower return than ideas and information.

Internet commerce is already altering the retail landscape. Egghead, Inc. recently closed its eighty retail outlets, changed its name to Egghead.com, Inc., and moved its entire business to the Internet. This trend is just beginning. In the future, as more business is done on the Web, with delivery through the mail, the demand for retail space will not grow as rapidly as economic growth alone would suggest. This does not mean that retail space will disappear, just that growth at the margin will begin to slow. The potential changes do not end there. They are endless. Think small, not big. Think soft, not hard. Think fast, not slow. The New Era does not need as much space as the Old Era and it wants to be mobile.

REAL ESTATE OPPORTUNITIES STILL EXIST

Although the New Era will not be friendly to real estate investments in general, some areas will perform better than others. As stated, retail space is not a growth industry; however, a whole new investment opportunity has opened in the suburban areas of the United States. The explosion in small business starts will continue and these businesses will move further from the city center. Much like the condo boom of the 1980s, office buildings are now being built so that they can be sold in sections to these small businesses. Investing in REITS, which build or manage these suburban office spaces, should provide a better than average return.

Another growth area in real estate will be in warehousing. The exponential growth in Internet commerce will require massive investment in new systems of distribution. Just-in-time inventory systems, trucking, air freight, and computerized packaging systems require a massive supporting infrastructure.

In addition, leisure activities from spas, marinas, ski resorts, theme parks, and gambling boats are proliferating rapidly. These investments add value to real estate through the provision of services. Although not all of these investments will prosper, some will. Unique properties near Vail, Jackson Hole, Disney World, and Cape Cod will remain good investments, but at some point, nonunique properties will see their profit margins erode. Hotels are springing up all over the country and all you need to do is look at the intersection of major roads throughout the country to see redundant investments. Many of these intersections have two, three, or more hotels today, where 10 years ago there were none. The price pressures from the competition will keep the lid on profits. In addition, gambling boats are spreading rapidly and as they do, the excess profits of the first boats are disappearing.

Another area reaching saturation is the housing industry. For many years now, housing activity has grown faster than demographic factors suggest are sustainable. In 1998, U.S. housing starts (including single-family homes, town homes, condos, and apartments) reached 1.62 million, while the total number of new U.S. households increased by just 1.5 million. Although many older homes are being torn down and replaced, and many Americans are buying second homes and many are moving to the suburbs, this excess of starts over new households cannot last for long. More importantly, in the past, when housing activity has climbed above demographic factors, price increases have slowed. This is already happening in the New Era and it should continue in the years ahead.

COMMODITIES AND PRECIOUS METALS

The same forces that are keeping the lid on real estate values will impact commodity prices as well. While economists have argued about whether deflation exists, commodity producers have no doubts. As can be seen in the following chart, the Bridge/CRB Commodity Futures Price Index in early 1999 was just one-half of its level in the early 1980s and very near a 24-year low. During the 10 years ending in 1981, the Bridge/CRB index rose by 10.8 percent per year. During the 10 years ending in April 1999, the

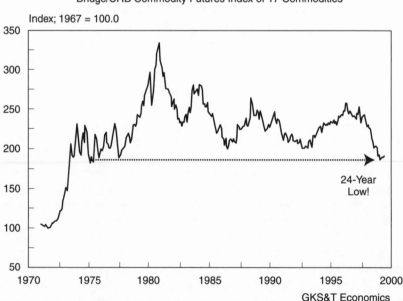

Bridge/CRB Commodity Futures Index of 17 Commodities

GKS&T Economics

Source: Haver Analytics

same index fell by 2.4 percent per year. Copper prices in early 1999, at roughly 65 cents per pound, were one-half of their 1995 level and unchanged from 1986. Aluminum in early 1999 was near 60 cents per pound, roughly one-half the price in 1988. Hardest hit have been agricultural prices. Soybeans at $4.65 per bushel in April 1999 were one-half their 1988 price and the same price they sold for in 1976. Corn prices fell to $2.05 per bushel in early 1999, 30 percent below their price in 1976, 23 years ago.

The decline in commodity prices has been a direct result of the five key trends of the New Era. In the 1970s, high taxes, regulation, and big government smothered the economy. The Federal Reserve tried to counteract the drag from big government by holding interest rates low. The combination of these two policies resulted in a surge in inflation. In the 1980s and 1990s, the size of government has shrunk, deregulation has swept industry after industry, and taxes are down. As a result, the economy has grown more rapidly. The Fed's response to this more rapid growth has been to hold interest rates higher than they should. The combination of these two policy shifts has caused a large drop in inflation. Add growing global trade and advances in technology to the mix and it is easy to see why commodity prices have fallen so far. For example, new drilling technology virtually guarantees that oil will be found at every new well. In addition, high-tech extraction methods increase the amount of oil that can be pumped from every well. Farmers are becoming more productive by the day and the combination of higher productivity and tight monetary policy causes prices to fall.

Interestingly, the continuation of deflation in the New Era does not mean that commodity producers will all suffer. Alcoa, Inc. has increased productivity and shifted its product mix so that even though aluminum prices are now one-half of their 1988 price, profits remain the same. Farmers, seeing profits fall somewhat due to lower prices, have partially offset those price declines with productivity. In each of these cases, while profits have been maintained by productivity, there is no overall profit *growth*. What this means is that the days of profits due to inflation are gone. Successful investments in commodities will require an increase in productivity. Some commodity producers will be able to implement new technology and shift production to higher value-added products, but on average, resource-based investments will underperform financial assets in the New Era.

Nonetheless, many investors continue to believe that inflation is just around the corner. In late 1997, it was reported that Warren Buffet bought silver. While the rumors spread like wildfire and silver prices jumped from under $5/oz. to over $7/oz., the investment has not paid off. Precious metals, such as gold and silver, are the ultimate hedge against inflation and the markets took Warren Buffet's investment in silver as a sign that the great investor thought inflation was returning. However, silver prices quickly fell back to the $5 to $5.50/oz. range in 1998 and early 1999. The lesson here is simple: Inflation in the New Era is nonexistent and trying to protect ourselves from it is a waste of time and resources.

As can be seen in the following chart, silver and gold prices shot upward in the 1970s as the United States devalued the dollar and inflation took off. However, since reaching peaks of nearly $800/oz. for gold and $40/oz. for silver, their prices have come down significantly and stabilized. In 1996, gold prices rose to over $400/oz., but in early 1999 they had fallen to under $260/oz. These declines in precious metals prices have hurt the stocks of gold and silver producers. The Philadelphia Stock Exchange Index of Gold and Silver stocks fell 3.5 percent per year over the 10 years ending in early 1999.

DEFLATION AND THE NEW ERA

It has been said that "inflation is too much money chasing too few goods." Deflation, therefore, can be called "too little money chasing too many goods." Many economists believe that strong growth causes inflation, but in fact, strong growth is deflationary.

A simple example can illustrate this fact. Let's say there are ten bananas and $10 in an economy. If each banana trades once a year, then each one is worth $1. Now let's assume that a new biotech approach to growing bananas increases the output of bananas to twenty each year. If the money supply is still $10, then the price of each banana *falls* to 50 cents from $1. If

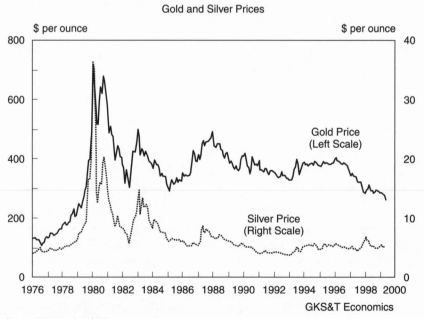

Gold and Silver Prices

GKS&T Economics

Source: Haver Analytics

the money supply increased to $20, then the price of bananas would remain the same.

The New Era is exactly like this example. The boom has caused a rapid increase in the output of goods and services, but because the Fed continues to hold money tight, deflation occurs. Like the Industrial Revolution, prices will continue to fall in the decades ahead. The Fed will continue to view the economy's strong growth as an inflationary force and will exacerbate this process of deflation. The impact of tight fed policy and higher productivity will be lower prices for goods, services, and real estate. Investments that get a significant part of their returns from rising prices will suffer. In the New Era, investors will see much higher returns by investing in ideas, not resources.

References

[1] U.S. Department of the Census. 1998. *Statistical abstract of the U.S.*, table 40.
[2] National Golf Foundation. 1999. *www.ngf.org*. From *Golf facilities in the U.S.—1999 edition*.

14

THE NEW ERA OF WEALTH IS JUST BEGINNING

To understand and profit from the New Era we must change our perspectives on economics and wealth creation. For too long we have been told that government is the source of wealth and that investors become irrational. For too long we have learned that the economy can only grow so fast, that unemployment can only get so low, and that the stock market can only go so high. The theories behind these ideas are from the Old Era and the New Era is proving them wrong. The perspective, which has been described in this book, suggests that the New Era is for real and that it is just beginning.

One of my favorite stories about differing perspectives involves four people—a young lady, her grandmother, a lieutenant, and his general. They all board a train together and are placed in the same car. When the train enters a tunnel and everything turns pitch black, they all hear the sound of a big wet kiss and then a loud slap. As the train leaves the tunnel everyone is wondering what happened. The young lady thinks, "Wow, what a great kiss, but why did my grandmother slap that general?" The grandmother thinks, "I am sure proud of my granddaughter, that lieutenant got fresh with her and she put him in his place." The general thinks, "I must have a talk with that lieutenant, he should not act that way, but why did the grandmother hit me?" The lieutenant thinks, "What a great day, I got to kiss a beautiful girl and hit my boss at the same time."

Like this story shows, perspective makes all the difference in the world and perspective is what matters most for profiting from the New Era. The five key trends of the New Era have created an environment for growth and wealth creation. They have ended the dark days of the 1970s and launched the United States into a 30- or 40-year boom. Strong growth, low inflation, higher stock prices, falling interest rates, and rising incomes will characterize the boom. Moreover, recessions will be fewer and farther between, opportunity will multiply, and the pessimists will continue to be wrong. Every industry worldwide will be altered by New Era technologies and productivity will rise dramatically.

The "increasing returns" of the networked economy will push the pessimistic arguments of "limits to growth" and "diminishing returns" onto the scrap heap of old paradigms. More importantly, the New Era is not anywhere near ending. We are in the second inning, not the ninth. It takes time for new technologies to reach their limits and the technologies of the New Era are just getting started. Today we are building the foundation of a fabulous future and as each day passes, the speed of change will increase.

Have you ever watched a skyscraper rise from an empty lot? It seems to take forever to dig the hole and lay the foundation, but once it is in place the building takes off. It may take months to get just 10 feet off the ground, but then every floor seems to go up faster. As the construction crew gets into a rhythm, the just-in-time delivery of beams and glass begins to accelerate and each floor is built faster than the last.

The New Era of Wealth is like this, but the growth rates are even more astounding. Every additional person who joins the Web makes it more valuable and as it gets more valuable, the benefits of joining increase. More importantly, as its value rises, the cost of joining falls. PC prices are falling and are approaching zero faster than DELL and Compaq (CPQ) would like. But even if prices for PCs were the same today as they were 2 years ago, they would be worth more. Cost and value (worth) are two different things. The value of owning a computer and being able to benefit from the information and possibilities of the Internet has increased so much that PCs are worth more today. Nonetheless, they cost less, which creates a virtuous circle of wealth creation. We have completed the foundation and now it is time to push to the sky.

VESTED INTERESTS AND NEW PARADIGMS

One of the most interesting things about the New Era is the slow acceptance of it by policymakers and many of our most stalwart and famous companies. Take Merrill Lynch (MER) for example. On June 1, 1999, after deriding online trading, Merrill Lynch finally capitulated. As a front page *Wall Street Journal* article put it, "It was less than a year ago that Merrill's brokerage chief, John "Launny" Steffens, publicly stated that 'the do-it-yourself model of investing, centered on Internet trading, should be regarded as a serious threat to Americans' financial lives.' Merrill instead found that scoffing at cyber-trading was a threat to its own health. "There's not a [broker] at Merrill who hasn't lost business to online brokers, a senior Merrill executive confides."[1]

Paradigm shifts are always hard for those with vested interests. It is very difficult for companies with thousands of employees that depend on the status quo to shift to a whole new model of doing business. However, the changes that the New Era will bring are inexorable. In a speech on May

26, 1999, to the American Iron & Steel Institute, Oracle Corp. (ORCL) President Raymond Lane told steel executives that the New Era was going to create a "brand new economy." He told those in attendance that "I don't believe that management is prepared for the changes" and that they should "plan for cannibalization." In other words, if you don't change and use the ability of the networked economy, someone else will. In the New Era, companies that don't find a way to evolve by using technology will be overtaken by either new startups or by those who do evolve.

Old Era companies will lose out to New Era companies and the gap between the New and the Old will widen as the next few decades unfold. Investors must pay attention to these developments. The potential of the Internet is nearly limitless and contrary to popular opinion, when there are finally no more people to get on the Web, the growth will continue. Information and access will boost productivity and reduce waste. Time is the most valuable of all commodities and the Internet is the key to conserving time. In addition, capacity is not a problem. There are only so many people that can fit into a retail store and there are only so many orders a clerk can handle at once, but the Internet has no such constraints. Only bandwidth (the ability of the telecommunications system to carry traffic) holds us back at this point, but bandwidth is expanding rapidly.

These forces are increasing productivity and erasing the impact of geography. Location is diminishing as a factor for success while access becomes possible from anywhere and at any time. New Era technologies are increasing access to information for everyone. As information and speed of communication increase, the world will become smaller and globalization will accelerate. The New Era empowers individuals like never before and those companies that either support or take advantage of it will reap huge rewards.

LUDDITES AND THE NEW ERA

There have always been doomsayers as technology has expanded our horizons. When mechanical looms first appeared, many people thought the looms would cause mass unemployment and poverty. The Luddites responded by raiding factories, wrecking looms, and protesting the proliferation of this new technology. Now, when we look back, we realize that the technology of mechanical looms, tractors, and mass production actually created wealth and opportunity and did not destroy it. The wealth that was created by these mechanical devices increased living standards for all citizens. In addition, the technology allowed many individuals to find more productive uses for their talents.

Today's technology is even more impressive. It is freeing up time and creating more opportunity than we have ever seen. While some people see these changes as bad, if we view them as positive we can truly benefit. Never before in history have so many opportunities existed. By embracing technology, our God-given talents will find outlets that we had no idea existed.

A MILLIONAIRE ON EVERY BLOCK

Already, wealth is being accumulated at an amazing rate. In 1999, "4.1 million of the 102 million households in the U.S. had a net worth of $1 million or more. That compares with 3 million such households out of 99 million in 1995, when the stock market really began to gain steam."[2] Between 1995 and 1998, the number of U.S. households rose by 3 percent, but the number of millionaire families jumped by nearly 37 percent.

If you follow the simple investment advice in the preceding chapters, remain optimistic, and find discipline about saving and investing you too can become a millionaire. Stocks in New Era sectors of the economy will continue to explode, interest rates and inflation will remain low, and financial assets will outperform hard assets. Invest in bonds and stocks and keep your exposure to most real estate and commodities to a minimum. Most importantly, stay out of debt. Despite rising pension assets, incomes and savings, debt has kept many from building wealth. In the New Era, debt drags us down while saving and investing will build riches.

IGNORE THE PESSIMISTS

In early 1999, as this book was going to press, the Asian economies appeared to be bouncing back, Japan was finding its economic legs again, and OPEC was cutting back on oil production. Fears of an overheating economy and future inflation had forced the Fed to raise interest rates twice and conventional wisdom had once again decided that the New Era was coming to an end. Interest rates climbed as these fears spread throughout the financial markets. Value stocks started to rise, especialy cyclical and commodity stocks, and thoughts of the 1970s were in the air.

At the same time a press release from InfoBeads was published proclaiming that as of January 1999, 67.5 million U.S. PCs were connected to the Internet. This figure was a 50 percent increase over January 1998, with business connections up 76 percent and household connections up 35 percent. This is the real story. Everything else is just a temporary step backward into fear and pessimism.

As the proliferation of technology continues to accelerate, the New Era is gaining strength. This technology explosion is raising productivity and lowering inflationary pressures, not increasing them. As outdated models of the economy flash inflationary warning signals, the price of gold has been falling and New Era companies have been expanding rapidly. With technology expanding and gold prices hitting lows, the fears of inflation are misplaced. Moreover, because the Fed has been holding short-term interest rates too high, inflation has become less of a problem, not more. Cartels, such as OPEC, cannot find long-term success in this kind of environment, and despite fears, the New Era continues.

Doubts will always find a voice, but the five key trends of the New Era are still in place. They will keep moving the world forward despite the doubters and those who remain optimistic will continue to benefit.

References

[1] Gasparino, Charles and Buckman, Rebecca. 1999. Facing internet threat, Merrill plans to offer trading online for low fees. *The Wall Street Journal*, 1 June, p. 1.

[2] Uchitelle, Louis. 1999. More wealth, more stately mansions. *New York Times*, 6 June, Economic View.

BIBLIOGRAPHY

Arthur, Brian W. 1994. *Increasing Returns and Path Dependence in the Economy,* 4th ed. Ann Arbor, MI: The University of Michigan Press.

Bartley, Robert L. 1992. *The Seven Fat Years,* 1st ed. New York: The Free Press.

Baumol, William J., Richard R. Nelson, and Edward N. Wolff. 1994. *Convergence of Productivity: Cross-National Studies and Historical Evidence,* 1st ed. New York: Oxford University Press.

Christensen, Clayton M. 1997. *The Innovator's Dilemma: When New Technologies Cause Great Firms to Fail,* 5th ed. Boston, MA: Harvard Business School Press.

Davis, Stan and Christopher Meyer. 1998. *Blur: The Speed of Change in the Connected Economy,* 1st ed. Reading, MA: Addison-Wesley.

D'Souza, Dinesh. 1997. *Ronald Reagan: How an Ordinary Man Became an Extraordinary Leader,* 2nd ed. New York: The Free Press.

Genetski, Robert J. 1986. *Taking the Voodoo Out of Economics,* 1st ed. Chicago, IL: Regnery Books.

Gilder, George. 1981. *Wealth and Poverty,* 4th ed. New York: Basic Books, Inc.

Gilder, George. 1989. *Microcosm: The Quantum Revolution in Economics and Technology,* 1st ed. New York: Simon and Schuster.

Hughes, Thomas P. 1989. *American Genesis: A History of the American Genius for Invention,* 10th ed. New York: Penguin Books.

Hughes, Thomas P. 1983. *Networks of Power: Electrification in Western Society, 1880–1930,* 1st ed. Baltimore, MD: The Johns Hopkins University Press.

Johnson, Paul. 1983. *Modern Times: The World From the Twenties to the Eighties,* 2nd ed. New York: Harper & Row.

Johnson, Paul. 1997. *A History of the American People,* 1st ed. New York: HarperCollins.

Kelly, Kevin. 1998. *For the New Economy: 10 Radical Strategies for a Connected World,* 1st ed. New York: Viking.

Keynes, John Maynard. 1953. *The General Theory of Employment, Interest, and Money.* 1st Harvest Harcourt Brace edition 1964. Orlando, FL: Harcourt Brace & Co.

Landes, David S. 1998. *The Wealth and Poverty of Nations: Why Some Are So Rich and Some So Poor,* 1st ed. New York: W.W. Norton & Co.

Lindsey, Lawrence B. 1999. *Economic Puppetmasters: Lessons From the Halls of Power,* 1st ed. Washington, DC: The AEI Press.

Maddison, Angus. 1991. *Dynamic Forces in Capitalist Development: A Long-Run Comparative View,* 2nd ed. New York: Oxford University Press.

Malthus, Thomas. 1798. *An Essay on the Principle of Population.* London: Malthus. Penguin Books.

Meadows, Donella H. et al. 1972. *The Limits to Growth,* 3rd ed. New York: Universe Books.

Mill, John Stuart. 1859. *On Liberty.* Published 1986. New York: Prometheus Books.

Mill, John Stuart. 1864. *System of Logic, Ratiocinative and Inductive,* 1st U.S. ed. New York: Harper & Brothers.

Novak, Michael. 1997. *The Fire of Invention: Civil Society and the Future of the Corporation,* 2nd ed. Lanham, MD: Rowman & Littlefield.

Peppers, Don and Martha Rogers, Ph.D. 1993. *The One to One Future: Building Relationships One Customer at a Time,* 1st ed. New York: Currency Doubleday.

Pilzer, Paul Zane. 1990. *Unlimited Wealth: The Theory and Practice of Economic Alchemy,* 4th ed. New York: Crown Publishers.

Rothschild, Michael. 1990. *Bionomics: The Inevitability of Capitalism,* 1st ed. New York: Henry Holt and Co.

Schumpeter, Joseph A. 1942. *Capitalism, Socialism and Democracy,* 35th ed. New York: Harper & Row.

Soros, George. 1998. *The Crisis of Global Capitalism: Open Society Endangered,* 3rd ed. New York: PublicAffairs.

Tapscott, Don. 1996. *Digital Economy: Promise and Peril in the Age of Networked Intelligence,* 2nd ed. New York: McGraw-Hill.

Wriston, Walter B. 1997. *The Twilight of Sovereignty,* 1st ed. New York, Replica Books.

Yergin, Daniel and Joseph Stanislaw. 1998. *The Commanding Heights: The Battle Between Government and the Marketplace That is Remaking the Modern World,* 1st ed. New York: Simon & Schuster.

INDEX